Alex Thomson was born in Basingstoke and spent his childhood setting fire to the local allotment sheds. He went to C??horne Comprehensive, which w??? ??? ??? ??? ???ently working as a TV documen???

Nick Rossiter was brough??? ??? ??? ??? ???ated at a very posh Catholic ??? ??? ???cars, exclusive dinner parties and is training to be a TV producer with the BBC in London.

ALEX THOMSON
and NICK ROSSITER

Ram Ram India

PALADIN
GRAFTON BOOKS

A Division of the Collins Publishing Group

LONDON GLASGOW
TORONTO SYDNEY AUCKLAND

Paladin
Grafton Books
A Division of the Collins Publishing Group
8 Grafton Street, London W1X 3LA

Published in Paladin Books 1989

First published in Great Britain by
William Collins Sons and Co Ltd 1987

Copyright © Alex Thomson and Nick Rossiter 1987

ISBN 0-586-08776-1

Printed and bound in Great Britain by
Collins, Glasgow

Set in Sabon

To Oxfam, for what they do

Illustrations

Acknowledgements

The authors would like to thank the following people for their help and support: Justin Pumfrey for his photographic help; Frank Evans and the staff at Oxfam in Cardiff; Alok Mukhopadhyay, Uday Gupta, Diane Crocombe and the Oxfam staff in New Delhi; Alajangi Swamy and Hiralal, Oxfam's driver in Nagpur; Jeff and Barbara Alderson, Pushpanath and everyone else at Oxfam in Bangalore; our sponsors, Air India and Sony UK Ltd.; Merlin Southwell for his invaluable technical advice in the face of our ignorance and the bicycle mechanics of India who made the journey possible.

Preface

By the end of October 1984 it was becoming hard to get through to Rossiter. He was absorbed, compiling lists of tablets, suppositories, inner tube vulcanizing kits and other items he insisted on taking to India without explaining what they did. He was out to cross the country by bicycle – lose weight and give up smoking.

With a week to go before our flight, I too became absorbed – in shortening Rossiter's lists, taking out items like sleeping-bags, gloves and a torch which I told him were unnecessary. The cartons of king-size cigarettes also had to go. Three days from departure preparations for the expedition were complete; seriously ill-equipped and in total disagreement, we were now ready to bicycle from one end of India to the other – top to bottom.

But then matters took off in India before we'd even reached Heathrow Airport. On the morning of 31st October, Sikh militants shot Indira Gandhi, the Indian Prime Minister, in the garden of her home in New Delhi. In the days that followed, riots swept through cities across the country as Hindus exacted a bloody revenge on any Sikhs they could find. The British High Commission in Delhi warned people not to travel to India unless it was absolutely necessary. The Sikh state of Punjab was completely sealed off from foreigners and journalists.

As foreigners and journalists intending to cycle straight across Punjab on our way south, the logistical problems of planning the journey suddenly leapt into a new league altogether. But strange events spring from adversity and now, against all the odds, we actually found ourselves in agreement on one thing at least – the journey was on ...

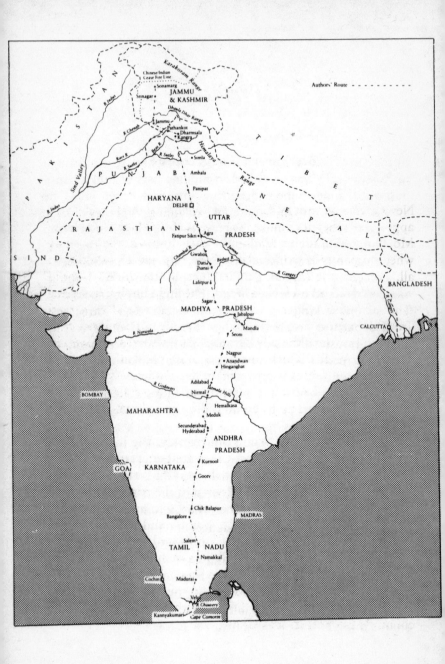

I

'Fortune, that favours fools.'

Ben Jonson, 'The Alchemist'

New Delhi is not what estate agents would call 'well appointed' when it comes to the international flight schedules. Most long-haul flights land in the early hours of the morning when humanity is working strictly to rule – if it's working at all. Tonight, the capital is under curfew after Indira Gandhi was shot dead here a few days ago. The flight has left us feeling dumped and bewildered in the grim warehouse of an arrival lounge. In theory two bicycles should come out of a black hole opposite me, onto the oily carousel. But we are not hopeful.

It is the smells which impress a place on you. That most underrated of senses is powerful in the suddenness of its surprise attack and now the mixture of bidis, stale urine and unseen snacks fried up by an invisible samosa-wallah root me in a daze to the spot.

Not so Rossiter. As I stare out blankly, the bicycles have arrived unharmed by the flight and are being re-united with their pedals. Unencumbered by the stalling sense of *déjà vu*, Rossiter has gathered the first crowd of the trip. Willing porters hold the bikes and lovingly stroke the foam of the handlebar grips while Rossiter twists, pumps and spanners them back into shape. He hurls their cardboard protection away with a flourish and it lands softly in a waft of dust on a huge pile of abandoned luggage. It is the first crowd of the journey, twelve porters or so, but as we are on the way to discovering, the crowd is to India what the hedgerow is to England – the country's essence, its way of life.

Delhi's way of life, though, is temporarily suspended. Riots and organized butchery have put the place into a communal state of shock. Only soldiers meet our flight and the customs men are giving yet another batch of foreign press a tired going over. Joining the queue we are about as inconspicuous as a Bank Holiday and we certainly come as light relief to the customs officials. All the interest is on the bicycles, and our bags full of cameras and recording equipment pass unsearched.

Still wondering whether we're innocents abroad or a step ahead of the hard news heavyweights still being searched behind us, we're suddenly ushered round a corner and then into a corridor lined with plastic chairs and soldiers eyeing us with extreme suspicion. One steps up to Rossiter, 'You are planning to take this into the city?' he asks, looking at the bicycle.

'Hope so,' replies Rossiter, patting the saddle with heroic optimism.

'Curfew is on. This thing will be difficult. You are requiring pass.' With that, he leaves and after half an hour it's clear he does not go to get us a pass.

Rossiter takes command at this point and disappears back into Customs returning in a few moments. It seems we need curfew passes but you can't get them here and if you go out of the airport lounge you can't get back in. The taxi drivers will not have rope to tie the bicycles onto the roofracks; they won't leave without a bribe and they'll drive without lights. 'All in all,' I can hear myself saying vaguely, 'this is no way to begin an expedition.'

'Cycle across India? We can't even push the bikes out of the bloody airport.'

'Let's go,' says Rossiter perfunctorily and we heave bikes and baggage out into what would be a car park, were there any cars about.

Over at the taxi rank it's not looking good. Although it's in the mid-sixties, the drivers are wrapped up in their cold weather 'clothings' which means a rough assortment of dark and dusty cloaks and scarves flung around themselves. Cloth sags and sticks out from them at random, and from each comes a silvery plume of bidi smoke, as an occasional drag lights up a black moustache. They look at us, uncommitted.

It is ten miles into town and I motion towards the nearest taxi. None of the nearest huddle moves. Glancing inside the Ambassador, I see it's quietly sleeping five tonight. Unwise to disturb them. I ask if anyone will drive and suddenly all is action. I can't think where else they thought we wanted to go – but such thoughts are left behind in the search for rope and a permit, to be had from the soldier asleep at the end of the pavement.

By some undetected process a driver is mandated and announces, 'Roping is very soon here! What is your native place? You are married, sir?'

In India people can shift from bald statement into a direct and totally unrelated (though usually much more interesting) question. It's a facility quite alien to British restraint and questions like these were to pepper us from one end of the country to the other.

'Roping' turns out to be two feet of rather sickly-looking twine but you somehow make do – even though twenty feet of rope had been necessary to get the bikes to Heathrow. The driver pokes one of the wheels by way of checking that they're secure, grunts 'Ram Ram' to his huddled colleagues, and jumps in behind the wheel. With two bicycles wobbling on the roof, three people, two spare wheels, nine bags and two ruck-sacks inside, we're finally on our way into town for the price of a five-pound bribe. Living in the crowd, though, Indians have perfected cramming into an art-form. 'This is lightweight load,' sniffs our driver airily.

Once into the leafy suburbs of south Delhi he insists we duck down below window level and he turns off the one headlight that was working. The richer suburbs are deserted except for cows wandering aimlessly or lying under the wide jamun trees that line the roads. Here and there the glow of a brazier glides by when I peep above the window level, chowkidars – the night-watchmen – sit by them and whistle to each other through the tense darkness. They seem immune to curfews.

The 'Hotel Bright' is anything but bright. Its plastic illuminated sign is half buried by hundreds of dead bugs attracted by the light rather than the accommodation. It has letters missing and reads 'Hotel B g t'. No matter, the driver wakes up the manager who instructs us to carry in all the gear over his staff and porters asleep in rows along a dismal corridor dotted with scampering geckoes.

'Good God ... Extraordinary ...' murmurs Rossiter, crunching in between the snoring dhotied bodies in search of our gloomy chamber.

'You see, there will be dust,' warns the proprieter, flashing us a winning smile.

There is indeed dust. The room is covered with it as if it's experienced a light snowfall. This is because the one small window of the place gives onto a cement works − and the window has been broken for several years, by the look of it.

'At your service, please?' says the proprietor and disappears with another smile. We never see him again.

Fortunately there is a power-cut so the full awesome dismalness of the Hotel B g t can wait till morning − a few hours away. We fumble our way into the damp, saggy double bed, coughing cement dust. Even though I can't see him, I know Rossiter has that black, insulted look on his face. Tomorrow we have to find a way to cross Punjab to reach the Himalaya, for the state is off-limits to foreigners, but right now I can't find a way to Rossiter to reach the bathroom. Bicycling seems further off than ever at this point, but we and the bikes have arrived, riots, curfew and tomorrow can wait. Lying here, with the sheets, I can hear the voices of friends back home: 'You're not still going with all that trouble out there, are you?'

The first sight of the morning is a puncture, mine. The second is of a blood-red cockroach, three inches long, trundling determinedly to the bathroom. Rossiter is up in a flash, springs out of bed and fills the air with a mist of cement dust. He flails wildly in the vague direction of the cockroach with an old copy of *The Times of India* but there's not a sign of the insect when the confusion settles. Rossiter paces about, naked, menacing, but we're forced to live with the fact that it is still lurking in here, alive and creeping ... somewhere.

In Delhi, opinion varies as to whether we can cross Punjab to reach our starting point in the north of Kashmir. In Janpath Bazaar a Kashmiri hotelier strongly resembling a pike, darts through the traffic at us: 'Habib! Habib!' he yells triumphantly, by way of introduction.

'Yes, jolly good Mr Habib,' replies Rossiter in his crispest Oxford accent.

'You go to Kashmir – I know this, sirs! You are wishing to stay on my houseboat, my Dal Lake houseboat, very best boat, sahib?'

'No,' says Rossiter unbendingly, 'we wish to bicycle across the Himalaya as soon as possible.'

Habib blows through his nose and looks momentarily pole-axed, but he recovers and smiles generously for us, very much the man who knows what we're after: 'I can give you hashish then. You are my friends. So, good hashish? You are wanting opium, sahib?'

But the only advice he can offer about Punjab is that we shall get our throats cut without a doubt and that 'a knife with buttons' will be necessary. We had long since decided that a flick-knife would more likely escalate trouble than allay it, though.

At the Government of India Tourist Office we are quite alone. The official takes off his pebble-glasses, leans forwards to us and confides: 'If we trust in God and think logically, all will be well. But any bicycle tour of Punjab state is most out of the question. Impossible.'

He subsides into his chair and beams at us both. 'You will both be most certainly arrested and imprisoned.'

It turns out that we are totally banned from Punjab but at the same time advised to take the Jhelum Express right through it to Jammu at the edge of the Himalaya. The tourist officer and railway officials cannot agree whether or not we are allowed to travel and keep speaking of unspecified risks in such a journey: 'What kind of risks do they think we'll run into when we start cycling?' Rossiter asks me in pure wonder.

But we have to get through the mountains and on the route south before the snows begin and the decision is made for us: we'll go by train to Jammu and detour around Punjab on the bicycles coming south, a detour that will take us back into the mountains but is plainly unavoidable.

One more call remains the day before we intend to catch the Jhelum Express: the British High Commission. It occurs to us that it would be courteous, and perhaps important, to leave our route and intention with somebody there in case of accident. Things get off on the wrong foot when Rossiter sees the Commission for the first time. When it comes to architecture, Rossiter is a sensitive creature who needs careful handling. Just before we left England he had almost crashed his car, swerving on a hill in Bristol to enhance my view of an old house. 'Vanburgh,' he purred, as the car mounted the pavement. He had notions that the Commission might reflect faded touches of the Raj and is no little shocked, therefore, when confronted with a diplomatic pile resembling an off-season Butlin's in recession: 'Is this really it?' he asks as loudly as possible, in the entrance hall. Our call raises some eyebrows but very little interest, and officials happily hold forth on how little they will do for us if we get into trouble. It seems there will be no telephone calls back to England unless, perhaps, we are suddenly taken seriously dead.

'We're having to cut costs just like everybody else,' a lady points out to us in schoolmistressy tones. Outside, in front of the fountains, a gleaming white Rolls Royce purrs to a halt and disgorges its diplomatic payload: 'But of course,' she adds tersely, 'you should realize that only the High Commissioner has a Rolls.'

On our last night in Delhi we get a sharp reminder that the city is still very tense. Misjudging the time needed to inch our way through the traffic of Old Delhi back to the Hotel B g t, we find ourselves in the magnificent afterglow of an Indian sunset with a rickshaw driver who refuses to go further because of the curfew, backsheesh or no backsheesh.

We set off on foot along streets normally lined with people bedding down in rows on the pavements – but all that seems to have changed with the curfew. A few hundred yards from the hotel, after thirty minutes' hard walking, the streets are quite deserted and we both decide to snatch an illicit recording of the eery peace the curfew throws over the city. All you hear are the crickets and the cows shuffling and muzzling each other in small groups.

Just as we finish, a motorbike with two soldiers on it comes suddenly from a side-road. With our usual commitment to teamwork I take one glance at the soldiers and run for it. Rossiter, however, looks like a parachutist crashlanded into a hi-fi shop. He stands rooted to the spot, fumbling with his headphones, completely trussed up in camera straps, microphone leads and tape-recorder baggage. I've already gone twenty yards or so before realizing he is immobile. The motorbike passes us, continues for some distance, then stops and turns as if coming towards us again. The soldiers have to have seen us, even though the street is unlit. I start to run again and Rossiter moves this time, earphones and leads flailing out behind him. I've no idea whether the soldiers see us entering the hotel – but at times like this even the Hotel B   g t is welcoming. They never come knocking on the door, at any rate.

The next evening we are on our way north at last. As in all Indian hotels, ours is populated with idle porters, lackeys and hangers-on, none of whom is in the slightest bit impressed by what we intend to do. This establishes something of a pattern. The idea of crossing the country on a bicycle simply does not excite people. What does impress the hotel entourage who alternately help and hinder us with our baggage, is the moment when Rossiter removes the front wheel of his bike with the flick of a lever. The entire company literally dances about and demands further demonstrations, thereby ensuring that the group of onlookers soon swells to a crowd. Eventually we have the bikes tied down (having invested in our own rope) on the roof of a taxi, settle the demands for backsheesh from the entourage and are blasting and hooting our way through the traffic to New Delhi station.

The excitement the bicycles are causing is ominous and we hope it won't be so bad in the country. What saddens me is that it strengthens the association between the West and techno-logical supremacy which you sometimes feel hangs over urban India like a vast, stifling deadweight. Jeans and digital watches still sell for inflated prices around Connaught Circus in Delhi or in the Bombay bazaars, because of the label and origin which have more cachet than Indian-made goods that may be just as good.

At the red-brick station there is a large notice which reminds people that: IT IS FORBIDDEN TO SLEEP ON THE PLAT-FORMS. The vast booking hall is nevertheless lined with people asleep and straggling queues which degenerate into scrum-mages near the counters. The ladies queue, by contrast, is a calm crocodile of multi-coloured sarees. Red-jacketed porters parade luggage about on their heads. Betel-nut sellers squat at their trade in odd corners along with ear-cleaners. A street-barber darts about touting for scrapeable clients for his stall outside. Peanut-sellers wander through with hot smoking piles of nuts on their head-baskets. Behind all of them, come Rossiter and myself, bicycles and panniers. Our second-class sleeper reserva-tion will get us onto the Jhelum Express, in theory. Bicycles are more problematic.

The 'ticketting office' is at the farthest end of the farthest platform. We trundle everything over the tracks to reach it, passing huge black steam-engines snorting and wheezing in readiness. On the way over there should be little chance of being electrocuted since the trains are either steam or huge rust-red diesels. There is some chance, however, because live wires lie exposed and crackling by one of the platforms. A cow wanders over to investigate, thinks better of it, with startling shrewdness, and ambles off down the track, in the direction of Varanasi.

I leave Rossiter, with his experience of playing rugby, to deal with the attack being mounted by fifty would-be passengers on the baggage-ticketting official, who can be heard behind the white-shirted siege, but not seen: 'Please, there is no problem and there is no need of pushings.' Rossiter emerges after some time, with a smeared and sweaty expression and two long forms which may eventually get our bicycles onto a train. Name, serial number, departure station, arrival station, date, time, father's occupation ... the forms fill two sides of A4 paper and are trophies in themselves. The bicycles are then decorated with a tin plate onto which all this information is lovingly painted by an official with superhuman reserves of patience. A boy appears, as they do in India, dead on cue and shows us to the luggage-car. You never seem to see boys of this type coming: they simply arrive, get paid some paise and are gone, palming a meagre living from pure, absorbed opportunism. But there is – as always – a system beneath the apparent chaos and the man who painted the plates is in connection with the man who launched back into the scrum with our forms; he in turn, has nodded to the boy who'll show us where to go. Like a million other sub-systems it's grown to fulfil the needs of employment and the need of corner-cutting through the myriad of bureaucratic ceremonies which festoon the simplest of processes in India – like getting onto a train. It works well enough, but you must pay a little and leave plenty of time before your train departs.

It's thirteen hours on the Jhelum Express from Delhi to Jammu, at the very edge of the Himalaya. Because of the recent troubles, tonight's train is total chaos and hopelessly overbooked. Our compartment is built to sleep six. You sit on wooden boards until bedtime when four more boards pull out from the walls to give two tiers of three wooden shelves. So much for the theory. Tonight, seventeen people – most of them soldiers with huge unwieldy rifles – are sitting, perching, leaning and squatting in our compartment just as they are in the whole train. It takes us more than ten minutes to muscle the twenty feet or so from the carriage-door to our compartment, with six panniers. It's going to be a long haul across Punjab on a night-train we're still not sure we're even allowed to be on; but so far, so good.

Curiously, I'm still not adjusted to the corollary of the Indian approach to cramming in the crowds, which is the fact that you do not easily offend people by pushing against them, squeezing past them or even treading on their toes. My breathless apologies during the fight to our (already occupied) reserved seats, meets with mild smiles when I knock into somebody: 'Please – no problem', or the current favourite, 'Mention not.'

The journey, then, is a tactile and food-sharing experience and we both somehow share our sleeping boards with a soldier, sleeping head to toe on the two-foot wide shelf. All in all, it's a long way from the bag-on-the-seat and retreat-behind-the-newspaper-to-avoid-the-danger-of-conversation routines of the English aboard British Rail.

The soldier on my shelf declines to take off his boots, which remain a few inches from my nose, creaking from side to side with the rhythm of the train, and liberally caked with the waste of an average Delhi street. The night airs are spiced with more than the scent of the soldiers' tiffin-boxes.

In typical fashion, Rossiter seems to be faring more comfortably. It has to be said that one of his reasons for attempting this journey was to reduce his present girth, but until then the poor man sharing his shelf has four or five inches of plank to sleep on before a six-foot drop to the floor, which is also covered in sleepers. The rest of the possible space is covered in prone Rossiter. And then there's the roll of the locomotive to contend with.

Our near-miss with the military in the curfew hasn't put us off trying to record in places where we should know better. As it is impossible for either of us to sleep – although everyone else is soon snoring away – the idea of recording some of the atmosphere was bound to occur sooner or later. Thinking that material from within the forbidden state is the stuff of editors' dreams, I ease out my recorder from the pannier I'm using as a pillow. As I do so, Rossiter looks over and whispers: 'You know what? They arrested a Canadian journalist here a couple of days ago. They caught one glance of his tape-recorder and that was that. Straight in the cooler.'

He's developing a fine talent for mis-timing these morsels of interesting and diverting information. But our luck's turning and nobody is disturbed by a faint whirr and hum from my shelf.

The dawn brings the first sights of the India we'll be bicycling through: the countryside, wide and endless, rising steaming out of the dawn mist on either side of us. Again there is the rush of excitement inside me at arriving in this place and the sleepless night is forgotten. From the glassless, barred windows irregular emerald paddies slip by. Bullock carts lurch along in the cooled-down dusts of the dawning plain. Two camels carrying haystacks pass and are lost into the mist. A huge and ugly hoarding rears up advertising SHIRTINGS AND SUITINGS. White, ghostly egrets stalk the edges of murky ponds. Water-buffalo are glimpsed, frozen, caught in the act of morning squelch and vanish.

Rossiter leans at his window in sheer amazement at the plains sweeping past and growing clearer as the mists lift and the sun climbs. An odd 'Extraordinary ...' passes his lips, his eyes are feasting on it all. At about an hour after dawn the soldiers leave in a heave of canvas, rattled weapons and 'Namaste's. Restored to something like its official capacity, our compartment is full of draughts and wide open spaces.

Leaving Jammu's spacious concrete station, we come upon two American cyclists pushing their machines towards the train. 'Hi,' says Rossiter, who once played rugby in the USA and still speaks a few words of American. 'You've been cycling much around here?'

'Naw, nat really. The roads are kinda rough around these parts, so we did most of our stuff over there,' says the male half of the couple. He gestures behind the station when he says 'over there', in the vague direction of Pakistan.

'Oh,' says Rossiter, 'Pakistan must be so interesting these days.'

'Naw, I meant Europe. We biked Europe before coming over here. Never bin near Pakistan.'

For a moment Rossiter is static, finding himself slammed full force against the American concept of the globe. Later, on the bus, he gives vent to the first in a long series of lectures on the present strength of the dollar: 'I mean to say, look at that couple we met at the station. It's extraordinary what they can just go and do. They talk about "biking Europe" as if it's a trip to Sainsbury's.' He gazes through the small hole in the bus roof through which we can see part of our bicycles lashed onto the rack. 'Well, anyway, I blame my bank manager. All that crap about standing by your pounds – the touts in Delhi wouldn't even look at exchanging pounds for rupees. The sheer indignity of it all. When I get back I'm going to my bank and I'll ...'

Ahead of us, there's a twelve-hour bus ride up from Jammu into the Himalaya and Kashmir. We're both keen to get up there as fast as possible and opt for the bus leaving the station in ten minutes, rather than resting up for the night in the town. According to the time-table, the bus should have left an hour ago but these battered old machines swear allegiance to train arrivals and not to anything so irrelevant as time-tables.

Even through the straggling bazaar at Jammu the road begins to climb and continues up for eight hours until we stop for the night in the high mountain village of Banihal. As the road coils and snakes its way up, raw, boulder-filled chasms and gullies run for miles off the edges of the lowest foothills. They're caused by the continuing de-forestation – the people here have literally torn their country apart by cutting down the forests which lined this road only a few years ago. Now only the highest slopes remain covered with trees. The lower bare hillsides have only the thinnest soil and cannot be planted, and only scraggy goats pick among the cacti for a scant feed.

At a higher level, some of the farther ridges and peaks still retain their cover of deodar and spruce and above that, by late afternoon, the first snow swings into view, perhaps thirty or more miles to the north. Ridge upon ridge, brown and then purple in the distance topped with blue rock faces and snows turned to silver in the sinking sun.

In the valley far down to one side of us, clusters of stone houses with huge stone-flagged roofs group in comforting huddles around their ancient, tiered paddies, below the vast valley walls. Macaque monkeys chatter and bounce about in excitement (maybe anger) as our old bus snorts ever higher.

At sunset it is chilly as soon as the sun dips below the far western side of the valley. In its bottom the sparkling Chenab river roars down from its source from glaciers already touched with the new snow of the autumn. We stop for chai at a roadside dhaba. Such places will soon be our life-support system on the journey ahead, with their squat clay ovens fuelled by pancakes of dried dung and rows of black-bellied pots simmering alu gobi, dum alu, chaval, dal and perhaps 'mutton' (that is, goat). There is also chai.

Despite a large, ambitious, hand-painted sign in English saying WE SERVE NESCAFÉ, nobody here knows what Nescafé is, but who cares? What you get to drink is invariably chai and more chai. This has nothing much in common with tea, which in India tends to be 'tray tea' where you can mix the ingredients of a good cuppa as you desire. Chai, on the other hand, works on the no-choice principle and is geared to the very sweet tooth most Indians seem to have. The largest available container is requisitioned and tea, buffalo or cow milk, sugar water, sugar and sugar are boiled away endlessly and the results ladled out to punters at fifty paise (about three pence) for a dirty cupful. No, this is not tea but I love it all the same and it's full of energy-giving, tooth-rotting sugar. Rossiter looks up at me over the chipped rim of his once-white cup. He is not fond of chai. 'You drink this,' he announces with complete contempt, and pushes the cup across the table through a column of ants who are busy transporting the remains of a past meal from one end of it to another. We watch them absorbed, enjoying the peace outside the rattling bus.

All too soon the conductor starts strutting about shouting, 'Chalo! Chalo! Chalo! Chalo!' with an air of great importance, even though all his passengers are sitting down a few feet from him. We are the only westerners on the bus, which is half empty. The conductor seems to be celebrating the fact by swigging regularly from a small green bottle and passing it to the driver who partakes with no apparent loss of his faculties.

For the overnight stay in Banihal we are directed to a large concrete bunker where our fellow passengers demonstrate the advantages of travelling heavy as people love to do in India. They all have thick woollen mattresses and blankets to see them through the night. We have nothing but thin sheet sleeping-bags. We have planned to beg or borrow bedding if we need it and as it's now midnight and very cold, eight thousand feet up in the mountains, it's time to put the plan into action. The chowkidar of the bunker looks confused by the idea of blankets, but this is perhaps my Hindi and the fact that, in this region, he probably speaks Dogri anyway.

Eventually, though, he does return with some much lived-in blankets which he has apparently found in the stone shack across the yard populated by a troupe of sexually uninhibited goats. The sounds of goat-ecstasy continue to pierce the night long after our arrival and the blankets have a strange and powerful odour, good for the imagination, hopeless for sleeping.

The next morning we are away just before dawn. The bazaar is full of goats and the slapping sound of the breakfast chapatti-makers at work all along the roadside. With chapatti, eggs and chai inside us the bus rattles and shakes us up to the Jawarhar Tunnel after a seemingly endless series of hairpins. We shall have to cycle all the way back along this road as it's the only way into and out of Kashmir. As we have been climbing in the bus for more than ten hours, it's beginning to look more than a little daunting.

In the tunnel I recollect reading a guide-book which spoke about how it takes you from the gaunt slopes of India into the green, lush and cultivated Vale of Kashmir. But we emerge into a waste of mist which clears when the bus gets lower to reveal drab brown paddies abandoned to the oncoming winter and a steady, cold drizzle: 'What? Is this Kashmir?' Rossiter asks, looking out in complete disbelief. 'I thought it was supposed to be beautiful here.' He stares in alarm through the dirty glass of his window at the desolate, semi-frozen paddy terraces.

'Ah well, you should see it in the summer, they say it's quite different,' I say rather weakly, as surprised by the change in weather as he is. In the bus-stand at Srinagar the rain is steady. The winter, the troubles in Punjab and intermittent unrest in Kashmir itself have dried the usual flow of tourists to a trickle. Srinagar seems deserted. No matter; the Kashmiris' enthusiasm for fleecing any westerner in sight is not dampened by political troubles or by the downpour. A group of hustlers and houseboat touts surrounds us immediately: 'Hello, my friend, you are wanting houseboat? I give you super de-luxe five-star grand houseboat. Very cheap. Dal Lake? Nagin Lake? You say. I fetch you.'

In the days of the Raj the British were not allowed to own land in Kashmir and so they came up with the stylish solution of living in long lines of houseboats moored in the glassy-clear waters of Dal and Nagin lakes. Inside, they all have the feel and decoration of Edwardian England and in the warmer months you can idle for weeks on these Himalayan lakes surrounded by the rising purple walls of the mountains. You can watch the buzzards and kingfishers, swim among the lotus lilies, wander through the Shalimar Gardens ...

'Thank you, but we have a boat we want to stay on – my friend Aziz's boat. Pala Palace is the boat.'

There is much ritual casting of eyes skyward and sighing with expressions of acute pain: 'Oh my friend. This is very bad boat. There are vermins in this place. C class boat and you are getting sickness at once. I give you luxury – you come?'

'No thank you. We shall cycle to our friend's boat. Goodbye,' I say to the more vocal members of the lobby, trying to look decided.

Unsure of his ground, one of the touts leans forward, hushed and conspiratorial, with the time-trusted formula. The rain is trickling down his moustache: 'Opium, there is for you? Hashish, good hashish from Kulu. You are wanting? You stay. I go. I bring and come for you. Ha!' He smiles, convinced that the minimalist sales patter is hitting home.

I grow firmer at this point: 'Look. You stay. We cycle. We go. Now.'

'So you are now wanting taxi, my friend. I bring for you.'

At the word a phalanx of uncompromising Ambassador-wallahs cruises into the bus-stand as if from nowhere. Again, as if this were a cue, the police who have been watching from their checkpost at the gates of the bus-stand choose this moment to wade in with their lathis, sending some of the more inoffensive touts squealing out of the compound.

'Do they always carry on like this here?' asks Rossiter with genuine disbelief at what is happening around us.

One of the taxi-men suddenly turns on him while the police manhandle the touts out of the way: 'My friend,' he glares, as if Rossiter were a life-long enemy, 'time is money. Money is business. Business is life!'

'Good. Jolly good,' says Rossiter. 'In England we have a prime minister who would be proud of that. But we'd like to go now. It's pretty wet out here.' At these words the taxi-driver spins on the spot and walks smartly back to the mouthpiece of his huge hookah lying sprawled over the front seat of his car like an evil, smoking octopus. He seems satisfied and evidently holds some sway around here since all but a few die-hards walk off in disgruntled groups.

In the course of running after our bicycles, one of the die-hards goes straight into an oncoming motorbike. As always, a crowd of stirrers musters within seconds to beef up the dispute – not that it seems in any danger of waning anyway. Nobody is hurt, fortunately, and we last see them busily exchanging insults and recriminations in the middle of the traffic on the Azad Road. The motorcyclist will need all the help of Allah he can invoke against a Kashmiri who has lost business and dignity.

It's a short ride down to the lakes to the east of the city.

In late November the rain is cold and steady. We can't see the mountains for mist and the houseboat we want is a wreck because it's being renovated for the summer. Aziz is pleased enough to see us and has his son Sherfi paddle us round the corner in the family shikhara, to his brother-in-law's boat. Mohammed's boat is a dingy, damp and cold affair but by this time we have had little sleep for two nights, are soaking wet and are willing to settle for anything with a bed in it. His boat just about fulfils this last requirement and Sherfi is soon lighting up the ineffective pot-bellied woodstove.

Within minutes we are both curled asleep while the rain drums on the corrugated-iron roof. Whether the bicycles have been damaged by the train and bus rides – to say nothing of being crammed in a shikhara – can wait till tomorrow. For the moment it's simply enough to have arrived in Kashmir. Everyone here laughs at our intention to go on up to Sonamarg to begin our ride, but that can wait too. Six thousand miles of travelling and we've not even started yet on the real journey. To cap it all the weather's just as it was when we left Heathrow.

2

'Anybody can ride a bicycle.
You just get aboard and pedal. Heh!'

Richard's Bicycle Book

It's 10.30 a.m. in the local bus-stand in old Srinagar, a much more shabby affair even than the inter-state bus-stand where we encountered the touts a few days ago. The 8.30 bus to Sonamarg still stands motionless in the large puddles of a compound full of brightly painted buses. We continue to wait in the bus as we have done for two hours. Outside, the conductor struts about like a farmyard cock, wrapped up in his ponchkai, with a bright red flowery scarf tied round his head. He delicately avoids the puddles fringed with muddy ice, throws back his head every few moments and crows: 'Sonnamarragg Sonnamarragg Sonnamarragg Sonnamarragg ... Hoooooooooey!!!' He pauses, as if for dramatic effect, then minces over to another dry spot a few yards away and lets fly again, pointing his unshaven larynx at the leaden sky.

He is not alone. All over the muddy compound, bus conductors are touting for trade like alternative prima donnas. To the other side of our bus the Gulmarg bus has been due out any minute, for the last hour. So: 'Goolmaarraag Goolmaarraag Goolmaarraag Goolmaarraag ... Hoooooooooooey!!!'

None of this has the slightest effect and we wait alone, bicycles tied to the roof. Suddenly, as from some unseen signal quite unconnected with the conductors, there is a last-minute scramble which fills the bus. Most of the passengers are from the outlying villages who've come in for the bazaar. Now they are heading home with hens, ducks, vegetables, candles and spices clutched in bulges beneath their ponchkais. One old man with a long hennaed beard has a bigger bulge than most – a goat. For some miles he wrestles with it before getting off.

As we pass out of the city beside the lakes and the huge fort overlooking them from its bare hill, our conductor continues to scream for custom while hanging out of the back of the bus, holding onto the open door with one hand as it ploughs through congested bazaars. I'm beginning to wonder if this isn't beyond the call of duty until I see an oncoming bus also trailing a wailing conductor from its back-end like some dirty out-sail.

Because Kashmir is strongly Moslem many of the women from more wealthy families are heavily veiled. They contrast starkly, in their sinister black bourkhas, with the golden weather-beaten faces of the mountain women from up the Sindh valley. Mingling in the crush of the bus is a group of tall, aloof old men with large, brightly coloured coil turbans resembling those of the Afghans or perhaps the Rajasthanis. Their long beards are dyed deep orange and all of them have thick golden earrings; perhaps they are descendants of the Afghan traders who once rode this track over the lonely passes to the bazaars at Leh in Ladakh, two hundred and fifty miles to the east. The Ladakhis say they were wild men – indeed they needed to be to make the journey at all, let alone to make it as a way of life.

Soon our rickety bus has swung eastwards, out of the Vale of Kashmir and on up into the narrowing Sindh Valley. We shall follow the valley as far as it goes today, to Sonamarg, at the foot of the mighty snow-blocked Zojii La pass. In many ways the cluster of wooden roadside shacks called Sonamarg is the last place in India. Nobody goes any further at this time of year and today we are the only passengers for the last, cold hour of the ride.

You exchange 'namaste' for 'salaam' when you come up into Kashmir from the plains of India. Beyond Sonamarg, over and beyond the Zojii La, you are into the high barren wilderness towering on into Ladakh, 'Little Tibet', and the greeting changes again to 'jullay'. In India, a vast country which recognizes 15 main languages and dialects out of the 1652 known, you can see, on occasions, how geography sets up stark language barriers.

At this time of year there is nothing in the Upper Sindh for anybody. Aziz told us this while hammering at his houseboat; the flower-seller in Srinagar told us this; the clerk at the bank told us this when he heard us talking about Sonamarg – and he wasn't even asked. For the last hour we remain alone at the back of the bus. Being alone on any form of public transport in India is an unnerving state to be in and when the driver unloads his last passengers beside us, he turns and stares at us as if to persuade us to reconsider. At this point the sun is still out but later the upper valley becomes a shadowy gorge into which the sun will not fall again until late spring.

'There'll be snow at road level by the time we get there,' says Rossiter, who has been watching the snow line creep down nearer and nearer to the road.

'Not a chance. I think it's in a gap where the valley widens out. You'll see. No snow,' I tell him.

'I'm cold as it is – look at it, snow's just above us now on the rocks.'

'Not a chance. It's only autumn,' I insist, very much the thinking man's climatologist. I'm damn cold as well but it's not good tactics to admit that to Rossiter.

Suddenly we are both slung sideways across the gangway as the bus lurches and drags itself up onto a long unsurfaced stretch of road. As if on cue, the sides of the track are fringed with snow, long icicles hang in a solid cascade from the granite walls of the gorge and the colossal boulders filling the churning river just below the side of the road. Rossiter turns to me with a fat contented smile.

'Snowballs.'

We get to Sonamarg late in the afternoon. Our arrival today swells the population by a hundred per cent. Both of the dirt streets are lined with wooden shops and summer workshops boarded up and padlocked for the onset of winter. The narrow pasture is frozen and mostly snow-covered; the herders and their goats have moved off down to the Lower Sindh and any paddies ended twenty or more miles back down the valley. The Zojii La pass into Ladakh is now blocked so this street has had its life-support cut off, and the 'sonamarg' – the meadow of gold – waits in suspended animation for the spring, seven months away in late May.

For the one and only time in the entire journey there is no crowd to watch us arrive and unload our gear, only the wind in our ears and the towering granite walls of the mountains flaked with snow and trailing plumes of silver cloud off their soaring peaks and ridges. In a few moments the sheer scale and silence of the mountains is pierced by the driver starting up again and turning his empty bus back towards Srinagar. Then we're left up here, at nearly ten thousand feet, in the most northerly accessible village in India.

On either side the mountains rise perhaps another five thousand feet with the snow clinging where it can to the grey pinnacled rock faces against the tireless wind. The peaks turn blue and then red and purple in the last rays of the day's sunshine. Moments later the sun has dipped below an intruding peak and the rocks now glower, deepening grey into the dark blue sky. It's evidently time to find a place to stay.

Near one end of the row of small shacks along the main road there is smoke coming from a squat stone chimney. For a while I had assumed the entire village had moved away but inside this hut an old man is sitting stirring a large pot full of hot water, chillis, a whole onion and twenty or so bobbing lentils. He is not the slightest bit surprised to see us. With him is a Sikh whose broken-down lorry stands on three wheels, indefinitely, in the middle of the deserted main road. He's wearing a huge black wrap-around turban and has the biggest kirtipan dagger I have ever seen, which he fingers suspiciously while the ancient beckons us in as if expecting us to drop by for chai on our way home from the office.

He warms us up with a blackened cupful of the chilli-sauce:

holding the cups warms our hands, the contents burn our insides. With a mixture of signs and Hindi we eventually get over the idea that we'd like a place to stay and so he leads us off the other side of the road up across the snow to a small wooden shack with a tin roof at the edge of the pine forest which drapes the lower slopes of the valley.

While Rossiter puts the bicycles inside and unloads the panniers I spend a frenzied half-hour ripping up pieces of wood and twigs frozen to the ground. Finally, after it is quite dark, we succeed in lighting the small heating stove in one corner of the shack. It gives out a feeble heat for as long as our meagre wood-supply lasts, which is about an hour.

By 6.30 it's quite dark and intensely cold, as I sit trying to warm myself over our candle, the decision not to bring sleeping-bags looms large and inescapable in my mind. There is only one consolation from being here (apart from the fact that we can start cycling soon) and that's the magnificence of the stars outside. Up here the Milky Way is so bright overhead it casts your own shadow against the snow and paints a gigantic ethereal swathe across the centre of the black night.

Apart from the pathetic stove, the only other objects in the hut are a rusty tap not connected to anything and two small charpoys with large holes in the webbing. Both our colleagues across the road have the benefits of kongris, ubiquitous devices in Kashmir through the winter consisting of small clay pots filled with live coals and covered with wickerwork, deftly tucked up under whatever you happen to be wearing. Because of this many Kashmiris have a look of advanced pregnancy as they pad around in the snow, often in sandals or even barefoot.

'Do me one favour,' I say to Rossiter in the freezing semi-darkness of our hut, 'please don't say anything about sleeping-bags.' In our concern to get the bicycles laden as lightly as possible this omission is clearly a mistake.

However, wrapped up in thermal underwear, jumper, spare shirts, trousers and track-suit, Rossiter is feeling much more positive and without warning launches into the finer points of the survival blankets he's insisted on bringing for nights like tonight:

'They're incredible,' he begins, 'the thing is, they're all aluminium foil so they don't let out any of your body heat. None of it. Clever, huh?'

'I haven't got any body heat at the moment.'

'Ah, but you will do, under one of these.'

'But they're so noisy it's ridiculous. One twitch of your toe and POW – there's this bloody great explosion of noise in your bed. How are you supposed to sleep with that?'

'Why do you have to be so damned fussy all the time? Think about it. They're designed for high altitude survival. Here we are in the middle of the Himalaya, sitting in a freezing shed half-way up a mountain and all you can do is worry about sleeping ... What are you doing now?'

'Spinning my rear wheel,' I murmur, leaving Rossiter to get on with his Scott of the Antarctic scenario. Thinking morosely I'm not in the mood for sleeping anyway, a wave of horror suddenly passes over me as I idly spin away in the gloom:

'Bloody hell, it's bent. My wheel's out of line,' I say, as much to myself as to Rossiter.

He explodes off his charpoy in a crash of the tin-foil sheeting under which he had been grudgingly surviving. He peers in silence at the wheel. Shivering by the light of one small candle, with the stove gone out and the journey not yet started, it is not a good moment. It's only fair to point out now a fact painfully obvious to both of us: neither of us has got a clue how you go about straightening a bent wheel.

'Get the manual,' says Rossiter, husky and death-like. 'Read it.' I read falteringly, with the wind trying to blow out the candle and whining under the ill-fitting front door.

'If ... the wheel is ... more than half ... an inch out ... pack ... the whole thing ... up and ... buy another ...'

A pressure-cooker noise comes out of Rossiter's head. 'Great. Bloody great. You see? That just proves what I was saying earlier about what an absolutely stupid throw-away society we live in in the West. No way would they tell you that around here even if they did have bicycles. As soon as something goes wrong we just ...'

'What are we going to do about it?' I say acidly, in no mood for a Rossiter state-of-the-nation lecture on western consumerism as moral decline. To his eternal credit, he stops in mid-flow, sniffs and glances straight at me.

'Buy another.'

We laugh in our lonely shack until we are almost warm, before huddling together with all our clothes on until it eventually gets light outside and we can stop crashing about under our tin-foil sheets.

Chillis and hot water is not the best way to start any day, I humbly submit, 'But,' as I say to Rossiter in the frosty dawn, 'it's better than nothing.'

'No, it isn't. Nothing is quite obviously better than that, to any vaguely normal human being.' My habit of eating anything anywhere is already sundering me from the concept of 'the normal human being' in Rossiter's estimation, as he is quick to point out. He, conversely, is much more fastidious and has eaten very little for four days now. I eat alone in the ancient's hut helping myself. As there's no sign of him or the driver, I leave something for the hut and food and collect Rossiter for a ritual photograph at the north end of the village. The lonely ceremony complete, we push off, bent back wheel or no, with an immense sensation of relief. We are on the road at last, even if it is rough and dotted with occasional boulders. As I fly into the first series of steep downhill bends on the road back to Srinagar, I shout for the sheer joy of it, going west with the wild dawn sun coming up on my back through a chink in the mountain wall behind me. My echo comes straight back at me almost as pure as its original.

The air is extraordinarily dry up at this altitude, as well as cold. Not having any scarves, we've wrapped our spare pairs of socks round our faces but after just a couple of hours both of us have wind-burnt foreheads and lips beginning to crack open.

After about ten miles, we pass through a military outpost where poor soldiers used to life on the plains are living in tents in the snow – though I bet they could sleep at night, unlike us.

Some of them are on a desultory early morning run in ludicrous, huge white snow-boots. They are extremely surprised to see us suddenly come freewheeling round a bend straight into their run. In fact, the whole exercise falls apart completely as all of them, including the officer in charge, stop and spontaneously applaud. They all yell 'Namaste' as we pass and then 'Ram Ram' as we leave them.

'Rarm Rarm,' yells back Rossiter, in true aristocratic style.

'You're getting good at that,' I tell him.

'Naturally,' says Rossiter, overtaking.

People say you can't escape gods in India and even 'Ram Ram' – the Hindu equivalent of 'Ciao' or 'Cheers' – refers to Rama, the ideal human being. When a group of men yell this at you, it sounds like a number of small engines revving up. When we yell it back there is always widespread mirth and general slapping of thighs – it's good to leave people laughing, either at or with us, we're never sure which.

For all the hassle of getting to Sonamarg, cycling down out of it is a wonderful way to begin the ride. For the first twenty miles or so we are freewheeling through the spectacular gorge the Sindh river has cut below our starting point. After an hour we are out of the snow, which eases our progress considerably. Although the snow is never deep on the road, it's often compacted and frozen hard and though neither of us comes off, it is slow going.

Along the narrow valley huge landslides have cut bare swathes through the large pine-forests which cover the lower slopes. Ancient tree-trunks lie embedded in the river and the road makes sudden unannounced detours round land-slides too big to dynamite.

By mid-morning we are meeting our first villagers, scattered goat-herders and then the first tiny terraces of rice-paddy stepping up and down the frosty slopes. Almost everyone who sees us, man, woman or child, 'Salaams' loud and heartily, with a broad smile. In the villages large poplar trees are all dotted with what look like huge birds' nests but are in fact small haystacks drying out the precious feed and bedding to see the goats, now creeping down the valley, through the winter.

By midday we are in Gund, a larger village and very much the main market for the produce of the valley with its vigorous little bazaar into which the local buses somehow cruise at considerable speed, klaxons blaring, before stopping to load up with people, animals and vegetables.

Finding a dhaba which is not completely crowded is not easy but we're hungry and determined and finally settle on a place serving up delicious golden omelettes and the richest, creamy walnuts I've ever come across. A crowd assembles to check over the bicycles. As always it's exclusively male, with small ragged boys muscling and squirming their way to the front. Usually there is an 'expert' on hand to put over the finer specifications for the good of all. Such men automatically assume the right to pull, probe and fiddle with anything that takes their fancy without even thinking of asking you. They are also, always, on the imaginative side of the truth in their explanations. Today's expert flicks a gear-lever, nods sagely at me and announces 'clutch' and unleashes a torrent of Kashmiri. Everybody murmurs. He also points out that the water bottles are full of whisky.

The laughable thing about this is not the ignorance – there's clearly no reason at all why anybody should know how anything so irrelevant as a western bicycle should work – but the way in which the self-appointed explanation-wallahs are so invariably wide of the mark. I often wonder if their audience is not actually better informed than they are.

As we move further down the valley towards the Vale of Kashmir and Srinagar we are repeatedly salaamed by little groups of old men sitting by the roadside, often miles from the nearest village. What they are doing there is not clear, since crop-farming in the valley has all but ceased for the winter. Perhaps they are literally 'sitting it out'. But we keep coming upon them, beneath a tree, on the parapet of a culvert, squatting around a hookah, in their baggy goats' wool pants, ponchkais and pill-box hats.

Rossiter is deeply puzzled after we stop with one such group for a while. 'This is really weird. Do you think one of them just wakes up one morning and says, "OK lads, how about going and sitting around all day at the dead tree eight miles west of here?" Or maybe it's India's covert line of defence against the Chinese – imagine legions of the People's Republic coming down over the Zojii La and running up against these guys – I'd be back to Beijing in a flash.'

The weather is growing steadily more ominous and as the road swings south into the Vale of Kashmir it finally breaks and begins raining a light, uncommitted sort of rain – but steady nonetheless. Coming through Srinagar by bicycle gives us a direct test of what urban riding is all about in India. In some ways it's quite a delicate matter of edging your way forward around and in front of rickshaws, goats, dogs, pigs and the odd monkey and getting out of the way of anything bigger than you – there are few rules of the Indian road but that might is right may safely be assumed to be one. Anyway, at least there are no cows wandering in serene immunity around the streets of Moslem Srinagar.

As a result of the recent temperatures – and it is cold now in Srinagar too – Rossiter is sinking rapidly into a heavy cold compounded by toothache and lips that the wind and dryness of the mountains seem to have turned inside out. He is not a promising sight.

So we decide to take a more comfortable houseboat on the Nagin Lake and rest up for a day to see if the cold improves – or the rain, for that matter. The trouble is that this comes up hard against my natural impatience, fuelled by bursting enthusiasm for the ride after such a fine run down from Sonamarg today. My impatience doesn't take kindly to minor considerations like personal health and the state of the weather. It ceases to register, for instance, the fact that we do not have proper waterproof clothing with us beyond a couple of ordinary cagoules. Because of these tendencies and a habit of connecting illness with unspecified general weakness of character, I lead us shortly and predictably into trouble.

Nagin Lake is usually a crystal-clear expanse with the Hari Parbat Fort looming up on its western shore overlooking the lake and the city. Tonight though the fort is a barely visible smudge in a steady downpour. The rain drums on the iron roof of our houseboat with a vengeance which Hamid, the boat owner, says will last for several days. 'Always at the end of autumn it is so,' he shouts against the drumming above. Hamid is a part of the ninety per cent Moslem majority in Kashmir and after he has brought us a sumptuous mutton and green bean stew (cooked by his sisters), he regales us with the story of his efforts to avoid the marriage his father is trying to arrange for him in favour of his own home-made choice. 'Many devices are necessary for this thing,' he whispers, very much the young conspirator, detailing how the girl he wants to marry has been strategically placed at family gatherings to allow the father to come round to seeing her as a possible bride, as if it were entirely his own idea. Delicate hints have to be dropped at strategic moments – though quite what the poor girl in question makes of all this, judging by Hamid's approach, is an irrelevant musing of a western infidel.

Later in the evening he takes us to his house to watch the Nine O'Clock News from Lahore read, strangely enough, by a woman and an unveiled one at that. The house is really one wooden room carpeted with rugs and wall-papered with old newspapers. With the thirteen members of Hamid's family inside it's very cosy – and there are plenty of kongris to spare.

After watching Lucille Ball dubbed into Urdu you know it's time to lie down and rest awhile. Back on the houseboat eight different bulbs in the main room can't provide enough light to read by because at this time of year the water-level is very low in the hydroelectric dams in the area – or that's what Hamid says at any rate. If this is the reason, Kashmir must surely soon grow brighter, for it is still raining hard when I turn in for bed.

It pours unabated all the next day. Rossiter salves his lips and drinks copious amounts of Kashmiri green tea seasoned with cardamoms and cloves, which he says is doing tooth and cold some good. He looks awful. So bad, in fact, that I have to get out, post off a cassette to the BBC in Delhi and buy two scarves for the coming climb over the Banihal Pass out of Kashmir. It takes a long time as I have to paddle myself across the lake and then into town along an intricate network of canals.

Back at the boat, the Supine One has a visitor. The visitor is not welcome. It is the flower-seller, one of many who patrol the lake like human-seeking missiles in their shikharas, waiting for someone innocent to home in on.

As I walk in the flower-man introduces himself. 'You are welcome to me, sir. I am Mr Bul Bul Far Out Groovy Flower Power Man,' and he gestures to his shikhara, ablaze with carnations, irises, lupins, roses and a large sign saying FAR OUT decorated with flowers.

Rossiter has had enough. 'Get rid of this guy, will you – he won't understand that I'm ill. He burst in here about five days ago and has been trying to sell me everything from sarees to saffron ever since.'

'I thought he's a florist.'

'He's a looney – get him out of here.'

But Bul Bul has disappeared only to re-appear seconds later festooned with large bunches of pink roses. For full effect he adopts a pose like Eros in Piccadilly while slowly extending a rose under my nose with a wormy smile. 'Ha! Man! Now you are smelling grooooovey scented roses, man. Yes?'

Mr Bul Bul is clearly a relic of what made Kashmir famous in the Sixties and an example of what troops of tourists can end up doing to people. I'm momentarily stunned by the performance. But he again vanishes before leaping in again sprouting irises out of all sorts of places on himself. Rossiter groans from a distant chair, 'Please, please do something.'

But Mr Bul Bul makes several more devastating entrances and exits before he's forced to concede he's run out of flowers. He stands still, looking dejected and deeply hurt. 'Please – for me, you buy?'

'Kill him,' moans Rossiter.

Something has to give in these situations and I end up buying some unpromising roses at an extreme price. Mr Bul Bul spins on his heels, launches into his shikhara and is off across the lake, a happy and richer man.

'He saw you coming a mile off,' snorts Rossiter in disgust from his chair. There are times when you just can't win.

Despite the fact that it is still raining the next morning, I persuade Rossiter to leave. He says he's feeling marginally better but I'm very soon forced to regret my impatience when the rain turns into a downpour as we leave Srinagar. By mid-morning we are completely wet, cold and dispirited, having made about fifteen miles. Rossiter's considered appraisal of the morning's ride is overwhelmingly accurate. 'This is a bloody drag.'

By mid-afternoon neither of us can feel our hands or feet for the cold and it has now been raining for about forty-eight hours. We pull in once more to shelter in a hut used for selling the cricket bats which are made in this part of the Vale. We have come about twenty miles all day on a dead flat road across the Vale, cycling only when we can't stand sheltering in the cold any longer. 'Rain stopped play – eh?' I suddenly remark, looking at all the new cricket bats hanging on strings from the roof of our hut.

I should know better. Rossiter rounds on me. 'God – you're an arrogant bastard, aren't you? I suppose you think this is going to toughen us up in some stupid way? The first place we find to stay at, we stay – and that's that. I've had enough of this and your madness to get going.'

He's dead right (of course, but there's no way I'm going to admit it).

As it happens, there is nothing until we reach Khanibal a further ten miles south – we are at least going south, I keep telling myself. Mercifully, I suppose, the rain eases off for an hour or so, but we're so cold now it's hard and dangerous to cycle with so little feeling in the limbs and my head feels like someone is cutting slowly through it with a blunt hacksaw.

At Khanibal there is a large Dak Bungalow for the use of

visiting government officials. To get a room, we need to talk our way round the chowkidar. We park the bicycles on the deep low verandah running along the front of the building and notice that there are two Mahindra jeeps parked outside. It looks as if the place could be full. On cue, the chowkidar mooches up to us flanked by evil-looking lackeys. 'Resthouse is full,' he announces in Hindi.

Having seen the office of the District Engineer opposite, I decide it's only fair for me to do the footwork and visit him to see if he can fix us a place to stay. Leaving Rossiter, I squelch through the flooded bazaar to the half-derelict wooden building housing the District Engineer (Anantnag) Jammu & Kashmir State. He is asleep.

His opening response to waking up faced with a soaking western cyclist, six feet four inches tall and looking like death, is tea. The prospect is deeply good. I slump around his wood-stove and begin to steam and fall asleep myself, while he is out seeing to tea. He returns and for some time we sit slurping in silence. He then opens, develops and concludes the 'conversation' in one verbal memo: 'You are requiring accommodation in this place. For your friend also. In Dak Bungalow there is none. Kashmir Chief Minister is there. All is full. I am assuring fully alternative accommodations for you. You are not married.'

The word certainly travels fast, when you turn up unannounced in these parts. How on earth all this information had got to him I have no idea – presumably from Rossiter speaking to somebody at the Dak Bungalow.

'Alternative' is certainly one way of describing what the D.E. has in mind for us. He shows me to a small stone room with just enough space for one charpoy, no windows, no light or candles and some peculiar damp slime growing down (or up) the walls. As I step in further to check that I'm not having some kind of cold-induced hallucination, a rat streaks out into the rain which has begun again.

'Thank you,' I say to the D.E. and leave for the Dak Bungalow.

43

Meanwhile, Rossiter has made friends with a rep from a Bombay drug company who says only two of the three rooms are taken. At times like this, that is all the information you need and in seconds we have shifted the bicycles and panniers into the middle of the third. If anyone turns up later on, freezing to death on the verandah beats staying a night in the 'alternative accommodations'.

Curiously, once we are installed, the attitude of the chowkidar, and thereby his lackeys, changes somewhat – they even vouchsafe to bring us a meagre supply of wood after an hour or so of heaping the stuff into great mounds in the room to which the Chief Minister will be coming. As we stand on the verandah a little after dark, enjoying the bliss of dry socks and normal foot-service resumed, the rain suddenly turns to snow. Immense soggy flakes of it, several inches across at first, then in the smaller, business-like stuff of which blizzards are made. In ten minutes the world has gone white and here we are, the wrong side of the Banihal Pass. The Chief Minister and entourage have arrived and muffled guffaws come from his room while the lackeys work in relays to satisfy his astonishing capacity to burn wood. On the white lawn outside an old cockerel crows in alarm at a world that grows white at night. 'Winter is come to Kashmir,' says the drug-man.

By morning the snow is well over a foot deep though it's no longer falling. Three buzzards sit bedraggled in the cedar tree in front of the bungalow, soggy with white caps of snow, shivering and losing some snow every now and then in irritable, uncomfortable shudders.

Rossiter is delighted this morning because he succeeds in getting some wood (stolen from outside the Chief Minister's door) to burn. But even the burning is extremely difficult, due to the design of these stoves which admit wood grudgingly though draw the line at oxygen as well.

'Glucose,' I say, offering him a biscuit by way of appreciation. A mittened Rossiter paw curls round the packet and begins to eat it from one end to the other.

'You see,' he blurts between munches, 'that's where we've gone wrong in the West. I mean, look at the chowdikar over there with his mates. There they are, sitting around the morning hookah, toking away on its leather tentacles and digging the dirt. You see so many people around here really taking time to get into the simple pleasures of life. Take the Chief next door – that's the sound of a contented man.'

Loud and regular snoring vibrates behind our bedroom wall as it has been for about ten hours. Rossiter harbours no ill-feelings about yesterday, indeed, in a way it is forgotten. He has a simple facility of moving from despair to contentment with great speed which is a huge asset on this journey. I watch his jaw moving rhythmically, pulping biscuits beneath his Kashmiri tea-cosy hat, as he continues his time-and-motion study of civilization.

It's five thousand feet up to the pass from here which will almost certainly be blocked, so we'll have to stay here a day at least. Overhead, a dirty leaden sky promises more snow. For a while we discuss the problem of being caught out by snows we were assured would not come until December and momentarily consider taking a bus before deciding to wait and attempt the pass, come what may.

During the day the weather clears and the snow begins to melt a little, but Khanibal is in the Vale, on the plain of Kashmir, even though it's still several thousand feet above sea-level. What is happening up on the pass is anyone's guess. I mean that quite literally, since every one we ask offers a different opinion with equal conviction.

However, the next morning is quite clear and we decide to risk it, feeling much rested and with Rossiter's cold on the wane. As we leave the chowkidar rushes out to demand 235 rupees for two nights stay with food. The food was good but £17 seems a little steep to say the least. We bargain fruitlessly on the verandah in the frosty air. When we refuse to go above 80 rupees, the chowkidar threatens to go and wake up the Chief, who is still in residence, still snoring. Thinking our anxiety to be out over the pass as early as possible in the day precludes getting entangled with the rudely awakened Chief, we pay up and immediately regret it, falling for what was almost certainly a completely empty threat.

While I sterilize our drinking-water, Rossiter has quite a lot to say about chowkidars. We pedal off into the slush, glad to be on the road again. Two thousand miles further on, Rossiter will still be finding new things to say about the chowkidar at the Khanibal Dak Bungalow.

From Khanibal to the pass is a long, hard pull of twenty-eight miles and with this uppermost in our minds, we decide to halt in the roadside village of Quazigund, which lies at the very edge of the Vale of Kashmir, before the climbing begins. As we enter the village, an old man, completely naked, is breaking the ice of a muddy pond for his morning wash. He has to compete feebly with some ducks and geese for the water, muddy and brown, with which he washes himself, vulnerable and alone.

We breakfast on omelettes, chai and stale glucose biscuits at a dhaba which calls itself 'The National Hotel' for reasons nobody can explain. Nobody speaks English, that's certain enough. Next door is the butcher's which smells foul even in the relative hygiene of a frosty morning. Every now and then a hand throws lumps of steaming entrails into the gutter for the dogs. No dogs though, this morning, so all the more for the ravens to descend upon, feathers glistening in the light, croaking with bloody satisfaction. It seems the butcher slaughters on the premises.

By the foot of the pass, the far side of the village, I count my ninth crashed lorry of the morning. They have run off the straight flat road into the frozen paddies, and this road is littered with them in various stages of decomposition, rust or cinders. It's as if the drivers lose all concentration after the hairpins of the passes on the way into Kashmir. But this whole stretch of road to Jammu is notorious even in a country where mass-killings in coach and lorry crashes are considered almost a routine form of death. The following is a small yellowing cutting which Rossiter, for some reason, keeps tucked close to him in his wallet:

Twenty-six people were killed yesterday and sixty-one injured when two buses plunged from the Jammu-Srinagar highway. The vehicles fell over two hundred feet into a ravine.

Unfortunately, bribes can take care of details like driving tests and licences and with no tachograph and huge delivery distances on poor roads, lorry drivers are often exhausted at the wheel. The same is often true of bus drivers.

For us, this means having swift reactions once we leave the flat and begin the long climb out of Kashmir. Fortunately, the road has been cleared of snow by the small army of gangers employed to do the job – it's a useful supplement for the long months when nothing much can be done on the land. Because the road is barely wide enough for a lorry to pass, we have to pull off into the snow banked up at the roadside. For the next hour we are constantly stopping at intervals. Finally we have to wait almost an hour for a colossal convoy of army lorries to pass, hammering their way back 'to India'. Thick black smoke billows out from each truck creating a long smudge as the convoy of two hundred or more snakes its way up the mountainside ahead.

When the last one has finally passed, we wait again to let them get clear and then begin pumping our pedals up the first of several series of hairpins. As we climb the Vale opens out behind us and the weather improves until the cloud has lifted sufficiently for us to see several miles down the intricate networks of contoured steps marking the walls of miles of frozen paddy. At one hairpin bend a lorry squeezes alongside Rossiter and a sinewy arm of a Sikh driver darts out with two apples for him, without stopping. We munch and watch the lifting cloud further reveal our last sight of Kashmir.

On the four-hour climb to the tunnel at the pass, the Beacon Highway Patrol (who are responsible for maintaining this stretch of mountain road) are beginning to wax lyrical about the dangers of driving along it. Large stone sign-posts, hand-painted, declare:

SPEED-KINGS MURDER AND KILL,
LEAVING FAMILY TO GRIEVE AT WILL

and, further up the climb, in more seductive mood:

RIDE SMOOTHLY OVER MY CURVES

Just before we reach the Jarwarhar Tunnel a large sign exhorts the driver:

IF MARRIED TO SPEED – DIVORCE HER!

I somehow can't see this approach going down too well on the verges of the M1 or the New Jersey Turnpike.

A little after midday, the road levels and we are faced with the twin entrances of the Jarwarhar Tunnel at the Banihal Pass, nearly twelve thousand feet above sea level. Fifty yards or so from the entrance, I stop and wait for Rossiter who has yet to appear round the last bend. I take out an old envelope and begin scribbling a few thoughts. We have reached the pass we last crossed by bus on the way into Kashmir and I can feel the end of the first palpable stage of the journey has been reached.

Suddenly, as Rossiter pulls up behind me, a jeep approaches from the direction of the tunnel. Then, after what seems like only a moment, four soldiers leap out and come up to us pointing their rifles. I hear the snow crunch beneath their boots. One of them, the commanding officer, suddenly pulls out a revolver, flicks the catch and levels it at my face. At once I feel warm and extremely heavy. Then another gun is pointed at Rossiter. Nobody speaks. We stand about looking at each other with the mist descending again, blowing in freezing clots over the tunnel entrance. I can hear my heart pounding in my ears.

Then, in a movement of pure and utter relief, the revolver is lowered and the officer steps up, grabs my envelope and throws it in a ball down into the snow. He motions us through the tunnel, still without saying anything and we need no second invitation to get out of Kashmir.

Still wondering what the hell is going on and why, we find ourselves half a mile into the tunnel without lights, quite unable to see where we are going. Stuck in here, there is no alternative but to go straight back to the soldiers who looked, minutes ago, as if they were going to shoot us. Rossiter is incensed and invisible. 'Told you we should have brought lights,' I hear him say, 'this is suicidal ... idal,' says Rossiter, echoing down the tunnel. 'Are you trying to kill us?' Still considering that one, I head back to the light and the soldiers.

By the time we emerge we are soaked and totally out of breath – a combination of altitude and fright. Fortunately, the jeepful of soldiers has continued its way down to Kashmir and those left to guard the tunnel are much less enthusiastic about weapons. In a few minutes we are able to hitch a ride through the tunnel in the second of the day's army convoys.

On the other side it's as if the fear, the greyness and the freezing mist of Kashmir never existed. Brilliant sunshine lights up the snowfields, dazzling against the high blue-black mountain sky. This physical change brings on the most overwhelming sense of deliverance and for a long while we sit in silence in the snow, tears in our eyes.

Relief changes into heady euphoria as we push off into twenty-seven miles of total, freewheeling, downhill beauty. On every bend a new view of the Chenab Valley opens below us, a gleaming mass of snow and rock cascading into the contoured ridges of the highest, abandoned paddies. Overhead an eagle screams, taut on the slide of a mountain thermal. The surface is good tarmac and the cold mountain air feels like it could file your face down to the bone.

After an hour or so we are down at the edge of the snowline. Water rushes over the surface in exuberant glittering flashfloods and on the valley floor herds of goats are mooching aimlessly across the bare brown winter fields, ant-like and absorbed. Between rocks as big as houses, some torrents are frozen into palaces and pinnacles of clear ice at the road's edge, waters caught in their last leap by the stealthy creep of winter.

At Banihal we stop but are unable to eat much for the sheer excitement of the last few hours. We bash out various theories as to why the incident happened the way it did at the tunnel and decide that guarding a tunnel (which is strategically important because it's the only land-route into Kashmir from the rest of India) must be mindwarpingly dull – and the temptation to throw one's weight around once in a while all but overpowering.

We continue downhill all afternoon, always close to the Chenab River which becomes more of a torrent the more it's compressed into a gorge as the valley becomes increasingly narrow. Between its rock walls trees hang out at precarious angles. All along these rock faces and among the trees, troupes of macaques are feeding – babies clinging to the bellies of mothers clinging to the branches of trees clinging to crevices for a roothold. It seems a precarious world – but the macaques are now almost constant companions for the next three hundred miles through the Himalayan foothills. As we near them they chatter nervously and flick the whites of their eyelids at us.

At Ramban, the map says, there is a P.W.D. (Public Works Department) resthouse. When we arrive in the dusty courtyard of this place, it's all a bit too much for the chowkidar and his cronies, who literally fall about the place screaming and gasping in fits of giggles the like of which I've never seen before or since in India. It's quite hard just to stand about, waiting until somebody has finished laughing at you. Eventually, he tells us in Hindi that the resthouse is totally booked. But, he adds, choking back eddies of mirth, we can sleep in his office if we like. And, naturally, there's not a lot of choice in Ramban.

The office lurks behind a wooden door that was once painted green in the good old days when it was attached to a hinge. It leans against the lintel and a chicken comes out through the gap this leaves. Rossiter goes in to investigate. There is the sudden, unmistakable sound of disturbed chickens. Rossiter emerges with feathers on his head and shoulders. 'Does this have to happen every time we try and find somewhere to sleep?'

'Well? What's it like in there?' I ask, giggling unwisely.

'It's full of chicken shit, that's what it's like. It's an office for chickens.'

But the chowkidar will have none of this. He leaps up to Rossiter and starts plucking feathers from him. He then gestures inside the office for us to look. He points out an old exercise book and says 'office' firmly.

'I don't believe this,' sighs Rossiter, carefully placing his sunburnt face in his dirty hands. 'Do these people do this kind of thing deliberately? We spend the entire day ploughing through psychopathic squaddies half-way up the Himalaya so that we can bed down in a pile of stale bantam guano when there are three perfectly decent rooms twenty yards away. I bet Rajiv doesn't have this kind of hassle.'

For some reason the comparison of himself and India's incumbent dynastic ruler is peculiarly satisfying to Rossiter in moments of duress and always seems to afford him immediate relief.

Anyhow, sheer dogged persistence drives the chowkidar to put us into a reserved room on the understanding that we'll move out if the reserver ever comes along. He never does, which awakens us to an interesting precedent.

Across the valley from our room, the ridges are quite soon in crisp silhouette against the greeny-yellow of the low western sky at sunset, which changes through purple and red to almost black overhead. After the sun has disappeared altogether a magnificent afterglow lights up the whole western sky bloody for nearly an hour. If things go wrong during the day in this country, there is always the grandeur of sunset to look forward to on nights like tonight, sipping tray-tea as the crickets begin to chirrup their way through the darkness.

Having been up over the highest pass at the tunnel, and two more in as many days since then, my rear wheel seems no more out of line than when we first discovered it in Sonamarg. Despite Rossiter's long and high eulogies on mountain bikes, our wheels do seem to be holding together so far, but the road has been tarmac since Srinagar except for landslide sections which rarely last more than a mile.

We leave the main Jammu-Srinagar highway at Udhampur and begin making our way east. At once we are out onto a road which varies constantly between being a rough track, an uneven concrete pavement and a patchwork of tarmac and potholes. It is also suddenly very warm, just two days after leaving Ramban.

Within a few miles we are into an area of barren hills topped with rock pavements, sudden hot gorges and cacti growing in clumps up the sides. In these gullies no wind or shade ever seems to occur and the temperature is well into the nineties. Already, still several thousand feet up in the foothills, water is becoming very important, and yet the sight of snow to the left, the north, is constantly with us.

In one of these ravines we suddenly come upon a troupe of about fifty macaques, most of which come bounding up to within a few feet of us, chattering and eye-lidding. As more of them arrive, I suddenly remember the pot-seller in Udhampur who warned us that the monkeys carry rabies. The money we forked out for rabies jabs is beginning to seem a more worth-while investment than it did in England. Realizing they're interested in the bananas in my front pannier, I hurl them as far as possible behind me. They are pursued by the assembled company and grabbed almost as they touch down, in a cloud of dust and scattered gravel.

The day takes us to Ramkot, at the end of which we have made a little over thirty miles in ten hours' 'riding', much of it pushing over stretches of rough road which is sheer drudgery – you can't even look at the scenery. All day the land has been very sparsely cultivated, a few stony fields of maize with cactus hedges and very few people along the road. We frequently stop and are left totally alone, which is not a common experience in India.

At Ramkot, Omparkash Kaguria – the village artist – is sitting under a large banyan (practically the first tree we have seen all day) as if expecting us. There have been only a couple of lorries on this road today and we are something of a novelty, as Omparkash is quick to point out. 'Never before white people in our place! Please – you are our guests in the resthouse,' and he gestures lavishly at the pink-washed stone bungalow covered in bougainvillea which overlooks the straw roofs of the village huts.

We follow him inside – no problems with the chowkidar tonight – and are just about installed when a good proportion of the entire village population drops by to see us and touch our fair (that is, sunburned and sweaty) skin. We know when we are in one of the more remote regions in India by the degree to which interest in our bodies overrides interest in our bicycles. Children – there are always so very many of them – crowd in at the doorway, fear of us overcoming curiosity only at the last moment.

Everybody in the village speaks Dogri, but Omparkash has a few words of English and some Hindi – but we can do a lot with a smile and with the fascination our size causes. I'm six feet four and Rossiter is, shall we say, losing weight already. In combination we must look to these people like something from a timewarp and so we're humbled by the kindness we encounter in places like this, so genuine and straightforward.

Later in the evening one of the villagers brings us a small pot of kuttar – the local relish – to eat with the dum alu and rice which the chowkidar cooks up. Kuttar is a relish of marrow and chilli boiled into a substance of extreme spicy heat. Personally, I love hot food, but tonight the kuttar is altogether too much and only the pot full of curd (brought out by the chowkidar in a move of inspired brilliance) saves our respective insides from turning into a molten mess.

'Mmmmmmm,' purrs Rossiter, tears in his eyes but an Englishman to the core, 'this is wonderful.' He nods appreciatively, whereupon another large dollop lands on his plate.

That night Rossiter sees more of the lavatory (the garden) than he does of our bed. I, however, sleep soundly through the night underneath the large fan-shaped web of a light-brown spider whose legs would easily outstretch a saucer. It is the first thing I see in the morning.

Whilst it is impossible for us to bicycle across Punjab, we are faced with the necessity of crossing two small areas of the troubled state to get to Delhi. The first of these comes the next day. By mid-afternoon we find ourselves following a huge nullah fanning its way ever wider onto the plains. We stop at Dyala Chek for some much-needed glasses of fresh-crushed sugar-cane: a clear, syrupy liquid, not exactly refreshing, but full of energy. At Dyala Chek we hit the main inter-state highway, which means a tarmac surface for the next fifty miles across a part of Punjab, but also means coming off the road into the dust at regular intervals to let lorries pass by without being killed outright. For the last two days we have been pushing the bicycles as much as riding them and the surface of the main highway is a much appreciated luxury.

Along the dusty verges of the road long caravans of camels are shifting stacks of hay and maize. From behind they look like a series of walking haystacks in slow-swinging procession. In the road itself, as if to underline the Punjab troubles, there are convoys of jeeps, armoured cars and huge field guns – anti-aircraft guns perhaps – all heading into the state from the border which is ten miles or so ahead.

A mile or two from it, we stop and ceremonially burn any documents we have relating to the BBC. With the bicycles, cameras and recording gear we could pass ourselves off as some odd kind of cycle tourists, at a pinch, but with BBC documents pointing out who owns our tape-recorders and why, we could find ourselves in trouble up ahead.

At the border, trucks stand in long, haphazard queues, their loads being systematically checked over piece by piece at the octroi post – a large tree-trunk barrier weighted by a stone to lower or raise it across the road. The octroi is the symbol of the vast network of local and state taxation-points which slow the speed of goods transport and put up the prices in the bazaars. In a sense it's a vision of the turnpike age or a glimpse at the type of system from which we're told the French Revolution grew. Be that as it may, we pedal to the head of the queue and are surrounded at once by soldiers who point their old Enfield rifles at us and order us to show our papers.

'Where are you buying this things?' asks one, pulling out Rossiter's small cassette-recorder.

'Tottenham Court Road,' replies Rossiter, adding helpfully, 'just up from Centre Point on the left-hand side.'

I wonder momentarily whether this is pure foolhardiness, but the soldier seems satisfied in a blank sort of way. He grunts at us and waves us on. We push off and have gone about ten yards when there is a shout behind us. The officer who seems to be in charge of border security waves us back to him. 'You will certainly be arrested if you attempt to stay one night in Punjab State. Please get out of this state before night is falling. Goodbye.' They certainly do know how to make you feel welcome. We get our heads down and bowl along the smooth, tree-lined road, green fields stretching flat on either side and we do not stop until we reach the noisy, cramped bazaars of Pathankot. Here, at last, I can get my rear wheel straightened out in time for our coming loop back into the mountains through Himachal Pradesh, to avoid Punjab.

Pathankot is a filthy, ugly, ear-splittingly noisy place full of screaming klaxons and diseased dogs. At the Charand B. D. Gupta Bicycle Emporium Showhouse there is a man who takes off tyres with his bare hands and behaves like he emerged from the womb with a wheel-truing jig in his hands. It's a form of cyclist's psychotherapy to stand and watch the man go to it. Soon we're friends with Charand and his sons while his wife (not introduced, of course) brings out large amounts of chai and samosa. Of course, there is a crowd of two hundred or more to watch us eat but on this kind of a trip you really do have to get used to the idea of eating in public. The same is also true of squatting in public, in a country where the performance of one's bodily functions is not a matter for modesty. Privacy is not prized in India.

We're both soon embroiled in a discussion of the problems of Punjab. People here are very keen to know what we make of all the problems surrounding Amritsar and now the riots in Delhi and elsewhere after the assassination. On this part of the ride we tell people we are students, partly because of the safe neutrality of the label and partly because journalists are banned in Punjab.

Meanwhile, Charand's mechanic has fixed the wheel and we put it back on. I'm certain he's never seen a wheel like mine before, let alone a ten-speed bicycle, but it hardly matters and the wheel is true once again. It seems to me that this facility of getting something fixed, made or patched-up is the essence of Indian streets, lined with tiny workshops often not much bigger than an allotment hut. How often do you see anything actually being repaired or made in England? And again, it's very unusual here to get the 'Oh, we don't do that here', or the 'That'll take two weeks', which is a way of life at home.

Charand reminds us that it will be dark quite soon and we have to be out of the state, so we make our goodbyes and roll off down the state highway, smooth and straight. At dusk, twenty minutes later, we are at the border. After the octroi post a man appears, pursuing a large black pig. I ask him if there's anywhere to spend the night near here. He gives up his chase with evident relief, leaving his pig hurtling remorselessly towards Punjab.

'At Chakki, resthouse there is,' he says.

'Which way is Chakki?'

'You turn here rightside and go straight, then leftside here,' he jerks his thumb towards his throat, 'do not turn here and there and you are coming to resthouse. It is very near this place. There is no problem.'

Sometimes the directions you get given in India take a little teasing out. It's advisable to ask several people and pedal according to the concensus. But the pig-man is all we have and we only have him for a moment before he is off in the direction of his pig who can be heard in the gloom attacking a banana-seller's stall further down the road.

Predictably, when we eventually find it an hour later, (having retraced our pedals in three different directions), the resthouse is full. It is quite dark and we are both very tired, happy to take the buffalo-stable the chowkidar offers us as an alternative to sleeping rough with the mosquitoes that are always with you on the plains, it seems. As an alternative to sleeping rough it's not exactly sleeping smooth to be in two decrepit charpoys, the air thick with your own sweat and the smell of buffalo dung.

No matter – the chowkidar is clearly taking us under his wing and comes across the yard with a wonderful mutton curry and the most gritless rice we have eaten for days. He looks like some weird old egret stalking towards us, his stick-thin dark legs poking out of his once-white dhoti, his mouth and its one tooth stained blood-red with betel.

He brushes aside our thanks and leaves as Rossiter sinks at once into a deep slumber, the bulk of him slowly slipping through a hole in his charpoy, almost as if he were melting. For some reason I can't get to sleep at once and lie listening to the crickets, the brilliant moonlight filtering through the chinks in the wooden stable door. I'm absorbed by watching the small rat who lives here gnaw in a frenzy at the door. Eventually I get up and open it a little and see him dart out across the dusty courtyard, lit by a great orange moon.

Omelettes, chai, chapatti and – wonder of wonders – the first bucket of hot water we have splashed on ourselves for a fortnight are on hand shortly after our gentle chowkidar awakens us unasked at dawn, around six o'clock. He will not hear of any payment for providing us with food, shelter and the hot water. Clearly, the extortionate cut-and-thrust of career-chowkidardom is not for him. We eat, crouching on the smooth stone slab which, relatively free from dung, acts as our table as well.

Across the courtyard, between ourselves and the resthouse, a very old man, who turns out to be the father of the chowkidar, is squatting at one end of a rotting tree-trunk. His legs, thinner by far even than his son's, are drawn up insect-like against his dhoti. It's as if he has been there all night and all year as he somehow squats motionless, drawing the smoke from a bidi-stub into his concave cheeks, his crabby toes splayed beneath the folds of his dhoti to grip the log, his head bound up in the coils of a huge turban. A mynah settles for a moment next to him, flicks its glance at him and is off again. He sits on.

As we leave I force the chowkidar to take a pair of fleecy snow-boots I bought at some expense in Kashmir. Rossiter observes, however, that we've already been caught out once by snow and is singularly unimpressed. Throughout the business of packing up panniers and putting sterilizing tablets in our water bottles or checking spokes, the old man is there on his log, abandoned completely to another world, one of a thousand such figures who squat and dot the landscape they are a part of, all across the country. Timeless and motionless.

After the brief respite of the national highway, our road today takes us immediately back into the climbs of the battered, heat-shattered ravines of the foothills climbing steadily all day towards Dharamsala. Ahead of us, to the east, the snows along the Dhaudalar range rise dreamlike out of the purplish heat haze which begins as soon as the eastern sun turns white from the bloody dawn, rising ahead of us. It is only a little while ago that we were cursing the cold and longing to see the sun again and yet now our faces, necks and arms are sunburnt despite using the new-fangled super-protection ultra-barrier suntan lotion somebody succeeded in selling to Rossiter while his guard was down. Furthermore, Rossiter's cold has left his lips bearing a striking resemblance to the country we are cycling through today: pitted with deep cracks and wild ravines.

As well as this I feel absolutely no enthusiasm for moving on and have to stop regularly during the afternoon to discharge the contents of my stomach. If this happens near a village – as it does on two occasions – there are pariah dogs snapping up fiercely what I've deposited by the time I can straighten up. This is no throw-away society.

By early evening we have made it to the steps of the Dhaudalar hotel in Dharamsala, perched up along a high spur coming out from the colossal, silent wall of the Dhaudalar Mountains that seem to rise vertically up into their snowfields just behind the main street. The climb up here has left me feeling extremely wobbly inside and out. We are both covered in the inescapable Indian film of sweat and dust, sunburnt, peeling and exhausted. I am aware that I cannot focus on anything as I walk unsteadily into the entrance hall of the hotel. I really think I might be unwell. I vaguely hear Rossiter introduce us to the bored receptionist confidently as the Trans-India Cycle Expedition. He watches with distaste as we advance across the hallway.

At this point, ten days out, I have no thought for anything but a bed. But Rossiter proves unflappable and within what seems like minutes has a room sorted out and suddenly appears with a huge bowl of steaming hot porridge. By sunset I find myself able to sit out on the verandah overlooking the huge, rippling expanse of the Himachal Pradesh foothills and out beyond them a sunset such as only India can produce. Beside me there is the soothing hum and cadence of Rossiter. Tonight, he has something to say about fibre value, slow-release energy: in a word, porridge.

3

'It is not now as it hath been of yore'

Wordsworth

Because burly macaques chase each other all night over the noisy corrugated iron roof of the Dhaudalar Hotel, sleep tends to be a hit and miss affair. We miss. Nonetheless, tired or not, a couple of days' rest gives my stomach a chance to resume normal service while Rossiter brews regular instalments of porridge, in between sorties up to Macleod Ganj – the Tibetan village that straggles a high spur of the mountains above Dharamsala. It's here that the Dalai Lama has made his home in exile and Rossiter spends most of these two days talking to Tibetan refugees whose present situation upsets him considerably. Hearing these people's stories of what the Chinese have done to Lhasa since the invasion and the cynical way they are now opening up the Holy City to (wealthy) western tourists, it seems the Dalai Lama will not be persuaded back by the P.R.-conscious overtures of the Chinese.

On several of the shops that wind up the main street of Dharamsala's winding bazaar, there are signs – many weatherbeaten with age – saying, GIVE TIBET TO TIBETANS. In one tailor's shop, a baby has the slogan carefully embroidered onto his thick woollen tunic, and it's apparent you make the slogans to last. The Tibetans know that occupations do not retreat with the same speed as they took place.

But life continues and the Tibetans seem to have assimilated themselves in pockets all over India. The mauve-robed monks down from the monastery in Macleod Ganj tickle and play-fight each other while shopping in the bazaar. On the second night in the town we eat in one of the many Tibetan restaurants catering for tourists, while the owner's family sit at another table engrossed in a Hindi soap opera on Doordarshan, the Indian state-run television channel. They have plenty of time to watch too, for after the riots across northern India the tourist trade is still not picking up.

We check out of the Dhaudalar Hotel at dawn the next day. In the cold, piercing light of the mountain dawn few people are about and our sudden appearance sends three kites flapping into the air from the empty bus-stand where they were cleaning up. We speed due south, each moment edging further away from the wall of the Dhaudalar Mountains which stand so close to the town that you could almost touch them at this hour. The grey, raw, towering rockfaces trail plumes of cloud from their tops, turning dyed pink in the dawn light.

As we freewheel downhill for perhaps eight or ten miles into the Kangra Valley, we lose sight of the snowline for the first time in the journey. It's sad in a way, but also a great psychological boost to be going south along a good road, so very obviously away from the mountains.

By this stage of the ride a distinct division of labour has grown up imperceptibly between the two of us. 'Sterotabbing' – the act of filling our water bottles and dropping sterilization tablets into them, has habitually become something I do. This is also, incidentally, our one rule of hygiene and so long as you like the taste of swimming pools, it seems to be standing us in good stead so far.

When it comes to punctures (only two to date), it is Rossiter who takes control, grunting, levering and calling for tools like an exasperated surgeon. It's up to me, therefore, to talk to the crowds which will appear within seconds of stopping for a repair, even when you are totally sure you are in completely secluded country. It's curious the way this involuntary demarcation arises, this making of habits and routines by instinct.

Through the Kangra, both road and terrain are kind to us and we catch up and swing past trucks on the downhill bends, the drivers hooting and waving. For most of the way down the valley the ravine is dotted with troops of macaques who chatter at us testily. Today though, they are far tamer than usual as this road is quite busy and they'll let us approach within a few feet at which point thoughts of bites, rabies and the incredible speed at which the average macaque can move, begin to crowd out our capacity for wonder.

Leaving the small town of Kangra, my confidence in our tyres takes a dent when Rossiter completely blows one out with an unexpected explosion. For some time Rossiter attempts to put on a new tube and spare tyre while lecturing the crowd that assembles on the finer points of vulcanization as a method of puncture repair. It's the same lecture as he gave me a few nights ago and although he does not quite seem to realize the extent of the damage, he wades in valiantly. It seems to me his message is not going home, but he is saved by the discovery that the spare inner-tube also has a puncture and soon the demonstration is underway: 'You see,' he says to the English-speaking contingent of one. 'It's just like welding rubber. Look at that now, you can't even feel the join, can you?'

The contingent strokes the rubber patch silently and intently. At once, as if in a conjuring trick, the patch comes unstuck, a gooey, glistening failure. Rossiter seizes it with a look of sheer disbelief. The sweat drips from his forehead in the midday heat. The small crowd has gone silent, for the sight of a grown man undone by his own vulcanization is an ugly one indeed. A Tibetan edges forward, offering Rossiter a banana, which he consumes while the two small boys who have wheedled their way to the front, paw and chatter over the sick tube. Rossiter fits another spare tube and for some miles to come has quite a lot to say about the man from the vulcanization puncture repair company who sponsored him on the journey with five hundred individual repair kits.

Early in the afternoon we reach Jawala Mukki where the Himachal Pradesh Tourist Development Corporation have erected a fancy new hotel largely to cater for pilgrims to the famous Hindu temple here. Heavy wooden doors embossed with the logo of the H.P.T.D.C. are in evidence and a great quantity of smoked glass. However, there is trouble in the lavatories and their smell in the restaurant is overpowering. To attempt to smother it, vast bunches of flowers have been placed on each table – but they have to go when the food arrives. Having talked only this morning about how much of a health risk meat could be, we're soon tucking into a chicken masala (having until now blithely eaten raw, unwashed vegetables in the salads dished up at any roadside dhaba we should happen across).

Food stops are always occasions for poring over our variety of inaccurate maps and on today's reckoning we'll try to reach Hamirpur twenty-five miles further on. It seems an easy distance until the road degenerates abruptly as soon as we leave Jawala. For the next five hours it is little more than a dusty track (often a little less) and it's inclined to kink and meander in deference to large boulders poking up through the ground in the middle of it, for no apparent reason. As we edge along a narrow valley cut by the Beas River below, the main traffic has become long caravans of donkeys loaded down with wicker panniers full of raw slates hacked in the tiny quarries that dot the valley side. The drivers yodel at us with an enthusiasm for our ride that we do not share, at times like this, when there is more pushing than riding to be done. And now we have come down several thousand feet from Dharamsala and are trudging along the sunny side of the valley, trapped in its oppressive heat.

Finally, by early evening, the road picks up into tarmac as suddenly as it turned to dust, and it's almost a relief to cycle up the series of hairpins that lead us up over a 'ghat section' before dropping slightly into Hamirpur. From the valley of the Beas River we climb into the cool of a magnificent old pine forest, so lush after the cacti and barrenness of the lower slopes. We get to the top of the ridge right on cue for the daily display of the sunset – only when the fiery afterglow sits low in the western sky and we are descending the other side, do we realize how tired we are after this afternoon's push.

At such times there is an unalterable law of bicycling which runs along the following lines: the distance between you and food, shelter etc. increases in direct proportion to the intensity of fatigue at the last recorded stop. Hamirpur demonstrates the principle unequivocally and we finally blunder into its candlelit bazaar more than two hours after dark.

All you can see in the main street of the village are those stalls still open and trading by candlelight or occasional oil-lamps. Pigs, dogs, goats and chickens seem to be running into things all over the place including my front wheel as we push the bicycles along. The soundtrack of a Bombay 'masala movie' screams out at ear-splitting volume from a trumpet-shaped loudspeaker. The cows are settling down to doze in the street while two ancient bullock carts become hopelessly entangled trying to squeeze round one somnolent cow. Recriminations fly, bullocks snort and stamp and the wooden wheels creak hopelessly.

At the road's edge, beyond the filth of the gutter, the scent of oil comes from huge shallow frying pans where samosas sizzle with tiny onions fried in spiced batter. Elsewhere alu-dum and alu gobi steam away in huge black pot-bellied cauldrons. The cooks hiss, cat-call and whoop to catch our attention, for few white people ever wander this way and business for two empty stomachs is brisk. We stop awhile at one of the stalls for chai, while Rossiter laughs at my attempts to get an omelette fried without any onion in it. This is considered the height of eccentricity by the chai-wallah and onlookers who know that onions are as indispensable to an omelette as eggs are.

Away from the chai-stall, though, there is little interest in us and the atmosphere of the town is oddly tense. We decide to find the resthouse as soon as possible as we're both very tired. I lead the way. In a moment or two I turn to say something to Rossiter and see that he is some way back surrounded by four men in civilian clothing. They are armed.

The one in charge turns to me when I approach. 'Good evening,' he says, fingering his holster self-consciously. 'We are from the Intelligence Service. There is election at this time. The situation in this area is currently very nervous. I am advising you to come this way please.' He motions up a dark alley and I stand still. Rossiter goes into the alley accompanied by two of the Intelligence in their loud checked jackets and high-waisted flares.

At this point it all looks suspect to me, but before I've time to say anything, the same Intelligence man who just spoke asks for my papers. The others stop in the alleyway: 'You show me your papers otherwise we don't go – you could be anybody.' I tell him without really realizing this is a pretty stupid way to carry on with four armed men, no matter where they say they're from. 'You are coming with us,' the same man repeats. For some reason this continues to look unreasonable from my point of view and when I again insist on seeing their papers they turn as a group and troop off. They say they're going to the police station and will see us later. We're amazed.

'Bloody hell,' says Rossiter, as we stare blankly after them.

Tired, filthy and now nervous, we eventually end up pedalling back out of town the way we came in, in order to try and get into the Circuit House. The resthouse in town is hopeless, occupied by the local Congress (I) entourage, in town for the election: candidate, fixers, jeeps, lawyers, hustlers, jeep mechanics and a cook. By some miracle the Circuit House has a benign and crustacean-like chowkidar whose kitchen is his shell. He's nervous anywhere out of it but happy to have two filthy, alien guests for the night. Why the Congress (I) are not here, I cannot imagine, for Circuit Houses are well up the pecking order of government accommodation and therefore prodigiously difficult to get into if you're as illegitimate as we are.

For the first time since the high passes my legs are really aching but tonight there is the unbelievable luxury of hot water – well, at least for a while there is. Goodness knows what state the bicycles are in after the day's battering. This will be one of those many nights when an examination of them will get left for the morning after.

An early night, however, is not to be. At the point of drifting off into delicious sleep with a clean body that doesn't smell, for once, we're startled by a loud knock at the door. In troop five total strangers followed shortly after by the chowkidar with tea. They're very curious about the ride and for about twenty minutes Rossiter and myself exchange anecdotes with them. Only when they begin to show an unhealthy interest in Sikhs does the penny finally drop in our brains: the Intelligence are back – only this time a more dapper and so I suppose more senior bunch. After about half an hour of banter it's abundantly obvious that we know who they are and why they are here. The boss takes a profound slurp of tray-tea and introduces himself at last: 'My friends. I must introduce myself at this moment. I am Mr Sengupta, Intelligence Service and I am congratulating you for your actions with my men earlier this evening. Very cautious. Very wise.' At this point he unveils his identification card. Apparently it is common for people in this area to go about impersonating the Intelligence in order to relieve people of their belongings at gun-point.

What they're really after is anything we may be able to tell them about the Sikh community in Britain, not Himachal Pradesh. Once again we are made aware of just how sensitive the authorities here are to the activities of the self-styled Khalistan separatists in Britain. With the activities of Mr Jagjit Chohgan Singh much publicized at home, I sit here praying none of them will show any interest in looking through our panniers containing BBC recording equipment and documents. The BBC is seen by many as a centre of anti-Indian sentiment for showing celebrating Sikhs in London after the assassination of Indira Gandhi. Many people have mentioned this to us in villages already and the Intelligence are not long in mentioning the organization by name.

Eventually, though, enough is enough of this and, having displayed complete political ignorance, we make noises about being very tired indeed. Mr Sengupta and the lads take the hint towards midnight and shuffle off much enriched by the news that there are Sikhs in Leicester and that Wales is not a district of London. They file out, wishing us well in turn for the rest of our journey.

It is a wonderful night's sleep – one of those where you wake up early but feel a sense of achievement merely by feeling so refreshed. We have turned east since we entered the Beas valley yesterday and today we continue east in what is really a vast and hilly detour to avoid Punjab. I suppose that on aggregate we must be dropping lower as we move away from the high ranges but there are still plenty of stiff climbs ahead of us.

By about nine o'clock we've come about fifteen miles along a fairly smooth tarmac-ed road, into a greener, lower area than Hamirpur, where tiny paddies step their way up the hillsides, the biggest of them still smaller than a tennis court. We stop for a breakfast of parathas, chillis and chai at a dhaba full of ancient charpoys, their hessian slats worn smooth by countless dozing bodies like that of the truck-driver snoring in the sun this morning. Inside, under the canvas awning, there are lots of very comfortable wickerwork chairs with high backs rimmed with old bicycle tyres. Whilst we eat, two camels wander by, on the scrounge, but the Sikh dhaba-wallah knows them of old and darts out hissing menacingly at the shambling duo. They stop and look at him for a moment, pouting and affronted, before wandering idly off, lofty, superior and apparently unowned.

One of the main hazards of the day – beyond aimless camels which continue to appear out of nowhere – is the numerous small tunnels which take our road through narrow ridges. All of them are, like the mighty Jarwarhar Tunnel out of Kashmir, completely unlined inside and because the terrain here is loose and gravelly it's common to see bits of the roof fall in in front of or behind you. On one occasion a pile of pebbly gravel and dust falls between Rossiter and myself as we pedal through. Hearing the crash much amplified by the tunnel, I can see nothing but dust behind me. Some time passes before the reassuring sound of a subterranean Rossiter reaches my ears:

'Good God! This is extraordinary ... absolutely something else again ... Amazing ... Hey! Are you still there?'

From now on, until we stop for food in the middle of the day, Rossiter has plenty of things to say about the state of tunnel engineering in Himachal Pradesh, not all of them complimentary.

Whilst eating what seems to be our staple diet in this region, alu gobi, rice and chapatti, the Indian speciality of cricket by transistor radio is much in evidence. One young man holds the radio high above his head at maximum volume while a crowd of forty, fifty or more gathers round as the First Test crackles away on All IndiaRadio, live from Bombay. By all accounts the Indian spinners are making mincemeat of England, which makes for much glee when we turn up unannounced to eat nearby. Even the crowd around the bicycles dwindles to single figures while the local comedian declares with an expression of mischief: 'Ah hah! Great Britain, but no longer Great!!'

Everybody laughs and with a flick of a switch the commentary is changed to English so that we can follow it to the detriment of almost everybody else present. Even in so small a village as this it's astonishing how many of the English cricket team past and present are known and loved. 'Jafferee Boycut' and 'Iyam Bowtharm' are bandied about, for our approval.

After a long conference with most of the village as to the best way to reach Bilaspur, we're on the road again. You very quickly learn in India that when it comes to direction it's the concensus rather than the personal opinion that you should follow. It's common for people to tell you what they feel you want to hear, rather than what is true. Never ask a question which can be answered 'yes' or 'no'. This is because 'yes' may mean: 'No, but you really are way, way out and I'm not going to be the one who gives you the bad news.' Or, it could mean: 'I don't have a clue.' It could very likely mean: 'Good God! What planet are you from then?' Finally, there's always the tantilizing possibility that 'yes' could actually mean: 'Yes'.

Having got the majority verdict we climb down over the early part of the afternoon to the Bakra Dam, one of the many recent super-dams the government have built in the Himalayan foothills to see people through the rigours of the summer and the fickleness of the monsoon that follows it – or should do. It's pleasing to see water after mile upon mile of brown, eroded hillsides dotted with patchy yellow grass, occasional cacti and herds of marauding goats.

The bridge that takes us over the lake created by the dam attracts a very great deal of hype from the Public Works Department signwriters who declare it to be the highest bridge in Asia at a little over eighty feet, which claim we both find a little hard to credit. Like many bridges in India, there are large notices telling you not to photograph the bridge or any part thereof and larger notices still, giving the passer-by great quantities of information about the bridge. I've often wondered if stopping and taking down the details lovingly given of date of completion, length, breadth, height, estimated and actual cost, name, contractor and so on, would constitute the same breach of security as the taking of a photo. But I've never tried it.

Pondering this, we rest on the bridge awhile, dropping pieces of banana for the macaques living among the supporting girders. Below them a large pied kingfisher sits taut and ready above the brackish green water. He ignores the clatter above, poised for anything impaleable in the water below.

At Bilaspur the chowkidar of the P.W.D. resthouse won't let us in under any circumstances and so we make a tactical retreat and attempt to telephone friends in Delhi to let them know we are still on the road. At the telephone exchange there are three rooms upstairs and a potter's workshop downstairs. In two of the upstairs rooms it is hard to make out much since everything is covered in thick brown clay dust. But in the third a clerk is haranguing a telephone receiver and hammering away on a morse-code button. He does not look up as we enter.

After ten minutes or so and no let up from his hand or mouth, I make a move towards one of the two telephones not in use. The telephonist freezes momentarily and then screams: 'Nahin, nahin, nahin, nahin!' with an air of not-very-latent violence. He begins shrieking down the receiver, banging it intermittently with his free hand whilst belting out the morse with the other. Perhaps some emergency is taking place, perhaps this is normal service.

After another ten minutes of this Rossiter can stand no more and asks, 'CAN I CALL NEW DELHI, PLEASE?', shouting to be heard above the remorseless noise of the operator. Another two minutes of tapping and bawling go by and then it's all over.

The telephonist leans forward, removes his thick black-rimmed spectacles and says 'No.'

In the time it takes for us to begin a reply he is back hammering and shouting. We beat the second retreat in under an hour.

Having eaten at a dhaba in the bazaar, we're feeling fortified for a second assault on the P.W.D. and this time encounter no problem from a different ostensible chowkidar who merely has us telephone the P.W.D. office to request permission to stay there. Local calls seem to work more successfully and we are soon showering away the dirt from a bucket we bring each other from the well, as none of the shiny new tap arrangements seem interested in delivering any water in our bathroom.

During the evening an earnest student called Malik calls on us. He says his cousin saw us arrive in the bazaar and he wanted to meet us and for some time we talk about his future prospects. He's from Assam in north-eastern India, left home after his mother died and came to Bilaspur to live with his uncle who knows people who work in engineering here and from whom, if Malik gets at least ninety-five per cent in all of his forthcoming exams, he might just be able to get a job.

'But my programme is very hard for me since I have to work from six a.m. until college at nine a.m. and from after college until midnight. It is necessary and there is no other way for me since I do not have money.'

'How would that help you in particular?' I ask.

'With money it is possible to achieve even highest marks. It is cheating, but this is the way for many people in this place.' He gestures vaguely out of the window. I feel as if we're intruding on his 'programme' but it's clear very early on that this is a healthy break from the drudgery for Malik and for us it's good to get beyond the endless question and answer sessions which are inevitable on this kind of journey.

We meet Malik again next morning as he's invited us round

for breakfast at his uncle's house (his uncle is away on business) which is decorated with very large posters of kittens with bows and a large array of representations of Krishna. It very soon turns out that the man who turned us away from the P.W.D. yesterday is Malik's cook – or rather his uncle's – and very sheepish he is too, to see us again in such unexpected circumstances. He circumvents the awkwardness of this by piling our plates with an immense amount of chilli-filled omelettes and a stack of parathas.

Malik assures us as we leave that all will be plain sailing today and that we can look forward to a smooth run down to the plains or as he puts it, 'Later you are looking from the ghat and all will be laid out before you.'

With that we are off into the thick morning mist rising slowly off the Bhakra Lake which comes close to the town. After only a few minutes an elephant suddenly appears on the road in front of us out of the mist, silent and ghostly. He plods past us in his unhurried, aldermanic gait while his owner – a Sadhu – perches on top fast asleep between his huge ears. The Sadhu is swathed in his saffron cloak up to his eyes and rocks gently from side to side with the elephant's motion, clinging like an enormous orange limpit. They go by and are engulfed in the mist while up ahead the first rays of the day's sun are penetrating the valley and its cloud, away in front of us.

After an hour or so of riding, we find Malik's grasp of the local geography is tenuous, to put it mildly. The road descends to a bridge now visible through the mist, about two miles ahead at the bottom of the valley. After that it crosses the bridge into a series of hairpins. I count twenty-three before they go into the hanging low cloud. Your mood dictates your approach to roads like this, I think. Sometimes you feel like getting your head down and pumping up the hairpins or again you may feel like taking it slow.

I favour the former today but Rossiter evidently feels like a gentler approach and pretty soon we're a long way apart, up the first zig-zags of the road. At the end of the first series of hairpins I'm surprised to see a chai-stall and a tailor's shop, miles from anywhere. I sit down for a cup, leaving my bicycle against an oil drum so Rossiter will see it when he comes by.

Ten minutes later he hasn't appeared. Twenty minutes go by, no Rossiter. After half an hour he has still not gone by, unless, just possibly, when I wasn't watching in which case he would surely have seen the bicycle. My first thought is that he's had a puncture – or something worse – to stop him. I wait by the road and stop the first two vehicles that pass, a truck and a bus – but they haven't seen him. I yell as loud as possible from the top of the hairpins and get two echoes back off the far side of the valley from which all mist has now gone. At any other time that echo would have been a thing of wonder in its clarity. Two Tibetan boys appear, ragged and covered with old sores, who point up the road. I have no choice but to believe them. I point at my watch but they can't tell the time. I begin pounding away up the next set of hairpins.

After a mile or so of climbing I meet a group of Tibetan refugees mending the road which now becomes an uncyclable track of dust more than a foot deep. Binding a tee-shirt round my mouth against the dust, I push the bike on after they tell me Rossiter is ahead. At every corner of a hairpin I yell ahead but nothing comes back and after two hours or more the combination of this and the dust makes me lose my voice. It's now doubly difficult to ask in my limited Hindi if Rossiter is ahead although all the roadmenders say he is.

They all say he's just a few minutes ahead but by now I'm beginning to feel that there's some sinister conspiracy afoot. Rossiter, meanwhile, is going through the dust as fast as I am, convinced for at least the first hour and a half of this that I'm ahead. All the time, in the back of his mind (as in mine) lurks the feeling that there's something ridiculously comic about losing each other on a mountain. At bottom, there's the utter stupidity of it – my fault – in losing each other in the first place when there are potentially so many other hazards to mess things up: it's my impatience again.

Three hours after I stopped for chai, I get to the summit of this mountain which Malik didn't seem to know existed. I'm so thirsty my tongue feels like sand-paper, my eyes are blood-shot with dust and the salt of dried sweat and my legs shake uncontrollably when I stop. Another gang of roadmenders comes slowly into my blurred vision – they're pointing ahead without me even asking. I reckon I must look a right state. Even now though, I refuse the lift to Swarghat which I'm offered when I stop a truck driver to ask how far it is, while resting a moment at the summit of the mountain. The idea of cycling across this country the whole way is evidently burnt rather deeply into my brain. Fortunately, the driver says it is only a few miles and now the road has stopped climbing, it is tarmac-ed once again. Rossiter has to be waiting there, he has to be.

The importance of finding him at Swarghat lies in the fact that the road divides here and the main part goes to Chandigarh on a metalled highway, the other fork goes off down a track to Hinganghat. If Rossiter takes the larger, more obvious road, he'll wind up in Punjab very shortly and in prison shortly after that when they find he's got a tape-recorder, BBC papers and a camera in his panniers. To make matters worse, I am carrying all our maps and most of our tools.

Suddenly the junction comes into view with its very makeshift octroi post – and no sign of Rossiter. I stop at it staring in blank despair and wondering vaguely, where on earth this leaves the whole expedition. As my brain begins to work hopelessly into the means of search and communication in a place a long way from the nearest local telephone, Rossiter suddenly catapults out of a banana-seller's. 'Shit,' he sighs. 'Am I glad to see you.' Rossiter has remained a little calmer than me it seems, or maybe has had time to cool down at least physically, if not emotionally. 'Look, come in here out of the sun where it's cool,' he motions to a stone-built shed by the octroi, 'I've got some walnuts here, there's good curd opposite in the dhaba and there's a guy up the road with some guavas which he might sell us – oh, and the boy from the shed next door is bringing chai in a sec – just brewing up. The soldiers here have got cold water if you want to wash.' It's music to my ears to hear Rossiter once again sizing up the food and wash prospects of some roadside shacks. For a very long time we sit about discussing how it happened and the infinite realms of the might-have-happened. The guavas are good and the soldiers' water is indeed cold and the sensation of relief is delightful, a physical sensation as well as emotional.

Finally, mid-way through the afternoon, we heave off down an awful (but correct) road, while the soldiers who had the water and were lazing about at the checkpoint with nothing to check – break into polite applause as we freewheel off down the broken-up road. We shan't forget Swarghat.

Losing each other in this way has, in fact, been curiously timed, for the relief we both felt when we finally met up again is suddenly mixed with the realization that the road down from Swarghat is the one leading us both at last out of the Himalaya to the great northern plains.

We freewheel carefully down the gravelly road overhung with odd, drooping pine trees quite different from the deodar of the higher slopes. Then from the top of a small series of hairpins, we can see the road snaking off out below us into an immense, flat plain completely unencumbered by hills. Out beyond the edge of the hills, the very limit of the Himalaya, gigantic nullahs fan out onto the plains in huge white deserts of rock and dust, the banks fringed with tall pampas grasses. To our left a long railway bridge crosses one tiny finger pressing out into the plain, toy-like from so far above.

In another direction an immense patchwork of fields shimmers away into the heat haze, pale green and yellow rectangles juggling and dancing far below us both. Nearer to us a herder follows his goats along the lowest slopes as if along the very edge of the country itself. Having talked together repeatedly about seeing the plains for the first time from the mountains, when the moment comes it's all too sudden, even after the last hurdle of climbing to Swarghat.

Together, we stand here in silence, sensing for the first time the idea of India, the scale of it. Was this what Malik meant by seeing it all laid before us? I will never know, but there is something cruel in the sheer immensity of this – the hint of size visibly before us, the hint of ever more land over every possible shimmering haze – for there is rarely anything so defined as a horizon. Twenty thousand feet and more of climbing and descent have not prepared us for this sight.

There is another element to seeing the plains before us, the statement they make about the size of the task ahead. Then, suddenly, somewhere overhead, an eagle shrieks out in the cloudless blue dome. Rossiter turns to his bicycle. 'Let's get on with it then,' he says, to himself as much as anyone else.

It takes a couple of hours to wind down and out of the hillside, the last one for hundreds of miles, and then at once we are into a series of nullahs cut and spread by the waters draining from the mountains in spring and monsoon. There is no way we can cycle across these areas – sometimes half a mile wide and the boulderous moonscape attracts and traps the heat. In the middle of these stretches it's so hot the dust burns our calves and rasps any flesh it makes contact with. Hundreds of tiny golden lizards flee for cover as we plod along, leaving tiny explosions of dust in the wake of their panicky scuttle for cover. But we are not alone in trying to negotiate the nullahs. Even though the way is only marked with occasional large boulders, the local bus bounces, revs and skids its way through from village to village. Social services may not be quite what they are in England just here, but they've got a bus service that actually meets the needs of villages despite whatever the terrain may throw up. I can't see this catching on in England.

By the time the sunset has begun doing its extraordinary things, we have reached Nalagarh – which Rossiter insists on calling Malaga – thoroughly exhausted by the day's events, but positively welcomed (for once) by the chowkidar at the P.W.D. resthouse. We spend a peaceful evening on the long verandah of the P.W.D. watching the geckoes hawk moths and insects along the cracked whitewashed walls by the light of the oil-lamp and reflect on the day's events. Losing each other made us push and cycle up six thousand feet of mountain in just a few hours; and by forcing us to see how much we rely on each other for the journey's success, the fiasco before Swarghat has also brought us noticeably closer.

Because we've not yet encountered any mosquitoes, nothing seems to keep us from sleep and we're developing the habit of getting up earlier because of sleeping early in the evening. Or, to be more accurate, I'm developing the habit of getting up and getting impatient with Rossiter who, it seems, can always do with that extra half hour. Really, he must hate me for this, but never mentions it, deigning merely to open an eye and sleep on.

Even so, the next day we are out along the road soon after dawn while the mist still clings, thin and scented, on the flat land. For no obvious reason we are suddenly into an area where the P.W.D. of the region has built bridges across most of the nullahs, which become smaller as we head south-east, with the wall of the Himalaya steadily falling away to our left. The bridges and the wondrous novelty of flat land and smooth road puts us both in a good mood, and far down the road behind me, I hear Rossiter singing in a melancholy warble, a sure sign that all is going well.

By the time we stop for food at midday we have reached the Grand Trunk Road, National Highway 1. It is the first main road we've been on since a brief spell from Dyala Chek to Pathankot. That marked the beginning of our huge and painful detour round Punjab and the superb Sikh dhaba which we eat in next to the N1 in Pinjaur, marks the end of it, at last.

As with most dhabas kept by Sikhs, this place is spotlessly clean, its beaten dung floor positively shining in the noonday heat. When we wash our hands to eat, the owner pours water over them from a huge earthenware pitcher in the tidy back yard. Near to us, a supply of Campa Cola bottles keeps cool in a stone trough where a clear spring bubbles from the ground.

Meeting the Trunk Road is, on the whole, a bad thing. It gets you along faster and the surface is (on the whole) excellent, but you're hard up against the might-is-right of the Indian highway code. The congestion is really worse than it might be: the road is single-lane so an unofficial dust lane has grown up on either side because smaller vehicles are always being forced off the road by anything larger. It's the 'soft shoulder' of India's answer to the M1.

Very soon we find ourselves in it, when a bus overtakes a truck coming towards us and forces us and a bullock cart behind us off into the dust. We're rather affronted by this, but by the time it's happened three times in ten minutes the rule has been made clear: if the only things in your way are smaller than you are – overtake and they will get off the road.

The central tool for all this is the horn which in some ways is an indicator of the driver's machismo. As Rossiter points out after several bursts from a bus behind us, 'You must feel a right eunuch around here if your horn goes on the blink.' Indeed, for the trucks, which have no mirrors, large signs across the back saying HORN PLEASE! are vital to safety on the roads. At the top of the 'pecking order' of traffic are the large, modern coaches that take the tourists from Delhi up to Chandigarh and Simla, tinted glass, videos and all. They have the loudest compressed air klaxons and you can hear them coming, even above the general row, for perhaps half a mile, blasting a way through, with the klaxon on almost continually.

Even the lorries get forced off the road by buses and the 'soft shoulder' is littered from here to Delhi with overturned vehicles, their cargoes of fruit or vegetables strewn about, the driver and his mate waiting serenely for something to happen in the way of help, burning parts of the load in the meantime to keep warm during the cold nights. On several occasions both of us nearly come off when having to dive for cover unexpectedly from the road into deep, soft dust.

Out of Pinjaur the country is totally flat. Across hundreds of miles of the great northern plains drained by yawning sluggish rivers like the Jamuna (or the Ganges of course), the land level alters by a matter of only a few feet. This flatness is as spectacular as the soaring of the Himalaya – though all trace of the mountains has gone from view now. On either side, square miles of maize, sugar cane, wheat, rice, rows of vegetables, rice, rice and rice are drilled out in regular fields behind the poplar and occasional banyans that line our straight, flat road.

Fifteen miles or so of this brings us to the Punjab border again where we might be refused entry, even though we are just passing through another ten-mile slice of the state. Lorries are queueing up for hundreds of yards before the octroi, their loads disgorged in preparation for a search. We slow to almost walking pace to let the soldiers get a good look at us, resolving only to stop if we are shouted at (or, I suppose, shot at). But at the border post they all seem interested in the lorries, merely staring blankly as we pass. Suddenly the border is behind us and we're in Punjab again. We get our heads down and go as quickly as possible.

Despite that, it turns out to be a very long ten miles and we finally decide to take a break. Feeling it would be unwise to leave the bicycles very obviously at the roadside, we push them off into a grove of small walnut trees which provides some cover. The only problem here is that every few feet or so, large funnel-web spiders have made their wide and silky fly-traps so it's virtually impossible to sit down without plunging into a web. The spiders themselves are indeed a mean-looking bunch, three or more inches across and sandy-coloured. They have no truck with us though, and dive into the cocoons they've woven at the back of their webs, listening, no doubt, as we talk in whispers and drink from our water bottles.

Along a main road like this, we can soon tell at a glance the places where drink as well as food is on sale. Every few miles there are small groups of lorries parked erratically, very often dotted with drivers staggering about the worse for a few bottles of Punjabi lager. Brands such as 'Kingfisher' and 'Dracula' seem to have particular cachet and once Rossiter and I are out of Punjab again, we decide to stop for a bottle or two.

Of course, once you've decided this, there is an immediate dearth of places and not until we are almost at Ambala do we find a distinctly illicit-looking drink-shop. Haryana is definitely not a 'dry' state, but all the drinking here seems to be done out of sight, round the back of the place where dusty green unlabelled bottles of God-knows-what are being sold at a brisk pace. Behind the dung-walled dhaba where the bottles are sold, there are a few benches of wood slung between some old millstones. This is the male-only Saloon Bar. If women drink in India, they are rarely allowed to do so in public.

At five in the afternoon many of the punters here are not going to last the course and we are greeted warmly and incoherently by several truck-drivers, one of whom falls into the dust in surprise when we appear round the awning of the selling hut. The lager (for it is that) turns out to be pretty good and a welcome relief on our dust-dried throats. Not so welcome are the dirty whisky glasses filled with what looks and smells like kerosene. After one gulp of this venomous clear liquid (which we are repeatedly pressed to drink), I can feel everywhere inside me where it has passed. I am sure this is not good.

'Holy shit ... ' breathes Rossiter, evidently with the same symptoms of internal laceration. 'Where on earth do they get this from? A cracking plant, I reckon.'

At intervals, various drivers veer unsteadily off towards their cabs. There is much uncertain fumbling for the ignition and with the night less than a couple of hours away, the lorries themselves will quite likely have no working lights, like the whole gamut of carts and bicycles (including ourselves) rolling darkly along Highway N1. Unsurprisingly, death along a plains road is considered as routine as being killed in one of the buses that regularly go off the winding passes in the mountains. I hope the road is less busy south of Delhi.

With about an hour's daylight left we reach the military cantonment of Ambala where the black smoke and horn-blasting of the traffic through the town's main bazaar is a vision of mechanical hell. Here, the road is dotted with the flattened, desiccated carcasses of those chickens, dogs and pigs that failed to judge their dodging quite correctly.

After some trouble we find the P.W.D. resthouse, an imposing bungalow from the Raj era in its own gardens, with a typical wide verandah running the length of the front wall. All of it is set back in green, shady gardens fringed with bushes of bougainvillea ablaze with blossom. 'Say no more,' I instruct Rossiter, viewing this tranquil haven from the rigours of the bazaar nearby.

But an unseen voice comes from the garden: 'Resthouse is totally full, sahib,' it growls. It turns out to be the voice of 'Tanktop', who wears what has to be the loudest combination of colours ever forcibly restrained within that particular item of dress. Then the sweeper appears and beckons us in – but Tanktop insists with such vehemence that the P.W.D. is full that we actually stop and listen to him.

'Understand one thing now please,' he says wringing his hands, 'there is no place for you in resthouse, sahib.'

'Are you the chowkidar, then?' I ask.

'No, no, no,' says Tanktop forcefully.

'Where is the chowkidar?'

'He has fled.'

I look at Rossiter but by the time I'm repeating Tanktop's last enigmatic statement he's already telling me where to go in no uncertain terms. 'You go to Deputy Chief Engineer's Office and there you are enquiring of him for accommodations in this place.' We've been here long enough to know the futility of pointing out that if it's full there can't be any point in asking officials for room. We get back on the bikes again.

Life is not running smoothly down at the D.C.E.O. (Ambala District) of the Haryana P.W.D. – or the D.C.E.O. of H.P.W.D. as the clerk who welcomes us in calls it. Life isn't easy mainly because the flight-path of the Indian Airforce Base goes right over the entire cantonment area of what used to be a colonial administration point. The jets of India's modern air force pour considerable scorn (and noise) on its once peaceful avenues.

We are shown to the Sub-Asst Engineer who may be able to help us. 'Good evening my friends. I am S.A.E. of this place but we are under the flights from I.A.F. base near to this place. I am telling everybody it is so difficult for us to work in such conditions. But what to do? You are hearing ... ' He raises an index finger in anticipation. For a moment or two it is not clear whether or not he is in need of medical attention – but gradually a smile of satisfaction creeps across his face as a distant thunder becomes a steady roar. In seconds it is so loud that shouting would be quite inaudible and S.A.E. positively beams at us across his tableful of ledgers and glass paperweights.

'F.C. of I.A.F.,' says S.A.E. with complete satisfaction. (Only in Delhi did we find out this meant Fighter Command of the Indian Air Force.)

S.A.E. is able to palm us off on to the E.E. who tells us, 'I am E.E. of this place. You are taking tea?' Tea would be most welcome, indeed necessary, as we're both tired out after a day's riding and this has the look of taking some time to achieve whatever we came here for. The Executive Engineer has a problem. He's every bit as uninterested in us or assisting us as anybody else here, but his immediate superior, D.C.E. (whom we thought we were coming to see back in the good old days at the P.W.D.) is busy. Ah! He is saved from having to speak to us by another jet for a moment or two. He has more glass paperweights than S.A.E., as befits his status – but as the fan isn't working they are merely fulfilling their use as status symbols until the fan is fixed. E.E. shuffles them nervously for some moments before settling down to ignoring us completely. It's strange how quiet it sounds in between the jets.

'Isn't it strange how quiet it seems in between the jets – or I suppose you're quite used to it by now, aren't you?' says Rossiter to E.E. who continues to scribble behind his rockery of paperweights and ledgers.

Silence.

'Yes,' I say loudly to Rossiter, 'almost eerie, you could say.'

Silence from E.E. except for barely perceptible scratching of his biro. I can feel eddies of suppressed laughter coming up inside myself and spend the next silent moment or two trying to avoid Rossiter's smirking face. We think we're saved when another jet approaches, except that when the noise is at its loudest a clerk appears at the door shouting something at us which is completely inaudible, as if nothing untoward was happening. This is too much for me and I'm convulsed with laughter while the clerk mouths in the doorway and E.E. scratches in, on a different cosmos.

The jet lands and without looking up E.E. says, 'You go now to see D.C.E. Please follow the clerk. I am happy to have been of some service to you.'

By some unseen communication, the tea actually arrives in the office of D.C.E. who has elevated beyond the realms of paperweights to the effortless possession of three telephones, which says more about you than paperweights ever can. Perhaps D.C.E. has made the grade because of his capacity to look at you and not speak in code. You can go a long way like that. And he has a name: Mr Patel. We're definitely getting somewhere here and the 'full-set tea' is excellent. By dint of lifting one of his telephones, dialling and saying, 'D.C.E. – accommodation for two persons in P.W.D. bungalow – expedite!' he secures us a place to sleep for the night, as well as plenty of time to sit and talk to him about our journey in which he is very interested.

Back at the bungalow, it may be dark but Tanktop is still hanging around under what auspices we cannot imagine. Why the actual chowkidar fled remains a mystery, though Rossiter suggests plausibly enough that he took to the Maldives to get away from this character.

Next day, at a little after eleven o'clock in the morning, the first serious mechanical problem of the journey happens as we are leaving the dusty junction town of Panipat on the busy N1. Riding two abreast in a rare traffic lull, Rossiter is holding forth, as is his wont, about the mesmeric effect the light falling between roadside trees produces as you travel along. Well wrapped up in his subject, he's relating to me the problems this has caused in southern France when there is a sudden twang in his rear wheel.

A spoke has broken and worse, a spoke on the block-side of the wheel. 'Oh no,' says Rossiter, 'No, don't do this to me please, please!' He glances vaguely skyward and is momentarily blinded by the sunlight. This is one of those difficult moments when it occurs to you that in a journey like this you may have bitten off not only more than you can chew but more than you could possibly shove into your mouth. Rossiter looks deeply at me. He takes stock. 'Well, this is it then, isn't it? Here we are stuck in the middle of bloody nowhere with a broken spoke. Great! And you know what? We don't have a clue how to mend it, do we? We really are pathetic, you know, absolutely bloody pathetic. And you know what else? I knew this was going to happen, I knew it – no way can we go riding around over mountain tracks for days on end and expect to get away with it. No way. I wish Merlin was here, I really do.'

'Well he isn't.'

'Oh well done, Holmes,' says Rossiter and slumps into the dust in a heap just as if his skeleton had suddenly dissolved.

It would not be the first time that Rossiter and myself would wish for Merlin, a life-long friend of Rossiter's who possesses the startling quality of being able to understand the mechanics and functioning of The Bicycle, just the sort of person to have at hand when funny noises happen to you on the Haryana inter-state. To worsen matters further, the inevitable crowd of boys appears in seconds, those boys, legion in India, who cannot be detected approaching, who do not come, but simply appear and adhere.

Eventually, we hitch a lift back into Panipat (and pay for it) and first of all sit down with two bottles of Limca, open the manual at the right page and concentrate very hard for ten minutes. The appalling gulf between manual-diagrams and mucky reality yawns wide and frightening at this point, but it is obvious to us both that the pathetic wrench in our tool-kit is not going to remove the block to make way for the replacement spoke.

As we begin asking for the nearest bicycle shop, it becomes clear that Mr B. K. Lal & Sons is the place to be – but how to explain about the pipe-wrench which we need? Explaining why we need it takes half an hour, as my Hindi is not up to it at all and on several occasions Mr Lal's son edges towards the derailleur cogs with a large rusty hammer. This is not good for our blood-pressure.

'Paprunch? Pop-righ? ... Pep pranch ... ' The words are tried, bandied about and rejected.

'No,' says Rossiter making lavish gestures with his arms, a despairing look on his sweating face. 'Pipe-wrench, it's pipe-wrench.'

Various helpers peel off and return with a multitude of spanners, hammers and pliers. One man evidently decides what we need is too esoteric and so brings back some chai, feeling the search will certainly involve that beverage. He's dead right of course. Finally, I think by a fluke, a pipe-wrench appears – but it is too small. No matter, it serves to illustrate and at once a boy leads me off to the back of a tailor's shop where, of all places, a mighty pipe-wrench is lurking.

Back at the Lals' at least a hundred people have assembled, spilling out over the shop into the street. The Congress (I) man has given up pasting up pictures of Indira Gandhi for the election and watches intently, as does a shoe-shiner who has shut his box up for the foreseeable future.

The mighty wrench does the trick, though a block tightened up across the Himalaya does not come loose without a fight. With that done we hand things over to Ravi (Mr Lal's son, minus his hammer now) who knows more about wheel-balancing than I suppose I shall ever do. The job done, he insists of giving both bicycles a thorough clean and oiling and presents us with a small plastic can of oil, as a leaving present. Try as we might, the Lal emporium will take no money, even though we have completely disrupted business for three hours because of the crowds.

Panipat, the most fly-infested place in India according to Moslem legend, has become a hard place to leave. As Mr Lal senior won't let us pay, we decide to buy his three sons tubs of ice-cream from a stall across the road. They seem massively delighted as we say goodbye, but from modesty they do not dig into their tubs until we are well down the road.

Although we are back on the road by mid-afternoon, we decide to make a short day of it and when a Haryana Tourist Development Lodge comes up on the right hand side after twenty miles or so, we pull in for the night. These places punctuate the main roads radiating through the state from the capital since the canny Haryana State Tourist Development Corporation have realized that, although there's very little for visitors in the state itself, there's rupees to be made by feeding, watering and putting up weary travellers on their way to more colourful places. They're the nearest thing in India to western motorway service stations and the H.S.T.D.C. have named most of them after birds so that large hoardings mellifluously proclaim DABCHICK LODGING 45KM and so forth, which all sounds much more inviting than 'Watford Gap Services'.

But actually sleeping in the Dabchick is not a great success due to the combination of the Grand Trunk Road twenty yards from our window, a generator that starts up at five in the morning and a cricket which I cannot locate, which has looked into the acoustic properties of the entire building and settled to sing in our bathroom. None of this matters too much, though, because when we get up, we do so in the knowledge that Delhi is around fifty miles to the south. We are off in good spirits by dawn.

For the second time on the journey we make the fatal mistake this morning of stopping near to a school when lessons are not in progress. It is quite hopeless. Boys swarm about everywhere pulling, fiddling and twanging anything they can get their hands around. We quickly abandon any idea about eating some breakfast in a promising-looking dhaba and pedal off down the road pursued by boys until they tire of the effort of sprinting and screaming their heads off at the same time.

Once we're away from them we stop for a (foodless) rest and Rossiter is obviously upset by something.

'Did you see those children back there?'

'Of course – couldn't really miss them.'

'No, not the schoolkids, the beggars. Two really small kids about four or five just standing behind the crowd of schoolkids looking really thin and covered with bites of some kind. I know we've seen children begging a hundred times before but it brings it all home in a way, seeing them just standing there, all weak with nowhere to go with all the other kids being kids like that. No energy or desire to mess about.'

We sit there, in the shade of a dense thicket of bamboo, staring out across the road some twenty yards away. Rossiter continues his thoughts about these beggar children. It's typical of him to have his attention snatched from our immediate concerns about crowds or whatever, to something quite different. 'Did you see what happened when they asked for some guavas from the guy with the fruit stall?'

'The one next to the dhaba we wanted to eat in?'

'Yes – the larger one just put out her hand towards one of the guavas and the stall-holder just swiped her right across the head. And you know what? She just didn't react at all, just sort of winced and plodded off holding the hand of her younger brother. And when there's a great crowd of kids like that there's damn all you can do about it. It seems to me they didn't have any home or parents or anything, just wandering like that and getting hit by bastards like that fruit-seller ... ' Rossiter's voice falls off, he stabs the dust repeatedly with a bit of stick, thinking.

We sit silent for some time. By this stage we have seen countless incidents of mean, struggling poverty, disease, of people just not ever quite getting enough of the basics, and now something which has pricked our senses again: a withered limb, a running sore, sudden pleading eyes, and you're awakened again to the size of the problem we're cycling through.

After three hours or so, a brown smudge comes into the distant air up ahead. As we move, it grows higher in the sky, spreads wider. The beginnings of ragged, straggling, unplanned buildings appear, more and more of them on both sides of the road. Low, dung-walled houses become mean, concrete rows, aimless streets wandering without beginning or end, nowhere.

Suddenly they cease on both sides and the sky all around is filled with hundreds of buzzards, crows, kites and huge vultures. In circles against the smog-stained sky they quarter the huge waste-tips on either side. We are at Delhi.

No city should ever be judged by the first you see of it, be it the airport, railway station or, in our case, the Municipal Dump. The scene on either side and overhead is surreal, almost unbelievable for a moment or two. On the ground thousands of kites and vultures flap, fight and tear over a sea of rubbish and filth. Hundreds more stand about in regimented rows, gorged, waiting. Stinking ponds are pelted with the birds' droppings while hordes of flies and bubbles of gas disturb the scummy surfaces. Away to one side, small trucks rumble over the drier parts and vomit more rubbish onto the heaps. Now and then large brown rats move nimbly from place to place, dodging the birds, knowing the country well. The stench hangs heavy in the air and into all of this go the scavengers – the human scavengers – picking and turning with sticks and a sack for any item that might bring a rupee in the back street bazaars, they must fight with the birds, the flies and the rats for anything worth the taking.

This is an awesome way to come into Delhi and for a long time we stand about, stench or no, spellbound by the movement and activity around us. From the dump, there lies ahead of us over ten miles of hot, dangerous and frustrating stop-and-start riding through the streets of Old Delhi until we reach the relative safety of Lutyens' New Delhi – which is not really a 'new' Delhi so much as the latest version the denizens of that much rebuilt city have come up with. Unexplained ancient walls of previous incarnations strike boldly out of the sandy ground here, run for a few hundred yards and stop before a modern roundabout.

Statistically, this is the most dangerous city in the world for road accidents and beneath today's thick brown veil of smog, we have ten miles worth of it to scrape through. Compressed-air bus klaxons blast a way through the chaos while trucks belching black smoke stand ensnared by bicycles carrying families of four. Auto-rickshaws shimmy and squawk for room to move, carrying silk-sareed ladies who press a saree-fold to their mouth against the fumes. Goats and black pot-bellied pigs trot about under marooned trucks and cars while thin children with matted hair dart out to demand backsheesh, fail and retreat exhausted when the traffic briefly heaves.

The ten miles takes about two hours to complete (without losing each other) and there's more than a little of a feeling of survival as well as arrival when (for the want of ideas and energy) we climb the steps into the gloom of the Hotel B g t once again. Over the last eight hundred miles the hotel has achieved a mythical quality in our minds, that of being 'fairly OK really, when you think about it'. But the pleasing fact is we are here, filthy, thinner but fitter for it, with a quarter of the journey completed. It's 1.15 p.m. on December 6th 1984, and time for a celebratory meal.

4

'Stand not upon the order of your going,
But go at once . . .'

Macbeth

The winter has advanced in the city since we were last here and jumpers are needed at night. Right through the day, although the temperature is in the sixties, the roadside hawkers are wrapped up in several blankets and what look like tea-towels round their heads in loose turbans. The sun is weak and pallid in this season, cocooned behind the brown haze of smog that hangs over the city in daylight hours. Here and there some work has at last been done to demolish buildings burnt down in the riots, gangs of labourers loading up donkey panniers with charred rubble.

Something about riding through the mountains to get here has fluffed us both up with absurd conceit, which surfaces as soon as we see tourists in Delhi, fresh-faced from the airport. Nevertheless, Rossiter has discovered an old school friend who has a flat in Nizamuddin, a suburb in the posh, south part of Delhi. Although he works in Calcutta, Rossiter quickly succeeds in contacting him and arranging a swift move into the flat – spurred on by thoughts of escaping the Hotel B   g t.

No sooner have we arrived than Rossiter settles into suburban life dangerously well. Within the hour he has arranged a short cultural trip around the city with one of the rickshaw drivers who hang out at the chai stall down the road. He's checked out the dhaba on the corner of our tranquil, tree-lined street and has even commissioned the local softloopaperwallah to deliver later in the afternoon – after he has had forty winks. Now he sits, feet on the railings of our balcony, cigarette in one hand, bottle of lightly chilled mango juice in the other. 'Ah yes,' he purrs, 'this is what the journey is all about, to be able to sit like this, watching the mynah birds, nice drink, nice smoke, pleasant sunshine – '

'Pancake and maple syrup with half-pound burger from Nirula's inside you,' I add.

'Of course, of course – even you must understand one must savour the delights of what the capital has to offer.'

'All we've done here so far is eat – and slag off tourists – I can't help thinking we ought to do something, somehow.'

'No, no,' yawns Rossiter, 'Relax ... observe ... contemplate ...'

And with that we both drift off to sleep in the hazy winter sun.

The plain fact is, the longer we stay in Delhi the more we remain in Nizamuddin, getting accustomed to life here, rather than involving ourselves in the life of the city. Around ten o'clock we get up – it's certainly cool enough to lie in – and wander round the corner to 'Anand's Loverlee' where, after two days, we're considered regulars with our own bench from which to tuck into rich cauliflower and onion samosas for our breakfast.

The Loverlee is a good vantage point to watch the morning's salesmen do their rounds. 'Tamata tamata tamata ta tama ta tama tahhhhhoooooooooooooooooo!' screams the tomato-seller, some minutes before his bicycle comes into sight, loaded down with wickerwork panniers full of tomatoes.

'Kelekelekelekelekelehhhhooooooooooooooooooooooooooo-ooooo' marks the arrival of the banana man. For extra effect he's constructed a turban out of his stock this morning, perhaps fifteen sweet green bananas balanced on his head as he rides along screaming.

During our time in Nizamuddin, Rossiter develops a flair for getting these men to sell him all manner of items. By the end of the week he's sitting in the marble surroundings of our flat, puffing on cigars. It transpires he's bought these by placing an order with the man who runs the elephant portering service outside the local station, across the square from Loverlee's.

For my part, I manage to get hold of some Indian spaghetti from the general stores. This place is the source of bitter words in Loverlee's since they've recently stuck a couple of wicker chairs outside and have begun selling chai. All at Loverlee's are outraged at this infringement on their business and there is talk of bribing the milkman so he won't take his cart there for deliveries of buffalo milk. But when it comes to negotiating a price to buy him off with, they can't reach any agreement.

Excursions out of our part of town are not terribly successful or frequent, and besides, if I go alone I never know what Rossiter will be up to, by now so at home in Nizamuddin I think he's forgotten what a bicycle is. Suspicions are confirmed towards the end of the week. Letting myself in, I discover him sitting in a brand new blue silk suit. 'Where the hell did you get that from?'

'The suit you mean?' he inquires, maintaining complete cool.

'Yes, it's er … it's really rather good, isn't it?' I tell him, impressed but baffled.

'Well yes, I'm quite chuffed actually – you see I've found rather a good tailor over at the Oberoi.'

'The what?'

'Oberoi – the Oberoi Intercontinental Hotel.'

'So we're on first name terms are we?' I say.

'You wouldn't understand dear,' says Rossiter, attempting to pat me on the head. 'No,' he continues, 'You wouldn't understand at all. Besides, you should see what he's running up for me to wear on the rest of the ride. I thought I'd need something a little more, um, *sportif*, shall we say, now we're down on the plains and things'll be getting hotter.'

'I don't believe this,' I tell him, burying my face in my hands. Rossiter can only be detected now by the swig of his lager and the whispering rustle of raw silk.

Three days later, he gets home from the Oberoi again. I should never have let him go. Just as I'm dropping off with the inner pages of the *Indian Express*, he comes through the door in an enormous pair of purple and blue tartan shorts.

'They are a bit loud,' is all I can splutter, burying my face again. 'You cannot possibly wear those outside.' I hope it may be a dream, or a joke at least. 'Seriously – you can't do it.'

'Why not, they're just the job. Like the vents?' he says, flouncing down an imaginary catwalk.

'Silk again?'

'No way – only the finest Indian cotton for Rossiter – the MacRossiter tartan, this.' He strokes the shorts endearingly.

'You're really going to wear those?' I ask.

'Sure am.'

'But they're even flared – on top of everything else – '

'For someone who squeezes into ludicrously tight, thick black cycling shorts in India of all places – you're hardly one to talk about what the well-attired cyclist should be wearing this winter, are you?'

Having got himself well and truly kitted out for evening wear and a hard day in the saddle, Rossiter now declares the next morning, against all expectations, that he's feeling recharged and ready to get going again.

It is now me who is so ensconced in the ways of Nizamuddin that the idea of leaving comes as rather a shock. Rossiter acting unpredictably again.

'But we haven't seen anything of Delhi yet,' I complain half-heartedly.

'I've been thinking,' says Rossiter, ignoring me, 'I've been eating and smoking far too much around here. It's high time we left Nizamuddin and got back to the bicycles.' He points at them in the yard below our window. They have faded under a film of Delhi dust during the days of non-use. Rossiter glances at me, checking my surprise at his sudden urge for physical exercise. 'Got a duster?'

On our large map called 'The Indian Subcontinent' you have to go about two inches south of Delhi – a hundred and fifty miles – before the green shading turns first of all light brown, then darker. After that, it doesn't turn green again for two and a half feet due south. That brown marks the Deccan Plateau, the vast dry upland of central India. I'm excited by the idea of getting into this whole area as fast as possible, ready for another change of country. 'Let's get the two inches out of the way first, shall we?' says Rossiter.

Next morning, after more than a week off the road, there's a palpable sense of relief, for both of us, at being out on our way south again, whirring through the misty streets of south Delhi at dawn. Soon we're moving out into the rice and maize fields as the first mynahs and roller jays are calling in the dawn haze. By the time the sun is high enough to warm us we are back into Haryana, crossing the second stretch of the state as it embraces the south side of the capital.

Gradually the randomly sited mills and sidings of the capital give out into the patchwork of flat fields. But only gradually: a tar-works or power station will suddenly loom up on the flat landscape just when we are thinking we have well and truly left Delhi. For some miles half-derelict paddies lie stagnant at either side, abandoned, as if in fear of the growing city, now just a brown smudge in the northern sky behind us. Near most of the villages there is an ancient-looking tank, usually with a small temple presiding over it and always with herds of black water buffaloes wallowing in the caramel-muddy water. They lie there, sometimes thirty or more, with a fog of steamy satisfaction rising off the gleaming black hides that part the bright green duckweed on the surface. Weed carpets their heads like some thriving mould as they rise up to watch us pass with expressions of ultimate vagueness. For some reason, many of the village women are today at great pains to wash these beasts. This seems a little odd to me since the buffaloes spend the greater part of the day slurping around in the water anyway.

Towards the middle of the day a likely-looking dhaba comes in sight, beneath a stately and wide-spreading banyan tree. Its bole is at least ten feet across and at the top there is a colony of twenty or so large and noisy cranes which land uncertainly in the top-most branches and clap their long bills at us in irritation. For a long way you can see them coming in to land, aiming delicately for the branches which have turned white with their guano over the years. At the last moment they beat their huge wings in reverse to try and slow down but this is more difficult even than it looks and often they get it wrong which means overshooting, banking high and wide of the tree and trying the whole process again. Needless to say, there are few leaves left at the top of the tree.

In the lower branches vivid green parakeets – like those that live at the Red Fort in Delhi – chase each other around the wide branches and a hoopoe darts into its nest like a huge black and white moth. At ground level, an ancient pheasant probes the roots for grubs, unsuccessfully. The tree and the birds it supports are a very welcome contrast to the vultures that have today begun to follow our progress from above. Every time you look up they are there, arcing as if they are surfing along unseen thermals, watching us, waiting ...

Half way to Agra, we spend the night in a spacious, pink-washed Circuit House. Such places – like the one we stayed at in Hamirpur – are intended for the use of the higher echelons of Indian officialdom and so are much more luxurious than the P.W.D. resthouses that are our mainstay. Nevertheless, although the enormous double bed has sheets and mosquito nets, there is the usual problem with the electric switchboard. As in most Indian buildings, the panels of switches display wild optimism. Twelve or more switches in a neat row operate one small bulb – well, at least three of them seem to. The others fail to activate any other lights or the fan which is a colossal affair much like a dead helicopter poking through the ceiling. Quite what the other battalions of switches are supposed to do is simply a question that recurs in almost every room you go into in this country. Perhaps the great national switch-on is just around the corner.

We are woken the following morning by the chowkidar's son who has somehow got hold of a Bullworker. He begins 'working' it at a very early hour and we are woken up by a piercing whine coming intermittently from the verandah of the building. Only after closer inspection do we realize this is because the contraption is badly in need of oil, and not the noise emitted by the boy exercising his considerable strength. For some time he exerts himself, straining in all sorts of positions which the human body cannot surely use in the normal course of things and smiling for our benefit when at the climax of each particular position. Then both he and the Bullworker assume their normal shape, the one whining painfully, the other gasping for air. At this point we are required to make noises of strong approval.

Here we are very much on the trade route for tourists going south along the circuit from Delhi to see the Taj. Because of that the road is excellent, and apart from the occasional tinted-glass 'Video Coach', very quiet. We seem to have left the horrors of the Grand Trunk Road behind. Now, there's time for a wave or a few words with the bullock-cart drivers, who are the main traffic here. A few words is all we have, though it's very funny to see these ancient carts holding up the odd DE-LUXE 5 STAR VIDEO COACH which can't pass till the carts shamble off into the dust.

Along the last stretch of road before reaching Agra, Rossiter breaks another spoke in his rear wheel. Luckily, there is a small bazaar nearby, where a boy of about ten is running a thriving bicycle repair business. Rossiter is beginning to ascribe a certain malevolence to his machine. 'You see?' he says, staring thunderously down at the wheel while the boy threads in another of our diminishing supply of spare spokes, 'You see if you were doing this bloody journey on your own you'd just climb into the saddle one day half-way up the nearest Himalaya and vrooooooooom! Next stop Cape Comorin with light refreshments served en route. No problem. But what do I get? Eh?'

'Er – I dunno,' I say, at a loss.

'No, course you don't. You'd just have no trouble at all. I get on my identical bicycle and it begins self-destructing from the word go. Really, this is so depressing.'

But, typically, Rossiter displays not the slightest sign of depression, he glances down at the bicycle. 'Chai?' he says, just when I am expecting more on the theme of bicycle as fate. By the time I've gone off to get some chai, Rossiter is already holding forth to the assembled crowd on the finer points of the derailleur gear system.

This latest little breakage makes one thing clear though: if Rossiter's back wheel continues the way it's started out – and there's no reason to suppose it won't – we will have to buy and carry a large pipe-wrench in Agra. Carrying a large wrench will be heavy but will save the infinite set of unforeseen problems that arise when you have to search an Indian village for a pipe-wrench when you don't know the Hindi for it and the explanation as to why you could possibly want it elicits nothing but mirth from villagers. As the tool we have from England for removing the back block of cogs is now very worn, we will also have to try to get a replica made in the city.

Before doing either of these things, it's as well to do right by the Taj Mahal. The building stands, as ever, in supreme peace, the bazaars around it only emphasizing its magnificent tranquillity. Across the Jamuna river, lost and stranded walls of a Moghul age crumble into the dust of the northern plain, half buried. Somehow, there is something of this stranded quality in the Taj Mahal itself, standing and gleaming out like this with no connection whatever with the world that now surrounds it and clicks SLRs at its pietra dura walls. Twenty thousand people built it in an age of autocratic splendour, an age long past, and there is today something sad in the splendour that remains so well preserved and so deeply removed. Meanwhile the visitors come and wander, the bees build long brown nests in the recesses of the marbled walls and the green parakeets call to each other across the domes.

Near to the hotel where we stay for two days, in a small shed at the roadside, a man with a lathe completes his replica tool for us in two hours. Its metal clasps fit perfectly into the grooves on the block and he charges us just fifteen rupees for it, less than a pound. Yet again, the adaptability of Indian mechanics makes us wonder.

Having got ourselves more or less roadworthy again and dispensing with the need to ransack entire villages in search of obscure plumbing devices, we decide to take another day in Agra, in the dingy hotel which seems to be mainly full of stoned Liverpudlians complaining about dirt, large insects and stomach upsets. This suddenly reminds us that we have now come about eight hundred miles relatively unscathed in terms of health if not bicycle wheels and spokes. Even with the wheel problems, now we are over the mountains, it does seem very difficult to get worked into a state of worry about anything – or that's what we think while sipping tea on the roof of the hotel, listening to the distant sounds of the town's bazaar half a mile away and the Liverpudlians ten yards away, discussing the pros and cons of going to Goa for Christmas.

Later on though, down in the gloom of our room, it is perceived by Rossiter that one of his front cogs is bent. As he has been complaining of a rubbing noise on his chain for several hundred miles, there seems to be nothing for it but to spend the rest of the day taking apart the more delicate, incomprehensible (and thus rather unnerving) parts of his machine. When the entire floor space is strewn with lots of parts that do not look anything like they seem to on the bicycle, I remark, 'It's funny how confident about everything we were up on the roof this afternoon. Oh, how the plains were going to be no problem for us at all!'

However, unable to sort out what could be causing the rubbing noise, Rossiter for once does not take things in his usual light-hearted style. He looks at me menacingly instead and draws a large mouthful of chai, then swallows hard. 'The fact is – we're completely inept. I mean mechanically we're a couple of complete illiterates.' He sighs despairingly and hits out at a mosquito.

'Come off it – we'll be OK!' I tell him cheerily, which

observation runs directly counter to all possible evidence on tonight's showing.

'Oh really? Really? You know what your trouble is? Probably not, as you can't see any trouble within you at all. But you just think that if we all sit around thinking positively everything will be all right. What you can't grasp is that we are both sodding stupid when it comes to mechanics. Stupid! God – I wish Merlin was here right now, I really do.'

'And,' adds Rossiter, 'we've got to go through the Chambal next, you know.'

No amount of positive thinking can persuade one from the significance of the fact that Rossiter's bicycle is giving us a crisis of confidence just before we have to ride through the most notorious region for dacoits – bandits – in the whole country.

In spite of some largely unspoken misgivings about the dacoits, we stay with our plan to go south via the deserted city of Fatehpur Sikri, about twenty miles west of Agra along the worst road since Ambala. Along the way the villagers are in the habit of darting into the middle of the road with dancing bears in tow. They attempt to block your way while prodding and generally being unpleasant to the poor bear so that it eventually rises upon its hind legs. This achieves what is called 'dancing'. Personally I call it cruelty, but then I do not have to make some kind of living out of a roadside village in Uttar Pradesh along which buses full of tourists pass on most days.

When the locals are used to doing this to stop a bus, you will appreciate that stopping cyclists – no matter how weird they might look – is child's play. And it is indeed children who lead out the bored bears in a number of villages.

Fatehpur Sikri itself rises suddenly from the ridge above the unending plain which is here ruddy and dry to the point of being Martian in appearance. The Moghul emperor Akbar began building here in 1570 – he was passing through when he was given the news of the birth of his son from an itinerant saint. He called in the surveyors at once and decided to build his new capital here. All went well for a number of years – but unfortunately only a small number. Soon the entire city was abandoned because the water supply was either too saline or insufficient, nobody now seems to know which.

Today it hardly matters. When you climb up the ridge you enter into a huge red ghost city, perfectly preserved by a climate so dry and hot for so long each year. Huge and complicated series of courtyards, mosques, stone screens, gateways and towers all stand in silence, given up for ever to the hot steady winds of the plain. Inevitably, there is something a little sinister in desertion on this kind of scale – even if it did happen more than 350 years ago. Strangely, the city is not overwhelmed by lizards, monkeys or snakes which can usually be relied upon to make the running out of human loss in India.

The main mosque here is based upon that of Mecca and you enter it through a huge gateway over 150 feet high. Just inside it there is this inscription: 'The world is a bridge, pass over but build no house upon it.' Which sends me into a reverie for a while, wondering whether they knew the city was doomed when they built it. I'm shaken from my thoughts by the appearance of one of the local maniacs who live in the small settlement outside the old city walls. He announces matter-of-factly that he will jump from the top of the gate's battlements, into the small slime-filled well which lies at the foot of the walls. Of course, he wishes to do so for rupees rather than for the advancement of Newtonian physics and as his side-kick organizes the whip-round from Rossiter and me, he disappears behind the wall, to appear at the top in a while, very much smaller, 100 feet up or so. As he looked to be at least sixty I'm not sure about financing this kind of thing and consider it the height of rashness to begin climbing before agreeing a definite price – very un-Indian, to be sure.

Rossiter delivers himself of the opinion that the man is bonkers after seeming to consider it for some time – but we pay up all the same. Seconds later the man catapults himself off the edge of the battlements feet first and smashes into the slime-covered pond at an appalling speed like a long brown torpedo, emitting an alarming yodel as he goes in, for full effect. It takes him ages to surface again: for a city with alleged water problems, this old well seems quietly sufficient. Soon the man is back, dripping and smelling strongly from the well, busily cleaning up the readies for his 5.6 seconds' work, with half an eye towards his next punters.

There is no mistaking when you enter the Chambal. These are India's Badlands where bandits have lived for over a thousand years. The road gives a short, almost imperceptible rise as the land heaves us away from the plains, studded with their occasional patches of scrubby fields and lifts us up into a barren and tortured moonscape. An area about the size of Wales is ripped and cut by entangled gullies where flash floods gash the sand and rock, leading eventually into the Chambal River. Sandy coloured lizards, some a foot long, scuttle for cover in these weird dry ravines as we approach.

For the best part (or worst part) of a thousand years the Chambal has provided cover for dacoits who attack travellers on the few roads that cross the region. Now we're amongst the ravines, we notice that all the cart-drivers are carrying shotguns or sometimes rifles and eyeing us, we're sure, with looks of astonishment. I find myself thinking frequently about the small knife I carry in one pocket, as we climb and dip through the gullies.

Dacoit leaders can become powerful men controlling many villages which provide food and shelter in return for protection from landlords and other dacoits. People here talk of dacoits with a mixture of admiration, fear and a touch of disgust. When we stop to eat in the late afternoon at the dhaba in Morena, a schoolteacher introduces himself and describes the festival atmosphere at the small town of Bhind when the dacoit leader Malkhan Singh surrendered to the police two years ago. It seems the surrender came after a year of 'dacoit war' during which the authorities shot thirteen hundred men whom they suspected of being or aiding the dacoits in Madhya Pradesh alone. 'But the dacoit peoples were also killing, robbing and burning many peoples,' says the teacher in hushed tones.

Apparently Malkhan Singh was in the habit of using headed notepaper announcing himself as 'Dacoit King' which he used regularly to correspond with the police, army, press, potential and actual victims. When he agreed to surrender, knowing that the army were closing in on his gang, forty thousand people came to Bhind, to the temporary stage, to watch him and his gang throw down their weapons. All India Radio and the national press covered the occasion. The Chief Minister arrived by helicopter and the ceremony was completed with a statement from the Prime Minister's son, Rajiv Gandhi, hoping peace would now come to the Chambal. To the hushed crowd, Malkhan Singh made a short speech, justifying his actions over the past years, from which he was wanted for more than a hundred offences of armed robbery, kidnapping and murder. He was then led off to Gwalior Prison. Whichever way you look at it, this was the end of one of the area's larger-than-life characters – many would say heroes – and for a while our teacher is lost in quiet thoughts, having told us of the surrender he had gone, like many, to witness.

The Chambal goes on, however, throwing up new characters to replace those who are shot or doing time at Gwalior. The next morning Rossiter buys *The Times of India* while the cook at a dhaba is frying omelettes and parathas for our breakfast. Inside, there is a small down-column story saying, in an unimportant way, that a bus was held up last night on the Agra–Morena road. Apparently dacoits had put up a road block to ambush the bus, shooting dead two passengers who tried to resist the men from the ravines. 'It's all right – we aren't targets,' says Rossiter to me once we are on the road again.

'I thought you were supposed to be against positive thinking?'

'Don't you worry – we'll be in Gwalior tonight, you see – and Gwalior's south of the Chambal.'

We duly arrive there just as it is getting dark, with the

dramatic boiling red sunset filling up the western sky to our right. As usual the afterglow lasts for a couple of hours after sunset, only fading at about nine o'clock. We stop for the night in a rambling old TORIST BUNGALOW. The place is designed for visitors going up to the huge hilltop fort that dominates the entire city.

In 1858 the British killed the Rani of Jhansi here during the Mutiny. A few years before that they had passed a convenient law confiscating any maharaja's property if there were no male heirs when he died. Not unnaturally, the spirited Rani took against this and led the rebellion of Jhansi, before retreating to Gwalior Fort. She rode out from beneath its fifty-foot walls and was killed by the British, thus ensuring her place in the pantheon of heroes of Indian Independence. In this part of the country she is remembered as something of a Joan of Arc figure.

Although during the day it is warm, the nights are still chilly – though not as bad as they were in Delhi and further north. Having left all our cold-weather gear in Delhi we have developed the habit of taking down the curtains (where they exist) in P.W.D.s and using them as blankets over our thin sheet sleeping-bags. We lie cocooned in the thick curtains, still attached to their heavy mahogany rails at our feet. At last we are into the brown shading on our large map, at the fringes of the Deccan Plateau in central India.

Gwalior, however, takes longer to leave than to arrive in, because the road south is blocked by fifty or sixty bullock-carts with solid wooden wheels, waiting to get into the sugar-cane refinery at the edge of the city. Each cart is piled high with cut cane and the driver asleep on top of his load. The refinery gates remain resolutely shut as they perhaps do every year at the peak of the harvest to cause maximum confusion.

We are edging our way along the queue when there is a familiar twang from Rossiter's back wheel. There is nothing for it but to wheel our way back into Gwalior to the main bazaar. The sun and the dust are both up by now – the dust only lies still where large pools of bullock and cow urine have stained it chocolate. Boys begin swarming again, jumping about and shrieking, 'Your good name?' as loudly as possible, knocking over each other and anything else in their path. It is exhausting just finding our way back to the nearest bicycle shop. Blinking the sweat out of my eyes I try to explain that spokes keep on breaking in the wheel and we do not know why – but the bicycle mechanic merely smiles and gets down to work once we have removed the block. There is nothing for it but to cross the street to the guava-seller's stall and munch several of his fruits with a dab of gritty brown rock salt in the middle – as refreshing as any drink, in these parts.

High, sun-bleached country stretches away on either side mostly without fields. Thorn bushes and the occasional spectacular cactus mingle with yellowed, coarse grasses. Grey and purple ridges hang suspended by the constant mirage in the distance and the vultures grow more numerous above our heads. Every now and then an unseen eagle screams out from above, but we can't look for it in the sky that the constant sun beats into a uniform, flaring whiteness.

Whenever we stop for a drink from our water bottles our vultures stop with us. This is actually quite comforting. The land is so deserted here that it's soothing to know that something at least is looking out for you – even if it's only to eat you. Water is becoming a problem and our four small bottles do not go far. They are also made of black plastic which means the sterilized water is very soon hot sterilized water. Rossiter has quite a lot to say about the designer who came up with black plastic. But such wide open country is the antidote to the noise and sheer hard work of Indian towns and cities. Out here almost the only sign of human life (beyond Rossiter's shorts and the odd goatherd) is the road itself. Trucks pass us very infrequently and there is always time to yell 'Namaste' or 'Ram Ram' as they pass, waving in frantic delight at coming across the two of us pressing slowly south.

By mid-afternoon we reach Dabra, where the normal chaos of streetlife has been thrown over the edge by a political rally held for the Congress (I) election candidate. In a way Dabra is Delhi on a smaller scale, with telegraph posts, walls, car bonnets, doors, buffalo-horns, rickshaws and people emblazoned with the hand symbol of the party. Even the clay cup I'm given full of chai made with rich buffalo milk has the Congress hand scratched into the surface. As there seems to be no food available in the town beyond some grey cold rice dotted with dust and dead insects, I eat that up while Rossiter looks away in disgust, only turning now and then to advise me that I've dropped some promising bits of insect in the dust.

A bus driver tells us there is a resthouse in Dhatia, so we decide to press on down there for the night, which seems quite feasible as the road is indeed as good as we were promised back in Gwalior. By sunset we are resting a few miles north of the town, gnawing stumps of sugar cane given to us by a passing lorry driver. A man comes into view pedalling his sturdy 'Hero' bicycle and gives us a warm and welcoming smile. 'Hello. Hello my good friends. I am welcoming you warmly to this place. You are coming from which native land?'

'From England.'

'Ah! Yes, yes, yes. You are both looking so very handsome upon your bicycles so I am feeling the need of passing the times of day with you.'

For some time we sit sharing our sugar cane and generally digging the dirt with Mr Praveen Chandra, one of an innumerable horde of Indian bicyclists who put us to shame on our fancy western machines. Praveen has already come seventy miles today and is on his way down to Jhansi – 'But not tonight of course. Ha! Ha!' I laugh, sounding as if I know what I'm talking about.

'Yes, yes. This will be quite possible,' says Praveen. A look of cold horror steals across Rossiter's face at this. Praveen's bicycle has no lights, no gears, no brakes, no mudguards and only part of a saddle. It is so big for him that he is forced to stand bolt upright in order to turn the heavy cranks, but evidently there is no need for concern. 'My good English friends,' says Praveen, 'I am always arriving at my destined place.' He smiles, happy with this reflection upon his dharma as well as his 'Hero'. There is no stopping Praveen, clearly.

Before we leave him he takes us off on an impromptu tour of Dhatia which snuggles comfortably inside its complete, ancient walls. The huge old sandstone blocks, worn and eroded at the corners have more modern 'Shirtings & Suitings' emporia built right up against them. Just to the west of the town, the deserted palace of Raj Birsingh Deo stands in eerie silhouette against the last glows of the sunset, while the chorus of crickets and bullfrog in the nearby tank begins to give the coming night its rhythm.

Praveen then takes us off to the Dhatia Circuit House and in his business-like fashion sorts out the chowkidar who is at first far from keen to have us stay. After Praveen has had some words with him in Marathi, the man is amiability at once – which makes Marathi look a pretty potent sort of language from our standpoint. Perhaps as a result of meeting Praveen, the chowkidar later comes in with a prodigious amount of rice and byngun – a spectacularly delicious dish of curried aubergines, followed by two large bowls of kheer, a kind of rice pudding with almonds, pistachios and coconut milk.

On many nights in lonely places like this Circuit House, built to house judges, there are mechanical problems to get worked up about or dust-choked parts and ourselves to be cleaned, or maps to go over which never seem to agree with one another, or water to be brought from the well for washing and sterotabbing. But on some nights, like tonight, with a full stomach for once, it is quite enough just to sit out on the verandah in silence, looking up at the galaxy of brilliant stars and to listen to the night's stirrings, chirrupings and raspings, the distant bark of a dog or jackal.

We have a vague arrangement to meet Praveen the next day at the huge Bharat Heavy Electricals works to the south of Jhansi, where he is a draughtsman. Having eaten some excellent stuffed parathas in Jhansi, by way of breakfast, we arrive at the factory entrance just as the night shift is clocking off.

Inside, the modern, low concrete buildings of the works stretch away indefinitely, shimmering in the heat haze.

Somewhere inside one part of this amorphous place, Praveen works and plots his emigration to Australia. (He proudly told us last night that his papers finally came through just a week ago.) As we are about to consign his invitation to the pile of other non-literal invitations we have received on this journey, Praveen appears at some distance in the crowd coming out of the works down the concourse towards us. He is pedalling his bicycle, still standing up to do so, which gives him a porpoising effect. He pokes out above the crowd of night shift workers going home, waving frantically at us, only to disappear again on the downstroke of his pedals.

The tour of the factory he has rather wildly promised is not to be, so we head off instead to the tiny canteen which Praveen insists is the works canteen – though it could seat about eight people, at a pinch. Like most Indians, the workforce almost all prefer the delights of a home-cooked and home-packed lunch taken from their shiny steel tiffin-tins, rather than any impersonal canteen-wallah's offerings. The canteen is therefore quite adequate to cope with a workforce of several thousand men. As I sit down, thinking of chai and jelabis, there is the untoward crunch of dead insects under my bottom. I get up a good deal slower than I sat down and begin smearing off a squashed cockroach from my shorts with an old newspaper, much to Praveen's intense consternation and Rossiter's mirth. Despite this less than appetizing beginning to things, the food is actually very tasty and we leave well refreshed. Our last sight of Praveen is his undulating motion, porpoising back to work down the main thoroughfare, into the Bharat empire.

The highlight of the day's ride is the Bedwa River which we cross in the middle of the afternoon – the hottest part of the day. It's one of the few perennial rivers in the region and the first opportunity for a swim since we began. The road bridge is not where it should be according to our large but imaginative map of the area, though that does not matter. Its squat concrete arches, visible at a distance, span a quarter of a mile of deep blue pools and lagoons, clear and fringed by enormous smooth grey slabs of rock, coming through the surface like schools of huge whales caught in freeze-frame for ever. So many of them that at this time of year, old men take the young boys from the nearby village fishing with small hand-nets in the pools on the far bank. Flocks of sandpipers flit across the shallows, a small heron probes the mud at the bank while green parakeets flash across the pools, chasing each other for the sheer hell of it. In the deeper water large fish pop the surface into radiating circles of water to disturb the deep still of the afternoon.

It is completely irresistible. Although the rocks are painfully hot at this time of day, we dance over them into the water, cold and wonderfully refreshing. It is a deeply luxurious sensation to feel ingrained dust wash away from your body, and to float about idly while small, unfearing fishes nibble your skin. Until we met the Bedwa we had been accepting an unpleasant film of sweat and dust on the skin as an occupational hazard and the relief from it – however temporary – is beautiful. Our swimming startles the fishermen and they put down their nets to come over and watch us wallowing about, giggling like a couple of idiots. It's nice too to know that we will not disturb their fish, because the river is so artfully divided up into pools by the rocks.

Waylaid by the charms of the Bedwa we are forced to ride about ten miles after dark to reach Lalitpur which seems a better option than sleeping out, on these cold nights. Cycling at night is not really very much fun here: the road has degenerated latterly and potholes, some a foot or more deep, come up in front of us at random. This means creeping along and squinting ahead to see what little surprise is coming next. And of course neither we nor the other road-users (thankfully very few) have any lights. I find myself getting fixated at times like this by the Rossiter Rear Wheel which, whatever else its shortcomings, has so far at least chosen convenient places to self-destruct. On these last particularly lonely and dark miles to

Lalitpur, I'm just waiting for that familiar twang and groan of despair to come from Rossiter's direction, a few yards ahead.

Finding a place to stay in Lalitpur is difficult and time-consuming. The business of searching out possibilities in new towns at the wrong end of a day's cycling and of producing official pieces of paper for unimpressed officials is agonizing when all you really want to do is flop down and sleep. I get to the end of my tether rather quickly in these situations, though Rossiter has a much bigger reserve of patience stacked away somewhere. My tether ends tonight in Lalitpur when the chowkidar of the P.W.D. resthouse will not let us sully his verandah by letting us sleep there when we realize the place is full up. Over at the Circuit House a mile away, the Janata Party election entourage is putting up for the night and the news is the same. Nonetheless, one of the Janata Party officials does finally point out that if we cross town to the Irrigation House we will perhaps find room there, as there seem to be no hotels in the town at all.

Somehow, the possibility of a bed and some water to wash in – however remote – will make you go rather a long way and shortly before midnight we are at the strawberry-pink Irrigation House. We only get there at all by dint of stopping to ask directions from an imposing man who turns out to be the District Magistrate. With calm efficiency after our floundering he shows us to the Irrigation House, rouses the chowkidar and gets us thoroughly installed. We wish him a hearty 'Ram Ram' and retire exhausted.

It is the D.M. who wakes us up the next day, introducing two 'friends' of his from the Intelligence Service. Rossiter catches my eye as the words come out of the D.M.'s moustached mouth – it will be some time before we leave Lalitpur this morning.

In the nicest possible way we are cordially invited to 'take tiffin' on the verandah and to 'talk' to them about our journey so far. 'We shall be most pleased to hear details of your programme across our country,' intones the fattest of the two fat Intelligence Officers. He speaks with the 'we' in such a way that there is positively no chance of turning round and telling him, Well, terribly sorry mate – got to be on our way! Besides, there's something very rude about refusing to chat with large men carrying revolvers – even at breakfast time. The real problem, though, is my intense sensation of guilt when faced with anybody in uniform, armed or not. 'Tell me,' begins the fattest Intelligence, his impressive handlebar moustache wafting gently as he speaks, dwarfing the D.M.'s version, 'We think you are both enjoying your tour by bicycle.'

Statement or question? I cannot tell. At once my mind begins racing over any possible misdemeanour either of us could have committed since flying into Delhi – both Handlebars and his slimmer colleagues are beaming away at us in a way that suggests they know something. Is it an offence to take down the curtains in government lodges? Are water sterilization tablets a controlled drug in Madhya Pradesh? Should we be cycling in public wearing only shorts? I fall silent, looking in vacant horror at the other Intelligence who begins stroking his gun idly while chatting away with Rossiter – who is capable of normal responses this morning, unhandicapped by my sudden guilt complex. He prattles away with them briskly while I sit, lemon-like, reading all sorts of subtle meanings into their amiable – positively avuncular – manner. For some reason they give me the impression that one loose answer and we could be exchanging notes on the Human Condition with Malkhan Singh in Gwalior Prison.

This is, of course, absurd. That the Intelligence actually do want very little more than a pleasant chat – well, not much more – is clear from the way that the next thing I'm aware of is Handlebars asking for a go on my bicycle. After some difficulty and assistance, his massive bulk is in place on the saddle, though not terribly stable. Unfortunately, the bicycle is in a pretty low gear and this, combined with the fact that Handlebars undoubtedly expected to have to push as hard as one would on an Indian bicycle, leads to disaster. With an almighty push of his huge right thigh, the poor man goes careering straight into a trellis of promising bougainvillea.

At once the second-in-command Intelligence is on the scene, straining to pull Handlebars out from the collapsed blossoms, dusting him down assiduously. Rossiter stands nearby with most of his face in the palm of his hand, making small trumpeting noises, his shoulders shaking desperately. I find myself biting my tongue very hard and staring fixedly at a distant point on the roof of the Irrigation House.

Handlebars, however, is at pains to lose no more of his dignity and brushes off his colleague's flapping behaviour with obvious annoyance. He advances to Rossiter, pushing the bicycle before him, very much the man in control. 'You should attend to the gearing system – it is too low,' he tells Rossiter who has shut his mouth tight against uncontrollable eddies of laughter welling up inside him. 'You better tell that to my friend – it's his bike and I've been telling him the same thing for days, but he won't listen.'

The road south from Lalitpur winds its way over large fields of mustard enclosed by hedges of cacti like those in the olive groves of Andalucia. The cacti look very old indeed and to my eyes it seems odd to see so homely a crop being enclosed so exotically. Some of the cactus plants are unfolding their rare, red flowers. But these fields are only occasional interruptions to the uncultivated face of the Deccan, where miles of pallid grass give out into low ridges of deep-brown boulders. It's an empty and vast landscape rising and falling away again, never quite becoming a desert though forever giving the harsh feeling that it will turn that way soon.

In and out of the brownish-leaved thorn bushes move straggling herds of goats, the only animals capable of marauding a living from such a land. The goats can be a problem, though. Besides continually trying to sexually assault each other they will also attempt to eat the more succulent parts of our bicycles if they get the chance.

On one occasion while Rossiter is answering a spectacular

and urgent call of nature, two goats amble towards my bicycle and begin munching at the foamed handle-bars. They look like they mean business and have already taken several mouthfuls before I notice them. I pick up a dead cactus and start laying in ... They are clearly impressed with my direct manner and trot off down the road with affronted dignity. I stand for a moment under the flaring white sun, looking menacing. Suddenly Rossiter emerges. 'Alex, is the heat getting to you?'

Having come down through the long tongue of Uttar Pradesh we finally cross the state frontier at about noon. Actually, 'state frontier' is a bit grandiose. There is simply an octroi made of bamboo-trunks lashed together and weighted with a bag of rocks. Beneath it, a small but brilliantly coloured tortoise is making for the more northerly state. He is giving it all he's got, neck strung out at full stretch, pulling his yellow striped shell along in a clambering low-slung waddle. It's as if he is expected urgently at the other side of the road later today. We have some time to watch him pass by, straining in silent determination. Fortunately, there is little chance of his being run over here, as we have not seen anything pass by us for the last two hours.

After crossing the frontier we enter one of the 'Ghat Sections' which are proclaimed with great pride by stone signposts. Such signs appear whenever the road has been put across one of the series of low hills that divide the Deccan and still retain remnants of the great forests that once covered the entire region. Over-ambitious signs draw the travellers' attention to tigers, barasinghas, leopards and a host of other animals which have probably not been seen in the area for a generation or more. The destruction of the forests in this part of the Deccan has had such an effect on the wildlife that you might as well put a sign up at Scotch Corner saying, 'Caution: Bears'.

At least there is always the good freewheel down after our climb of a mile or so to the top of the ghat section. At the end of it we find ourselves in a particularly calm and neat village with an enormous well at least twenty feet across. Inside it, plate-sized bull-frogs croak in alarm at the splash of the descending bucket they just can't get used to living with. Most of the people here seem to work in the large quarry at the southern end of the village where the granite is hacked away at by an army of quarrymen working by hand. The employment seems to be steady and the children look noticeably better fed than is usual in the villages we come through along the road. Here, that strained, taut expression in the children's dark eyes is relaxed and their legs are not quite so thin around the knees.

'With the stones there is enough for us, but it will not last us for ever,' says Dinesh, who used to work in the quarry until an accident left him crippled and bed-ridden. As we talk at his bedside – a straw mattress on a stone bed – village children come nearer and stand with us.

As the older men of the village assemble to have their photo taken, Dinesh translates the village's wish that we stay and eat with them, and relays some of our experiences to the men who gather to listen. As always, there are never any women in such crowds and even small girls form only a tiny part of it. For these people, the journey up to Lalitpur – roughly forty miles – is a major undertaking, even though this village is right on the main road with very occasional buses and trucks to take them there. Delhi though is totally foreign, a vague place of government where the people speak an incomprehensible tongue. As for Kashmir, well, Kashmir is simply an idea that takes a good deal of explaining to the older men.

As in every village, without exception, we are struck by the sheer numbers of children out and about. Only in India, Rossiter says to me, does he suddenly realize how few children he sees at home. The difference is, indeed, quite marked, and many times I find myself wondering what will happen to them all in the future. Even in a prosperous village like this, children are the only available insurance against the hovering shadow of poverty that never quite retreats.

*

At Malthone, about twenty miles south, we decide to rest for the night in the lonely one-roomed resthouse that stands out in its gleaming whitewash and red pantiles, in the harsh scrubby landscape. Malthone strings along the road for about a hundred yards and then gives itself up into the empty Deccan. From the higher ground on which the resthouse stands, we can see the next ghat section, a shimmering purple line far out beyond the tiny town, perhaps ten miles to the south.

Down at the roadside there is a tiny dhaba made of bamboo with a roof of dried cacti which looks like an extremely chaotic thatch and means very little smoke can escape from the huge clay oven below it. Sitting in the intense heat and smoke of this place, it takes some time to detect that there's nothing but old congealed rice to eat. As the owner is putting more dung into the oven to heat it up, I catch sight of a chicken outside, looking if anything more desperate to eat than we are. The idea of an egg seizes me and I run into the road. For some time I follow the bird trying to find its owner and it conveniently returns to its yard some way back.

I go in – it appears to be an only chicken – and find the owner. For some time I stand there making constipated gestures in an attempt to explain the concept of an egg to him. It is not easy. After a very long time he suddenly stands bolt upright and says, 'Ha ... Ha ... ' and taps his forehead. It seems he understands and I return to the dhaba. 'It's OK,' I tell Rossiter who hands me a chai, 'eggs on the way.'

Eggs, however, do not appear and after a while we give up and eat the old rice the dhaba-wallah has been boiling away, while giving us hopeful glances. As usual our eating draws a large crowd who seem reassured to see us eat and afterwards relieve ourselves.

A fair number of these people follow us up to the resthouse where we're forced to lock ourselves in until even the most persistent have left. Early in the evening while we're sitting on the verandah, I'm surprised to see the chicken man arrive after disappointing us earlier. He's brought a bag with him and points to it saying, 'Ek ... Ek ... Ek ...' by which I reckon he means eggs at last. I nod triumphantly at him. He lunges into the bag, there is a muffled squawk and he pulls out the chicken I'd followed earlier. With astonishing speed, he wrings its neck and begins plucking it before we've realized what's happened.

'No, no ... eggs!!' I yell at him, pointing hopelessly at my bottom.

'Eggs on the way – eh?' says Rossiter, appalled at the fatal turn things have taken. The air is now thick with feathers, and the chowkidar has appeared from nowhere to cook the 'Ek'. I've realized too late that 'ek' means one, that is, one dead chicken. Rossiter is beside himself: 'Honestly, with all your environmental pretensions, you ought to be ashamed of yourself. Wait till the R.S.P.B. hear about this one – you'll get nicked!'

It appears that our food, this evening, is chicken, or 'Cok' as the chowkidar has it. I have to admit, I've a real passion for chicken – even starved chicken – but Rossiter is disgusted.

'Mmmm ... gorgeous ...' I mumble, trying hard to enjoy it. 'Want some?'

'Huh, you tuck in, I'm not eating the village mascot. Look at the poor thing, it's more like a curried starling – '

After about an hour's riding from Malthone the next day Rossiter comes to a stop without pulling off the road. He stands extremely still while I catch him up, presuming he's seen a scorpion or snake up ahead. In fact his gaze is fixed on a man rolling over and over along the road, tumbling steadily in our direction. As he rolls head over heels, his companion walks along beside him with the luggage, a brass pot four inches high.

He is a Sadhu – a type of Hindu Holy Man who has decided to give up his job, (a bucket-making business in Jodhpur), and begin a series of penances on a massive scale, believing his more earthly business has reached its maturity. To do this has meant leaving his wife, his eight children and his house but he tells us between rolls this is the only way to improve his karma – a kind of Hindu law of cause and effect relating one's good or bad actions to types of possible reincarnation.

The Sadhu measures his progress at the end of each roll by sitting upright and carefully placing a small marker pebble he carries on the broken-up tarmac of the road. Rossiter is transfixed. 'Holy shit ...' he breathes, hit between the eyes with the fact of another human being completely outstripping both of us in terms of physical endurance and, if the expression on his face is anything to go by, enjoyment. The Sadhu sits up and smiles at us, a bead of sweat drops from the end of his foot and a half of beard and rolls down his chest which, like much of his torso, is grazed and cut up by the rigours of rolling. He tells us he's come all the way from Kanpur and is now on his way back there – two hundred and fifty miles to the north, at least. He then looks to his friend and groans at the brass pot. Rossiter takes the hint and places ten rupees in it, and on the Sadhu rolls with a quiet 'Ram Ram'.

For a long time we watch the two of them growing smaller as they go north, the Sadhu rolling and marking up his progress, his friend with the easier but mindbendingly tedious task of walking along with the pot containing the backsheesh. India has armies of fake Sadhus and sidekicks who do very nicely thank you extracting money from gullible foreigners. But they are found in likely places around temple sites like Khajuraho or Madurai – not along lonely stretches of road in the poorer parts of Madhya Pradesh.

Watching them both disappear sets me thinking of our journey, the problems of which look gloriously unimportant set against rolling. Our problems – like the Sadhu's – are ultimately self-inflicted, since we chose to come here and ride bicycles, but when things are going badly it'll be comforting to think that we could always be rolling naked along the road instead of trying to cycle down it. Broken spokes look much better in that light.

As soon as we have recovered our rhythm again, which tends to mean me cycling a few hundred yards ahead, I am stopped by the sight of a horde of vultures squabbling over a buffalo carcase at the side of the road. The huge birds – white-backed vultures – can be seen coming in to land for miles around, dropping in gliding descent off their look-out thermals. They take about twenty yards to stop, having touched down, flapping wildly with their long pink necks stretched out. Around the carcase, in their black gowns of feathers and white collars, they look like a gang of unruly lawyers hissing and squawking to gain access to the choicest offal.

As these great birds devour the buffalo, a strict pecking order soon becomes apparent. The prime birds have first choice and jump up, extending their necks up into a bloody hole in the buffalo's belly, their hooked beaks snickering away rapidly, gobbling the entrails. Every few moments they pull out their heads and sit, soaked in blood, fierce black eyes blinking away the flies with an expression of complete amazement. If a lesser bird approaches, these leaders run at it, hissing like wildcats.

In their manic enthusiasm to convert the dead beast into guano as fast as possible, some birds eat so much they are temporarily incapable of getting airborne again. They run, flapping desperately for fifty yards or so before collapsing bewildered into the dust where they sit panting, covered in flakes of dried blood.

As there is no food available in any of the villages in this area we decide to press on to Sagar – not that there's much choice. It is a deeply alien experience to find oneself in an area where there simply isn't surplus food for selling to passers-by. All we can do is find a well, fill our bottles and keep going.

We reach Sagar at about four o'clock. Both of us should know by now that many people in this country nod their heads meaning 'No' and shake them to say 'Yes'. A simple mistake (which at this stage of things we ought not to be making) sends us the wrong way in Sagar after we have stopped to eat some dal, rice and fried eggs. We eventually get shown the right road by some enthusiastic boys on bicycles who reunite us with our road hard by the absurd, bright yellow parish church. Otherwise a perfect replica of a Perpendicular original in the Cotswolds, standing on what ought to be its village green, because

Sagar is on the Deccan it is a village brown but a group of men and boys are doing what one should with it, setting up stumps of various lengths for a game of cricket.

The man who prepared the food for us says there is a resthouse in Surkhi, twenty miles south, so we have to leave the cricketers and get on our way before really having the chance to embarrass them with our devastating lack of skill. Between Sagar and Surkhi the land gets as near to desert as it has yet come, great swathes of sand barely concealed by the thin grass struggling to bind to it.

In Surkhi itself – a village of a few hundred people – the Baratiya Janata Party have just finished their day's campaign which has evidently been accompanied by liberal amounts of the local charas being smoked. We are 'invited' to stop by one of the casualties falling across the front of Rossiter's bicycle, bringing both of them to the ground. By the time poor Rossiter is upright again we are separated in a crowd several hundred strong with numerous unco-ordinated arms around each of us pulling us into the nearest dhaba for chai. This is not very welcoming. Nobody has any particular wish to say anything to us – they all simply want to stare and laugh, with glazed red eyes and gurgling giggles at us. Sometimes you're just not in the mood and this is one of them but the crowd has that volatile, excited edge to it that we feel at once. We are un-settled, threatened, and decide it would be unwise to decline any 'invitation' to take chai.

Our drinking does actually calm things a little and people seem slightly less prone to fall over one another than when we first arrived. Most of the villagers are wearing B.J.P. badges and insignia distributed by the campaign party, though few show any idea of why or of what the party is about.

Very slowly and deliberately, we announce the fact that we'd like to go to the P.W.D., which means that eventually room is made for us to depart without feelings of hurt. It also means, of course, that advance parties of small boys tear off screaming and yodelling to announce to the chowkidar that he has guests. The poor man was evidently asleep and is deeply shocked that we should want to stay in his spotlessly maintained but little-used resthouse. He later brings us the inevitable ledger to fill in, which tome informs us that nobody has stayed here for three years.

'Yes, the resthouse is very small,' the chowkidar tells us in Hindi, as if that explains things.

Much of the evening is taken up throwing small boys out of the doors and windows of the resthouse, none of which locks and which provide easy access to sneak in on the Englishmen and see what weird things they are getting up to. Of course they treat being ejected as a huge joke – so much so that their fathers and elder brothers come along to watch the fun, smiling quietly.

We seem to have hit a seam of crowd problems. Partly this is because we are following the B.J.P. lads as they party their way through M.P. State (Sagar District) but it is also because of the large numbers of men in the towns along this stretch of road who do nothing except smoke charas most of the day. Instead of this inducing a state of catatonic stillness, it seems to make them edgy and excitable.

By the time we arrive at Deori the next day we are very tired: the road having entirely disappeared into rubble and dust three miles back, giving Rossiter a puncture. Pushing heavily laden bicycles in India the dust gets in your hair, your eyes and your nose. It films your tongue until you feel like your mouth is full of gravel. Although we are now both very tanned my face is peeling for about the fifteenth time this morning and every time I wipe the sweat away from my face the film of dust rasps off more skin, worsening the raw red patch that used to be a nose in the good old days.

The rally by Deori B.J.P. is still going on, megaphones blasting into the ear-drums of a crowd of men in white pyjamas topped by a sea of black hair, listening only vaguely to the candidate shrieking at them from an upturned oil drum.

Things are evidently not going too well for them either, since about half the crowd of several hundred decides to follow us rather than be screamed at. Were we not tired, filthy and hungry this would be funny and we should no doubt be making clever comments to each other about how this reflects on the electoral standing of the B.J.P. But it isn't like that. The boys swarm round inevitably. A hundred times 'Native place?' and 'Your good name?' are asked, often by the same ones who can say it and are not bothered that you have already answered it. Suddenly, a small stone hits Rossiter in the back as he pushes his bicycle a few yards ahead of me. It does not hurt him but makes us both put our heads down and march the bikes as fast as possible into the nearest shelter from the crowd, the noise, the dust and the heat which are all becoming too much.

An empty-looking shack comes up to the left of the road next to a pot-seller's stall. We go in without waiting to check if anyone is there and barricade the door with my bicycle against the boys. While Rossiter goes to work on the puncture I fend off the more truculent boys trying to pull apart my bicycle, climb over it, come in through the flimsy roof or squeeze through the tiny side-window.

We feel like circus animals, caged in this boiling iron shack where grasping fingers poke in from every crack at us through the hot tin walls. I suppose you can't expect to ride into Deori as if it's Tunbridge Wells and not be noticed – but this is ridiculous. I can only say it's astonishing that boys like this calm down when they grow up, as much as they do. When the tyre is mended we barge straight out into the crowd, abandoning any hope of eating or washing ourselves. For some distance elements of the manic crowd run alongside us, grabbing us and the bikes and shrieking hysterically.

There are few villages along the road south of Deori, and after a couple of hours we cross the River Narmada and take the opportunity to wash some of the day's dust away in its low and brackish waters. There are fishermen here, but they use lines rather than the hand-nets we've seen. They crouch, holding them in the still, shallow waters, hunched like old, white herons, thin brown legs tucked up beneath their dhoties. They do not acknowledge our presence.

A few miles south from the Narmada, there is a rare instance of two major roads crossing each other. To the right, the sign points off along a deserted road trailing away into the rock-studded plain, to Bhopal, a name that has assumed new and sinister dimensions since the chemical disaster there earlier this month.

At the chai-stall that owes its existence to the crossroads, a truck-driver from Gujurat tells us we can stay at Kareli, but it is dark by the time we bother to leave the peaceful group who either work or hang about at the stall.

Our attempts to get to Kareli are distinctly half-hearted and we end up putting the bicycles against a cluster of large rocks which are the only shelter in this treeless countryside. Wrapping ourselves up in the few clothes that we have with us and our thin sheet sleeping-bags that used to be white, we settle down in the dust between these large smooth rocks.

Several hours later, having been too hot for most of the previous day I can stand the cold no longer. 'You awake?' I ask Rossiter, dimly perceived on this moonless night, looking rather like a minor rock heaving with sleep. There is no answer so I assume his more padded frame can keep out the cold better than my skeletal body does. As I sit shivering, occasionally getting up to run on the spot or jump about in a half-hearted attempt to get warm, I start wondering what people at home are doing. I get quite far down the road with this, inventing all sorts of scenarios, until I light a match to see my watch. It is so near dawn here that most of the people I know in England will be asleep now. My speculations evaporate and I spend a lonely half hour before the eastern sky begins to light up and the stars start fading overhead.

We actually reach Kareli at about eight o'clock and can see no sign of a place to stay. 'You look pretty rough,' Rossiter tells me as we drink coffee in the small bazaar of the town, 'I'd say you're looking every one of your twenty-four years.'

'My God – I'd completely forgotten –'

'Here, take these,' Rossiter says, with one of his ultra-benevolent smiles. 'Happy Birthday.'

He gives me a small paper bag made from an old newspaper, full of delicious fresh cashew nuts, which go extremely well with the strong coffee this dhaba is selling. For some days now I have pressed upon him, in my sternest way, that birthdays are irrelevant for us here in central India. He has ignored my lectures predictably and though I'm not going to tell him, I'm touched by the Rossiter sense of occasion.

I do not know where or when he managed to get hold of the cashews, for buying very much in the way of food has been something of a problem over the last few days. We have been living off chillis, rice and occasional dal, morning, noon and night which very quickly saps your energy. Because of this problem, we decide to try to push on and get down to Lakhna-don today if at all possible.

At midday we stop for some shade and to fill our water bottles, having made good progress all morning. A strikingly tall man wearing a large dagger and a Rajasthani coil-turban comes over to us from the herd of goats he is driving along the road with a boy.

'My friends – you are British peoples I am suspecting! Ha!' He roars with laughter, fiercely. 'I am a freedom-fighter against the British! You are welcome here in my country. Come – we shall eat together.'

Amjin Singh Patel is manifestly not the sort of person you turn down on such an offer, which comes with the force of decision rather than suggestion. He strides off without waiting for us as we gather the bikes and follow, leaving the boy without a word, to cope as best he can with the goats.

His house turns out to be a short distance up the road back in the direction we've just come. From it, he farms tracts of land with his sons for a wide distance around, partly because the land is only intermittently capable of growing anything with any success and rocky, barren areas intersperse the small fields of cane, maize and wheat. Partly it is because he is a wealthy man, doubling up as the local money-lender and legal adviser for anybody who needs help and is prepared to get themselves further into debt with him.

In his forthright manner he takes us on a rapid tour of the farmhouse with its one huge communal bedroom upstairs and the row of enormous clay pots used as a granary – each one ten or twelve feet high. We eat on the shady verandah in front of which is parked Amjin's pride and joy: his gleaming Triumph Herald.

Wooden trays are placed on the earth floor where we're sitting and onto them are piled rice, papadums, chutneys, dals, parathas, a large dollop of byngun and another of kheer with a sesame-seed biscuit by way of a sweet. As soon as any pile or dollop shows signs of diminishing, Amjin's wife or daughter rushes out to replenish it. We eat with our hands, and my eyes overload my shrunken stomach. Afterwards, we cross the field at the back of the house to wash our hands again, just as we ritually washed them before the meal. Coming from the well, Amjin takes us to his own tiny temple set into a room about the size of an average wardrobe but filled with a healthy representation of the Hindu pantheon.

The temple is dominated with a large bronze Brahma with his four Vedas, flanked by Vishnu. Hanuman, the monkey god, is also perched above the others in an attitude of engrossed concentration.

Amjin lights up two joss-sticks, stoops and picks up a small book lying in one corner of the temple. 'Please, take this for your anniversary: it is Bhagavad Gita.'

Between Mr Patel's farmhouse and Lakhnadon there is another unexpected ghat section towards the end of which I'm forced to eat my words about the unlikelihood of seeing any wild animals on such roads. On the long freewheel down the far side of the ghats, a wild boar brings us both to a sudden stop in the dusky light. He is up ahead of us about a hundred yards away. He trots into the road, stops and sniffs the cool evening air in our direction, before making off into the thin forest on either side with his taut muscle-bound trot. We wait for a respectable interval before going forwards, trusting to an instinctive feeling we have that he was alone. All that remains are his trotter-marks, clear in the undisturbed dust at the roadside.

Finally, more than two hours after dark, we reach the bazaar at Lakhnadon and sit about drinking mango lassi until we can face going up the hill to the resthouse. It is just as well that we rested before doing so since the chowkidar is of the uncompromising school who insists with all the usual vehemence that the place is not merely fully booked but that both rooms are actually occupied – in direct conflict with all visual evidence of two large empty rooms.

'But there's nobody here, can't you see that?' cries Rossiter, not unreasonably. A bead of sweat drops off his nose onto the floorboards of the verandah, with an audible tap.

'Nothing is possible for you,' replies the chowkidar with tired finality. 'You must see the District Magistrate.'

'Where does he live, then?' I ask.

'It is near to this place,' says the chowkidar, sensing it's time to play 'Hunt the District Magistrate'. But he is dead serious. I'm dead beat, and in no mood for this kind of business. We leave him and find the D.M. ourselves by the brilliant device of asking a more positively disposed human – which means almost anybody else in Lakhnadon.

Like most of the D.M.s we have so far come across, the Lakhnadon edition is immensely fat – but he is also surprisingly fast-moving and fairly races us back up the hill to the P.W.D. when we have explained our predicament over the mandatory cup of tray-tea. Within seconds he has secured us a room in the resthouse but does warn us that the place is full tomorrow with extra D.M.s arriving in town to make arrangements for the coming election on Christmas Eve – or 24th December as it is in India. The chowkidar shows not the slightest surprise at seeing us again, nor the slightest hint of losing face in any possible way, true to his school. All is apparently as he expected and he now goes about his business with an air of smug self-satisfaction.

Although we've already eaten in the bazaar we're invited to eat the 'Cok' with two of the D.M.s who have arrived to organize tomorrow's polling. The 'cok' is the same one which we heard the chowkidar inexpertly killing earlier on – but even after Malthone I'm not losing my stomach for under-sized chicken. In any case, when a D.M. asks you to dinner, you do not refuse. In the course of eating, the conversation comes inevitably round to the imminence of Christmas. 'So this time will be a big Festival for you?' says the larger, obviously more senior D.M.

'No,' I tell them at once.

'Yes,' says Rossiter.

'Will you be taking a rest from your cycle programme, during this festival?' asks the senior D.M. At this point Rossiter drops a bombshell.

'Yes indeed. I think a week at Khana would be a perfect Christmas holiday – it's so near isn't it and I know Alex would love to see a tiger. You know all about Khana, don't you?'

'Where?' I say, confused.

'You know – one of the wildlife parks where Project Tiger is based. It's supposed to be really spectacular. With all your rantings about the environment, you must know about it.'

'Eh?'

'Well,' sighs Rossiter to the D.M.s. 'My friend would enjoy it, I know, and it doesn't take long to get there does it?'

'Ha!' says the less fat D.M., looking glazed.

'Tigers! We have preserved them for the world, and you must surely see them on your special festival. It shall be arranged, I am speaking to Mr Lal on this matter – all is possible.'

5

'No mountains infringe on the curve.
League after league the earth lies flat,
heaves a little, is flat again.'

E. M. Forster

'Please, you do one thing,' says the District Magistrate Mr Lal the next morning, as we sip tray-tea on his expansive verandah, listening to a bul-bul bubbling away unseen in the distance. 'Please, you will visit our doctor here in Lakhnadon while I am making arrangements necessary for your visit to Khana.'

'Thank you –' says Rossiter, but he is cut short by Mr Lal frowning.

'Please, you must be careful with our doctor's speaking. He is having very strong accents and sometimes he is being difficult to hear with correctness. I am thinking he is not from England.'

With that, his man appears and bundles our bags and bicycles into the Mahindra jeep and speeds us down to the bazaar, trailing a cloud of dust behind us. We turn right, out of the bazaar, and climb a short hill out of the town to the place where the low, whitewashed houses give out into the cacti, thorn bushes and washed-out dullness of the Deccan. In front of the last building of gleaming whiteness is a sign in English: 'Lakhnadon Mission Hospital'. Ganesh dumps us and our belongings unceremoniously before screaming off to help Mr Lal make arrangements for voting in this region. He has an air of puffed-up importance about the task, which we get in the way of, rather irritatingly.

Clearly, this is one of those subliminal Indian arrangements whereby you only find out what is required of you when no other alternative is apparent, a system which avoids a good deal of ambiguity but does sometimes put you squarely on the spot. So there seems to be nothing for it but to barge in and introduce ourselves. As we cross the courtyard we are both transfixed by a female Edinburgh accent. 'Good morning,' says the voice as if we'd been expected for some time. 'Are you looking for Doctor MacDonald by any chance?'

The voice belongs to one of the two Scottish nursing staff who help Dr Donald MacDonald run this mission hospital in the middle of a particularly barren and lonely stretch of Madhya Pradesh. It is not the most likely place on earth to find the influence of the Free Church of Scotland. We are shown through a small wicket gate under a cascade of bougainvillea in very full bloom, across a garden of mango and guava trees and into the sitting-room of a family house all set up for Christmas with cards decorating the walls, an improvised Christmas tree adorned in tinsel and a tray of hot mince pies coming straight from the oven in the hands of Joan MacDonald. Suddenly, with the smell of the pies and the sight of the cards everywhere and the warmth of the welcome we get, we're acutely aware of how far Christmas with all its family connotations has dropped from our minds whilst we've been on the road. 'Donald's operating just now – it's only a cataract so he'll be here in a few minutes. It'll be quite a surprise for him to see you both.' Not half as big a surprise as running into a family of Scottish Christians in festive mood is for us, I'll bet.

When Dr Donald MacDonald appears, it's been a routine sort of morning so far with three operations completed in his tiny theatre as well as rounds of the hospital itself. After a quick cup of coffee and a mince pie he is back out again to do another operation, having done his level best to get us to stay for lunch with the family, ably assisted by the three young MacDonalds home for the Christmas holidays from their boarding school in Ooty, more than a thousand miles south of here. Having disappeared for a moment, he is back a few minutes later to take his large torch into the operating theatre, where electricity is not something to be relied upon.

Although it is tempting to stay, we know that the only bus towards Khana will leave in thirty minutes (in theory) so it's time to return to D.M. Mr Lal to see what arrangements he has come up with.

He has, in fact, not come up with very much. To be honest: nothing. We explain to him that the MacDonalds have been kind enough to look after our bicycles for us, so now we have walked back here and are ready to go to Khana to look for tigers. This has very little effect on Mr Lal at all, who sits in his creaking wicker chair, pats his rolling belly contentedly and smiles at everything that passes. Finally, as the bus is about to leave, Mr Lal takes it upon himself to write a note to his colleague Mr R. K. Singhai in Nainpur who, he beams, will surely be of the greatest possible assistance to us in arriving at Khana.

The whole idea of leaving the bicycles to go somewhere entirely different is deeply peculiar when bicycling southwards has rather become a way of life for us both. On the bus – which is like a furnace and smells overpoweringly of petrol – Rossiter is in euphoric mood. He regards his pointing out to me the existence of Khana as a cartographic triumph and will not let me hear the last of it. More than this though, an experience in the MacDonalds' house has put him in a great frame of mind. Squeezing his frame into the tiny space allowed for one's body on Indian buses, he turns to me. 'Did you see what they had in their bathroom? Did you? Did you see it – you know what I mean?'

'No,' I reply, disappointingly.

'Oh dear, oh dear, oh dear,' laughs Rossiter. 'They only had a western loo, that's all. Oh the bliss of not having to squat at the edge of some paddy with half the nearest village watching to see how you function. Mmmmm – was I glad to set eyes on it. Shame we can't take one around with us, really.'

'Oh, I don't know. I quite enjoy squatting, in public or otherwise.'

'That's because you're a latent exhibitionist,' says Rossiter with an air of finality. As his bowels have been acting in fairly spectacular fashion for some time, the relief of a loo must be welcome.

The problem with tiger sanctuaries is that, by their very nature, they do not happen to be close to anywhere. Although the reserve is not seventy miles from Lakhnadon, getting there is not easy. After a couple of hours on this bus, which stops every few hundred yards, we get to Gunsor in the late afternoon with seven hours to wait till the next narrow-gauge steam train passes through the town's tiny station. We decide to drown our sorrows at a small evil-looking counter where lethal, green, unlabelled bottles of spirit are being sold furtively by a man with a severe hare-lip. This brew makes arrack or Tibetan chang taste like Earl Grey tea. We agree it must simply be ethyl alcohol or perhaps some left-over meths from a poor year. One small green bottle is, we find, enough.

Gunsor is unusual in being the first place we have seen where the Bharatiya Janata Party seem to be scoring a hit with the electorate. It is their posters that dominate here and not those of Congress (I) and the inevitable megaphone blares to an evidently converted audience.

After our drink we are in dire need of somewhere to sit in relative peace and are glad of the free seats offered by the local video-cinema-wallah. Inside the 'video-tent' (ladies on the left, gents on the right) the audience is being treated to the familiar fare of a Bombay masala movie. Plump villains and plumper heroes and heroines tread the tightrope of a plot which is lost on both of us but contains the inevitable wet-saree scene wherein the heroine contrives to get a soaking and thus stoke up the film's content with something erotic. Almost everyone of any significance bursts into song at the most unlikely of times, including one poor fellow about to have his eyes put out by an overweight heavy with a large ring through his nose. But you know everything will be all right when the baddies have been inexplicitly done to death and the portly hero and ample heroine end up singing at each other half-way up the Himalaya against the setting sun. The audience is stamping, cheering or crying with relief that it's all worked out against the odds.

Judging by the weight factor and the need to sing, Rossiter says we could make it big in Bombay films. On reflection though, the sight of Rossiter serenading his heroine wearing some lavish kurta and warbling in Hindi may not be quite what the audience is looking for. All in all though, the film is a stylish change from the Hollywood guns, guts and grunts approach to heroes.

The journey to Nainpur is made in the tiny two-carriage train at a little over walking pace. It is quite cold by the time the train leaves just before midnight and when we get to Nainpur it is freezing – I suspect we must have climbed in altitude in the four hours we were in the train. It takes some time to wake up the one rickshawman at Nainpur Station and persuade him to take us to the P.W.D. resthouse.

It is three o'clock by the time we get there and after shouting 'chow-kee-daaar' for what seems a very long time, he appears wrapped in blankets with the long stake and lantern that all chowkidars sprout when the sun goes down, looks at us standing and shivering and refuses to let us in. Flashing our (by now distinctly tattered) pieces of paper does no good but the chowkidar finally decides to extend one bony hand from the dark blanket that cocoons him, and raps at the door of the second bedroom to wake a Police Inspector who seems to be staying there with his young boyfriend. Presumably this is to have us both arrested, which is preferable, frankly, to standing here shivering all night, but it is merely to ask if we can be put into the room next door to which the Inspector immediately assents, telling us to come and see him in the morning. That part of the deal makes no impression on either of us as I am bitterly cold and Rossiter is both cold and ill.

We duly troop next door in the morning, pretending not to notice the boyfriend hiding, ill-concealed, in the cupboard. The ridiculousness of this is awful, almost overwhelming, when at one point the unfortunate man is overcome by the desire to sneeze whilst the Inspector starts to talk about our journey IN A VERY LOUD VOICE. Having made it quite clear that he is doing us a big favour by not arresting us both for causing a disturbance and interrupting his night's, er, sleep, he lets us get to the door before saying, 'But – you are not offering me any present from your country?'

'I'm sorry,' I tell him, 'we carry very few things – we have only money.'

'You have pounds sterling for me?'

'Well no,' I lie, 'only rupees.'

'You will give me rupees.'

Suddenly we're put in a difficult position. We realize he thinks he can extract backsheesh because he can say we've made a noise in the middle of the night – which is true. On balance it's best to offer fifty rupees, claim that is all we have and get out. It works.

Much better things await us at Mr R. K. Singhai's. Mr Singhai is absolutely at a loss as to whom Mr Lal of Lakhnadon is, but 'overjoyed' to see us both anyway and 'delighted' that we should like, eventually, to get to Khana (a destination beginning to seem more and more remote). R.K. sees it as not the slightest imposition that we should turn up out of the blue at breakfast time and soon has the wonder of hot water for us to wash in and a breakfast of fried eggs, omelettes, boiled eggs, parathas, apricots, mango chutney, chai and cashews. R.K. believes in going to work on an egg (or six). Unfortunately, Rossiter keeps telling me he's feeling dreadful, which information even I am beginning to take more seriously. I have to eat a great many eggs this breakfast time.

As luck would have it – or is it all part of some unfathomed arrangement? – R.K. is going to Mandla today and will drop us off from the jeep with his friend Mr Mopatra who is working there for Project Tiger. 'Surely he is willing to assist you in reaching Khana. There is no problem.'

Once you have got yourself locked into this kind of chain-communication you might as well go along with it, so we climb into the jeep and are covered in dust within minutes along the dirt road to Mandla, wondering where we'll end up next with little hope of it ever being Khana.

But both R.K. and Mr Mopatra are as good as their respective words and late in the evening, having taken about thirty hours travelling over two hundred miles to reach a place only seventy from where we started, we are in Khana.

Arriving late at night at a national wildlife reserve is not a very good idea – but it happens to be the only time we could get a lift with one of Mr Mopatra's jeeps. Because visitors are not really encouraged in this reserve there are only a few small bamboo huts to stay in, in the forest – or at least you can when they are not full of Bombay sewerage engineers on a works outing.

This, of course, is our own fault since the whole concept of getting to Khana is based on the principle that the only sane way to do it is to come via Jabalpur to the north, where you can book a hut in the small area of huge forests into which humans are allowed. Since nobody would be so stupid as to approach from any other angle due to the sheer hassle of it, we now find there is no room for us. The burden of coming from the south-west instead of the north can be very onerous at Khana. 'But you must have somewhere,' I plead. 'My friend is ill – anything will be all right.'

'No it won't,' mutters Rossiter next to me, slumped against a bamboo wall.

'I shall try to do my best,' says the man who seems to be sorting out such matters. I have a vague feeling of having been either an unwonted burden or a straight pain in the neck to almost everybody we've met since leaving our bicycles in Lakhnadon. But again, nobody takes it amiss that we arrive from the wrong place and wrong direction at the wrong time of day.

'He'll get us a room – I know it,' Rossiter breathes, confident as ever, in sickness as in health.

I am now able to say that it's surprising how well two grown men can sleep together under some old sacking on a thin charpoy with large holes in it, even given that one of the two has decided to underline his statements about feeling ill by staggering off into the jungle all the time to be violently sick. I keep telling him this kind of thing will get us nowhere but he doesn't seem to take it in – perhaps he's feeling ill.

When it gets light enough to see by I gradually realize that the intermittent rasping and snuffling sounds coming from the forest a few yards away are the sound of the chital – spotted deer – a small group of which graze unperturbed near our hut under the huge sal forest. Above them, a family of silver langurs leaps along the highest branches, making them bend and spring as they catapult themselves from one tree to another with offhand grace. Now and then they stop and eye the ground nervously, as the rising sun brings off the dew in clouds of steam. The parakeets are cavorting and crying out in the lower branches and, far off, a jackal barks shortly on his way home to rest. The first rays glint through the rich green undergrowth lighting the spiders' webs, a hornbill glides past, intent and silent. Somewhere in my head, as if at a great distance, a voice reminds me that it's Christmas Day.

Rossiter, however, is not enthusiastic about the date or anything much beyond a continued desire to avoid eating. He has now eaten nothing since he left the MacDonalds'. It is me, therefore, who eats both lots of kheer served up for breakfast in a large bamboo hut across what is visible in daylight as a compound in the forest. After that I spend my Christmas morning sunbathing while Rossiter sleeps with a whole charpoy to himself. Luxury.

By the afternoon he reckons he's feeling well enough to try and organize a ride out into the jungle at dawn tomorrow. Although the Chief Warden of the reserve tells us that nobody has seen any tiger here for almost three weeks and adds that this is not at all unusual, we are keen and optimistic about finding even the odd pug-mark – anything to make the reserve live up to the reputation Rossiter has been building for the place ever since he sprang its existence on me in Lakhnadon.

When I get back to the hut after trying to arrange this, Rossiter is sitting in the sun wrapped in a blanket (even though it is hot; maybe he really *is* ill?) and wrapt in conversation with the wizened telephone engineer who was last night attempting to unravel cables at the reserve office, to no apparent avail. 'The problems have grown beyond my capabilities here,' he says tiredly. 'I am calling for the Chief Sub-Engineer from Jabalpur.'

'By telephone, eh?' I suggest, unwisely, and the engineer then spends a great deal of effort telling me why this is not possible because of the cable.

'But I am asking your friend here for a picture of Mister Michael Faraday, but he is telling me he is not carrying such a picture. You have a photo of this man?'

I have to tell him the awful truth that I, too, am travelling so light as to have neglected my photograph of Michael Faraday – that goes in with the sterilization tablets the very next time I head for Heathrow Airport. All we can do is promise to send him such a photo upon returning to England, along with the rest of the list of similarly unlikely cravings in need of satisfaction from others we have met along the road.

When the engineer goes, Mr Sinha – the Chief Warden – arrives and tells us about the reserve (evidently old hat to Rossiter, who seems to be staging a recovery). It was not for tiger that these two hundred and fifty square kilometres became a reserve in 1955. That happened to protect the Swamp Deer or Hardground Barasingha hunted for centuries in these sprawling, lush sal and teak forests that line the Banjar Valley. The barasingha stand over five feet tall and with stags carrying antlers of fourteen points or more they sound very impressive. But Khana is more than a place for hunters in the past, for it was here that Kipling wrote *The Jungle Book*. That was not in the Rossiter list of facts, and adds to the atmosphere of the place considerably, especially as it gets dark and the spotted deer begin to edge out from the fringes of the forests onto the stretches of grass that surround our small huts.

Peculiarly, in the dead of winter, the forest is actually quieter at night than the paddies, hills and scrub we have been travelling through. It is also a good deal darker, and after we have gone across to the kitchen hut to chat with the cooks, eat eggs for Christmas dinner and warm ourselves, we cannot find our way to Mr Sinha's hut which would be the only one with electricity if the current were working (trouble with the cables, no doubt). Mr Sinha had invited us over to hear the Queen's Speech at 8.30 in the evening – the absurdity of this coming live into the jungle seemed far too good to miss – but instead we find ourselves trailing about with no moon, unable to see anything away from the glow of the fire in the cooks' hut. 'You know something,' I say to Rossiter as we thrash about in the undergrowth. 'If we'd bothered to join the Scouts we'd have a torch or something on us now.'

'If you'd bothered to look after the torch we once had it would have lasted us further than the Punjab.'

'I think that's being –'

I get no further. A low, throaty growling comes from the undergrowth. It does not appear to be very close, so far as we can judge it, but one thing is clear: the growl is up ahead and the light of the kitchen fire is behind. We turn and run.

Fortunately Mr Sinha is sitting round the fire when we charge in and warns us not to go anywhere at night without the large torch he helpfully produces for us to use whilst we're here. With him and it for comfort we go to his hut – in a totally different direction, discussing the noise we have heard, which intrigues him greatly. 'I think perhaps this is a dog,' he says after some time.

Whatever it was, we had enough of it and it is comforting now to sit by candlelight drinking Mr Sinha's plentiful supply of whisky and hear the Queen crackling out into the jungle on BBC World Service. Rossiter seems unmoved by the whole performance, beyond the sheer incongruity of it, as am I until it comes to the national anthem which, for the first and probably the last time in my life, seems absurdly moving, blasting out of the radio, rolling through the open door with its mosquito net drawn back, out into the huge black beyond. However much I try to ignore the significance of birthday and Christmas, events conspire to give them more the more I try.

At dawn the next day, before six o'clock, we climb up into the howdah of one of the three elephants kept at the camp – the only way of going into the jungle away from the dirt roads. Wrapped up against the frosty cold of dawn in the blankets from our hut the huge animal lurches us off along a tiny path. As we shamble along, the first jungle-fowls stir and the doves begin to call to each other, unseen in the dense green foliage. The mahout climbs up along the bended knee of his elephant and perches behind her ears, steering by a nudge against right or left ear as we swing along. This mahout is keen to inform us that the Duke of Edinburgh sat upon this very beast when he came to Khana and could we possibly get him a picture of the event? We make a mental note of this under the Faraday assignment, on our list.

The huge elephant is able to plough along, through or over almost anything and the mahout nudges her across sudden deep nullahs full of grasses twenty feet high or into dense bamboo thickets. The hinges of the howdah creak to the swing of her huge brown back. Boar, chital and jackals cross our path and skulk off before the huge beast. After walking for perhaps two miles or more the mahout brings the elephant to a stop at the edge of a wide nullah thick with golden grasses at least as high as we are.

She raises her trunk to filter the morning air, dewy and cold. Now and then there come from her trunk huge sighs, steamy and smelling of cow dung, as she edges her way slowly and delicately down the steep banks of the nullah. All the while the mahout nudges behind those incredible ears and whistles softly, almost to himself. Down in the nullah she moves more cautiously, almost expectantly.

After perhaps a hundred yards, she freezes. Without panic she holds herself utterly still, ears straight out and motionless. 'Tiger,' whispers the mahout, pointing down to our left. For a very long time neither of us can see anything down there but grass stems, hissing quietly in the cold dawn light. Then, as the mahout grows impatient with us, there comes a low muttered growl from the grass ten feet away. I peer into the grass, and the symmetry of a tiger's face suddenly takes shape, staring back at me: an unblinking stare and jaws parted just enough to let that terrible noise escape. Now we know when we heard it before — last night near the huts.

Even at this distance it is impossible to make out more than the face and part of the neck, so perfect is the camouflage. There is no doubt in my mind that you would tread on a tiger out here before you would see one.

But we cannot linger. As the growl fades the elephant moves off unprompted in one mighty lurch through the grass stems. She has had enough and in a second the tiger is left, melted away into its surroundings to do what tigers do best, nothing. 'You bring luck to Khana,' says the mahout when we are clear of the nullah. Over the next four days in the reserve we find ourselves being 'lucky' on two more occasions including one sighting of a tigress in much more open country, splayed out at rest beneath a thicket of bamboo in a wide clearing covered with leaves. All of this is a testimony to the success of Project Tiger in preserving these animals from possible extinction in this part of India – even at the expense of human beings. It is also testimony to the training and aplomb of the elephants which crunch through the jungle. I cannot say if tigers at rest resent being disturbed very much – but I do know that hearing a tiger growl sounds much less frightening from the back of an Indian elephant.

Our return to Lakhnadon turns out to be far smoother than our arrival – it could hardly have been less so – but one never quite knows here. We take a bus from Mandla – near Khana – to Jabalpur. It is a bad ride. Because the front part of the roof has become rusted away and is roped down, the engine vibrates the whole sheet of metal giving the impression of someone attacking sheet-metal with a pneumatic drill two feet away. We are near the front where the noise is loudest. There is also a gaping hole in the gangway where the rusted floor has caved in and been left unpatched for ventilation purposes. As we are about to pull away from the Mandla bus-stand an enterprising chicken pops up through the floor-hole, rides a few yards for the sheer hell of it, then slips below, emerging out under the back of the bus unscathed.

Money is rarely a straightforward matter in India but the ticketting on the bus is a whole scene to itself. Rossiter pays our fare (six rupees each) with a twenty note, plunging it at the conductor's hand as the bus screams and belches black smoke to cruise at about ten miles per hour.

'Nahin, nahin,' shouts the conductor, squashing the note back into his hand, nodding vigorously, yet looking through the grimy window.

'I have no change – please take it,' Rossiter shouts.

'Nahin.'

'Please!'

The conductor takes the note, now gone limp with palmy sweat. He checks it, sees a small tear and looks down at Rossiter as if questioning his sanity. 'Nahin,' he patiently repeats, with much nodding. He continues looking out of the window, glancing down to check on us every now and then. It is all part of the national game, played right across the country, whereby nobody wants to part with any change. Everybody claims they haven't got any because there's a shortage and nobody will accept torn notes – which are thus difficult to palm off on people as Rossiter is trying to do.

There's nothing for it but to offer new money, which gets us round the tear problem but takes us to round two: change. The conductor simply dredges a handful of coins and small notes (some torn) and dollops it into Rossiter's hand uncounted. You then have to refuse the torn ones and hold out for more change since the original dollop is deliberately never enough (but it's just possible the customer might not notice). Even if it's not the conductor's money, the game will still be played with relish. He changes the torn notes. We hold out for more change and the conductor – preferring not to lose more change than necessary – scribbles Rs. 2.60 on a morsel of paper, by way of IOU. He then heaves out sheaves of delightfully coloured tickets and tears and stamps one for each denomination of coin and note we eventually manage to give him. Such is the scope in the Madhya Pradesh State Road Transport Corporation for spicing ticket-collecting with that most tasty of Indian ingredients, bureaucracy.

It is nothing but pure relief to stagger down from this bus at Jabalpur, the noise of it being such that even the bus-stand here sounds quiet. The bus-stand is, in fact, ringed with megaphones blaring out victory songs on behalf of Rajiv and Congress (I) now elected with the landslide victory everyone expected.

Jabalpur was the town from which the indefatigable Colonel Sleeman worked away to stamp out the practice of 'Thuggee'. For a very long time before Col. Sleeman arrived in town, the Thugs had been in the habit of strangling their victims with a silken cord in order to appease the goddess Kali, the fiercest of the Hindu gods. With her garland of skulls she is wont to ask for sacrifices and the Thugs delivered them in this region with particular zest. It took well over fifty years to stop the practice, in which time Sleeman had set up a 'School of Industry' in which to hold and occupy the hands of suspected Thugs with 'constructive labour' — not, one presumes, rope-making.

After one night of luxury in a small Jabalpur hotel where the hot tap works, we're both itching to get going south again. In the middle of India I am assailed by the notion that now Christmas is over something 'normal' ought to begin happening again, like work. With our thoughts turning to the bicycles again, we decide to try to telephone Indian Airlines in New Delhi to arrange to have the spare wheel we have left there freighted south. With the Rossiter rear wheel shedding spokes at its present rate we shall be lucky if our supply of spares lasts us even to Nagpur — let alone beyond.

Having got through to the Air India office from the telephone exchange with very little trouble and left a message, we go straight to the bus-stand for what promises to be another painful ride back to Lakhnadon. As it turns out, it's almost pleasant, with the vehicle half-full, the roof in place and wall-to-wall flooring. The ride is much enlivened by a feeble-looking man with one long and pointed tooth, who gets on with a small pig. Although its front and back legs are trussed up, it squeals, butts and fights the man for ten minutes before they both get off and continue the struggle at the roadside. The driver's reaction is to light a sixth large joss-stick and calmly fog up his end of the bus even more in an effort to ignore his cargo.

It is strange, on a journey such as this, to return to the same point you were at just a short time ago, but the MacDonalds are pleased to see us. 'Did you see any tigers?' asks their son Colin who comes pedalling up the dusty road to meet us (there are so few buses it is easy to guess which one somebody will arrive on).

In the house, Joan is getting the roast beef (buffalo) ready and has a suggestion for us, as she hands us cups of tea. 'If you want you can go in and see Donald when you've finished your tea – I think he's doing a stomach ulcer just now.'

'It's OK just to wander in and watch?' I ask.

'Oh yes, just take off your plimsolls,' she advises us, surveying the wreckage of our baseball-boots which must, somehow, last to the Cape.

In the small operating theatre, Donald's two assistants are pointing torches into the patient's stomach. 'The – ah – the electricity's off again,' Donald explains, straining to tease God alone knows what into position inside the glistening red wound. From the start, Rossiter is completely engrossed by what is going on but I have little stomach for this kind of thing, if you'll pardon the expression. I am not feeling too good; indeed, it's getting hard to focus and my head is becoming hot and heavy. Suddenly the patient starts talking to Donald, who has his hand buried inside the man's insides.

'He's . . . um . . . he's talking, isn't he?' I point out, trying to believe this isn't happening to me (let alone to him).

'Oh yes – he's just had a spinal. Can't feel a thing, you know.'

To my spinning brain, this seems like giving somebody an aspirin before removing a major limb. I would never make a surgeon, much less an anaesthetist.

Rossiter though is peering over for a better view and then I am vaguely aware of him saying (while I concentrate on not blacking out), 'Er, do you think, I mean, would it be possible for me to, ah, to interview you whilst you're doing the op? Sort of describe what's going on? I think people would be quite interested.'

As I stagger out in search of fresh air my last sight is of Rossiter, microphone in one hand, camera in the other, peering into the man's insides and saying, 'Is that his pancreas then?'

That situation contrasts totally with the conversation over lunch and during the tour of the hospital we go on later. The problems of bringing up a family in this situation must be huge when the children go to school a thousand miles away from parents themselves five thousand miles from home.

Nonetheless their three children seem happy enough, undemanding of and unfettered by all the paraphernalia of the West. Colin would like a bigger bicycle, true, and like boys everywhere is keen on throwing pebbles at the huge old toad who lives in the well. As we wander out from the hospital into the small fields, Donald tells us it's hard to raise a sufficient crop from the thin, sandy soil here when he can only afford to pay low wages for piecework in the fields. We stand there not knowing quite what to say to all this, wondering how it could be possible to run a farm at all when you are already running a hospital.

When we finally set off down the road in the late afternoon sun, Colin pedals furiously with us for a mile or so, wearing a horse-riding hat and red tee-shirt. Then with a small, shy 'Bye then' he turns and we watch him become a shimmering red blob in the heat haze, floating north above the liquid dust.

It is curiously comforting to be back on the bicycles again, even a relief in a kind of way, and, as if to return us to old times, the road gives out pretty soon into jagged lumps of tar and potholes. It has been smashed up by some contractor who has concluded, evidently, that the job is done and has upped and left the road in ruins. Parts of the wrecked surface are now being worked smooth by the indestructible buses and trucks that come piling over the debris every now and then. For those with vehicles of more sensitive disposition it's back to ploughing along on foot or at walking pace in the dust of the roadside for about two miles.

As we push along we come upon three old-looking vultures perched on a naked, blasted tree, silhouetted against the white of the sunbleached sky. They do not fly off as we pass them but merely bend their necks low to get a look at us, beaks gaped wide in an attempt to keep cool, while flies buzz around their gape, attracted by the stains and scabs of their last meal.

At Lakhnadon we had joined National Highway 7 a single-lane road much like an English B road. About half a mile after the surface resumes unbroken, a signpost to Kannyakumari suddenly appears on the left of the road, facing the oncoming traffic. The NH7 winds its way from the Hindu temples and Ganges bathing-ghats of Varanasi for nearly 1500 miles to the temples and sea-ghats at Kannyakumari, our destination at the tip of India. According to the signpost there are 1969 kilometres to go and we really do not know whether this is good news or bad. It's good to see Kannyakumari actually signposted but they could have left out the bit about the distance, just to spare our feelings a little.

It's still over a hundred miles to Nagpur, our next port of call and reputedly the hottest city in India. Neither Rossiter nor myself is capable of thinking in terms of kilometres even after cycling over two thousand of them laid end to end. It's curious how aspects of the life you're used to persist strongly against all the odds – or perhaps they persist because of the odds. As we left the MacDonalds' house quite late on we decide to stop at a Dak Bungalow which conveniently appears after a couple of hours, at Seoni Chapara.

The bungalow is left open, the two doors to its bedrooms off a deep wooden verandah gaping wide in the pinky light of sunset when we arrive. At first there seems to be absolutely nobody about and we edge cautiously into one of the rooms. Just as we do so a large scorpion edges its way out – we give way to it, fast. After giving the room a thorough going-over for any other such sitting tenants, we move in for the night. Only when I am moving my bicycle in do I notice a small man squatting at the other end of the verandah. 'Are you the chowkidar?' I ask, in Hindi, rather optimistically. He stares back at me in complete amazement and shifts one of his feet, both of which are encased in huge Rajasthani slippers of brightly embroidered leather and pointed, curled-up toes. I ask again. He looks, if anything, more amazed and Rossiter nods approvingly as he always does when my attempts at Hindi meet with stunned gazes. 'Anyway, they speak Marathi here,' I point out, spying a possible defence.

What really proves that this old man is no chowkidar is the way he refuses the money we offer for the room, or rather, not the way he refuses but the fact of refusing money at all. Chowkidars do not refuse money. Later on, as we sit on the huge unmade bed and I attempt to swat mosquitoes, the old one suddenly appears at the window staring in at us, silent, his head shrouded against the night in his dirty white cloak. For some minutes he stands peering into the candlelit room from the blank darkness of the night outside. This is profoundly disturbing and is just getting to the point when we're about to leap up and get rid of him when, of his own accord, he disappears from the window. Instantly we spring up to make quite sure he has left, glimpsing him disappearing into the night in his dull white cloak.

For some time we are silent, watching the candle's flame. 'You know what I'm thinking?' Rossiter says after a while.

'Yes – I think I do,' I say huskily.

'What?'

'That this could be some kind of . . . a kind of trap.'

'Yeah. I mean why would that guy just sit there when the place is wide open and then come and look in on us like that – as if he was checking up on us. Everywhere we stop there's always people hanging around or coming to look at us, so why not here – the town's only a few hundred yards up the road, half a mile at most. I really don't like this at all.'

'Me neither.'

'So what shall we do then? I'm really not into staying here at all, not after seeing him suddenly peering in at us like that.'

'There's nowhere else,' I say.

'Could keep going, couldn't we? We've not done much today and personally I'm not at all tired.'

'Nor me – but you know what it's like trying to go at night here – what happens if the road goes back to being broken up?'

'Sleep out again – we're already pretty well bitten by the

mosquitoes here. In any case I really am not keen on staying here at all, are you?'

'No. Let's get out of here.'

And with that, we stuff what little we'd taken out of the panniers back into them and wheel the bicycles out from the verandah onto the road, in the moonless dark night.

It is, of course, almost impossible to cycle along the road, which is cracked and pitted, as it had been ever since it stopped being totally broken up. But we are thoroughly jumpy now and do not stop until we have cleared Seoni Chapara by several miles to the south, where a likely looking patch of rough grass presents itself at the edge of a sugar-cane field. In fact the grass turns out to be yellowed, tough and spiky so we end up trying to sleep at the edge of the canes, being bitten on our knuckles and faces by mosquitoes and wondering if we are being paranoid or not. The fact that we both had an identical feeling about the deserted Dak Bungalow seems enough to swing the case for us – Rossiter and I very seldom have identical feelings about anything at all.

Really, 'sleeping' on Indian roadsides has very little to recommend it. When the dawn finally comes along we are both cold and horribly bitten. The only benefit of this is that we are reminded that the coming day will be a Sunday which means that, for once, we do not forget to take our weekly malaria tablets. When there is enough light to find them, we munch them in silence for breakfast, with a mouthful of chlorine-flavoured water from the bottom of one of our bottles and a bit of raw cane to chew from the field around us.

At least we do get going good and early, though it is well over ten miles before a dhaba comes in sight where we wolf down rice, dal and curried cauliflower with endless cups of chai by way of late breakfast – even though it's well before seven when we get there.

Because of the previous night's experience, the chowkidar who snarls at us that evening at Khawasa is a pure delight. He really is a chip off the old chowkidar block and frustrates our attempts to enter after a day's bicycling, exactly as he should. Indeed, we only succeed in getting in by dint of agreeing to let him kill a 'cok' for us – for which he will no doubt extract an extreme price for us in the morning. Once bribed, the door is opened, the 'booked' officials vanish into thin air, we can put away our important-looking pieces of paper and put behind us the previous night.

Despite all past experiences I'm still a devotee of 'cok' and after eating this chowkidar's delicious (if tiny) bird with the customary rice mountain of EEC proportions, I fall into a deep and much-needed sleep to the sound of Rossiter speculating on the likelihood of my dying soon from overconsumption of malnourished fowls.

True to form, the chowkidar darts up to us after a morning chai, ledger in hand. 'Eighty-three rupees,' he smiles, his pencil doing irrelevant sums in one column of the page.

'No.'

'Cok there is forty-five rupees, chaval and sabze, rent for room there is . . .' he continues at high speed in fluent English.

'There is this there is that – there's quite a lot really, isn't there? Too much we are thinking,' Rossiter suggests, to move the discussion along.

It's a pleasant enough way to spend the time between loading the bicycles and setting off and we eventually leave thirty rupees for the chowkidar and his fleet of sub-chowks who appear for the Grand Settlement Summit – still a good deal more than we have had to pay in most P.W.D. resthouses and far more than any government official would pay, as the ledger testifies.

Much refreshed by the night's sleep and the morning's haggling, we freewheel along the road to the octroi and the state frontier between Madhya Pradesh and Karnataka State. Around the post there is a permanent-looking group of bored soldiers who occasionally rifle through the contents of trucks pausing to pay tax at the octroi. As we sit and drink another chai for the hell of it, one of them comes across to us, approaches my bicycle and without a word or look at us, flicks

144

one of the gear levers murmuring 'cycle clutch'. This seems to do him a power of good and he returns to his bored colleagues, with a hint of swagger in his stride, having put us both right about a thing or two.

Later on, as we are beginning to look out for a village with a dhaba in it, the Rossiter back wheel gives its familiar twang. Hitherto this has always happened close to a village or town, but our luck has to run out eventually – like now. 'So what happens now?' says Rossiter, as we squat by the road sharing a guava and sterotabbed water.

'Either we hitch a ride when a truck comes up along the road or we press on with the bust spoke, I suppose,' I say at last.

'You know we can't do that,' Rossiter says, idly spinning the rear wheel. 'Look at that – it's warped already. See?'

'Well, we may as well just try threading the new spoke ourselves then. God knows – we've seen enough ten-year-old kids doing it. It can't be that hard – even for us.'

'Oh no?' Rossiter smirks. 'Don't ever underestimate our incompetence.'

'Let's get the manual and see. I can't see as there's much choice. There isn't even a car on the road today, let alone an empty truck. And,' I say, glancing into the hard blue sky, 'the vultures are massing for us.'

Predictably, the spoke has gone on the block side of the wheel, which means we can at least do the first part of the operation in our sleep. 'I could do this bloody job in my sleep,' mutters Rossiter as he goes to work on the wheel, for once underlining my train of thought. 'But what I don't understand is why, oh why this keeps happening to *me*. Why is it? What am I doing wrong? There's somebody up there who's got it in for Rossiter –'

'Relax – it's just that there's something wrong in the wheel – we'll get the new one in Nagpur – rely on Indian Airlines – our crates will be there.'

'Something wrong with the wheel, eh? Absolutely brilliant. Bloody marvellous. I suppose that little incisive analysis completely solves our problem then, does it? Your trouble is you just think if you ignore a problem long enough it'll go away. Well, I'm telling you – it won't.'

'I just reckon there's two sorts of mechanical problems: noises that go away and noises that don't.'

'Well, my bicycle's very, very noisy then. Give me the manual.'

You can tell which pages deal with spokes – they're completely smeared in oily thumb-prints so you have to peer into the diagrams through great smudgy clouds of grease on the page. 'This is useless – can't make out a bloody thing here,' Rossiter says, peering down at the page and smearing it further with his blackened hands. By now, the inevitable group has begun to form, materializing out of the empty countryside as people do in India. The several early arrivals are then supplemented by a bullock-cartload of people going north to harvest the sugar-cane but with plenty of time to stop and watch the fun.

As they circle in close around us, one man barges forward, almost stepping upon Rossiter in his effort to view the proceedings. He catches sight of the manual. 'Your book is totally dirty – I am afraid a completely new book will be necessary for you.'

I glare back at the man with a look of ill-concealed violence which is entirely lost on the bibliophile, who calmly nestles in at the front of the group, folds his arms and settles down to watch.

As ever, I get steadily more and more impatient to get going as the numbers swell. Rossiter, squatting in the dust, succeeds in threading the new spoke quite quickly in an act of pure mechanical inspiration. It does not seem to need any filing either, which is lucky since we do not, of course, have a file.

The wheel holds itself together for the ten miles or so to the nearest village, which distance takes us down to lower, greener, cultivated land where it is also noticeably hotter. We are dropping down towards Nagpur at last. We sit under a thatch awning made of palm branches and leaves and listen to the commentary on the Test Match from Calcutta while yet another seven-year-old genius trues up the wheel a few yards away. He will take no money for his work but readily accepts a leaf containing freshly fried chillis and onions in batter which, with some warm, stale goat's milk, is our lunch today.

The gradual descent continues into the outskirts of Nagpur – or Snakesville, as people called it in Delhi ('nag' meaning snake in Hindi). No such reptiles are in evidence though, as we edge towards the city through the tired-looking cottonfields on either side of the road. There is no sign of the orange groves for which Nagpur is famous, but the fruits themselves are everywhere in the bazaars, a treat when we have had only guavas or nothing at all in the way of fruit all through Madhya Pradesh. They are lovely big oranges too, with thick, loose skins, bigger than the largest grapefruit and bursting with juice. With the skins so loose you can peel them in seconds and chuck the rind to the pigs and goats always doing the street-cleaning under your feet.

Between our stop for oranges and the centre of town we are confronted by brightly painted truck convoys with lavish pictures of voluptuous goddesses on them, apparently transporting loads of black dust across the city. The last thing anybody could possibly require in India is dust of any colour, and the lorries are so laden with the stuff that great clouds of it trail off them as they wind and chunter along the busy streets. From a distance they look as if they are on fire. Everything gets covered by it, and before it occurs to us to put on tee-shirts we are covered too. Because we're already covered in sweat our skins turn black in a matter of moments and it is days before the last of this dust is gone from our scabby mosquito bites.

The elegant lady in a silk saree at the general post office is most surprised by the look of us. As we have only one clean tee-shirt each it seems a shame to put it on now and because of our unpleasant appearance the Chief Sorting Clerk has to be called in, while we attempt to prove who we are in order to get our mail from the Poste Restante. He shuffles our passports, very suspicious, before asking us disarmingly, 'Why are you like this?' gesturing at our blackened faces and bodies.

When we have finally been positively vetted, there's the rather mixed discovery of six letters from England for myself and nothing for Rossiter. The lady pushes the wad across the counter, adjusting her saree at the shoulder with that characteristic flick you see here every day. The confidence we both felt as we edged our way into the city – the half-way mark of the ride – is now strangely dented by the fact that only I have any letters to read. When we have been accustomed to sharing experiences, this produces a feeling of disturbing imbalance, and for some time I leave the letters unopened, only beginning to read out the absurd, intimate details of home when Rossiter asks me to. He can now smile at the stories of England, as we lie here covered in grime beneath the palm trees on the lawn outside the Nagpur G.P.O. in the noon heat of New Year's Day.

6

'Miles to go before I sleep;
and miles to go before I sleep!'

Robert Frost

Finding somewhere to stay in Nagpur is more difficult somehow than finding a place out on the road – or so it seems. The
main reason is that a gigantic mass wedding is scheduled to
take place tomorrow on the Public Open Space behind the
Officers' Colony near the centre of the town. Presently, the
Public Open Space is being turned into a Private Closed Place
as a series of huge shamianas is put up over the dusty, flattened
grass. Several hundred poor couples will be wed here tomorrow in such a way as to preserve the dignity of ceremony and
feasting without having to saddle the brides with the often
crippling expense of dowries. Of course, several hundred couples means several thousand friends, relatives and hangers-on.
'Hm,' says Rossiter after some searching of various dingy
establishments. 'We seem to be in a no-room-at-the-inn situation. The trouble is, there's not many inns here in the first
place, are there?'

   The fact is, Nagpur is a long way indeed from almost
anybody's tourist itinerary and we end up in a vast (and almost
full) block of flats built in the centre of the city to accommo-
date the families of civil servants for those months of the year
when the entire State Government of Maharashtra ups and
leaves Bombay to come and give Nagpur a piece of the action.
Our one grey concrete cell has unplastered walls and an evil-
scented drain that gurgles menacingly every few minutes in the
corner of the concrete floor. Whilst clearing its throat in this

endearing manner, it splutters filthy ooze onto the rough floor for a moment before sucking it down beneath the grille, leaving only a brown stain and the smell, thick and heavy in the air. Still, it is a room.

'No it's not, it's a bunker,' declares Rossiter roundly when I grow over-optimistic about its potential. Outside, as the evening approaches, we're both aware that the cloud and humidity have been steadily building up. Inside, the taps are not working, the drain gurgles on and the stickiness of it all is getting too much to handle.

Later, during the night, the storm breaks – a huge relief since until then it's too humid to sleep at all. Besides, in the last half hour before the rain finally falls in huge drops, there is almost continuous lightning with no thunder at all. I keep on saying to Rossiter that this is against the rules. 'You know – this really is against all the rules. I mean there should at least be some thunder thrown in somewhere.'

'I wish you'd stop telling me that, I understood the first time.'

'But it is weird if you get thunder but no – '

'Will you shut up? I'm trying to watch this happen in peace. This is the first bloody rain we've had since we left Kashmir and all you can do is go on and on about the lack of thunder. You're never satisfied, that's your trouble. It's appalling, you and that sodding drain burbling on and on and on. Just repetition and smell.'

'I can't help that – there's no clean water in here.'

'Not you – the drain,' murmurs Rossiter, cupping his face in his hands. 'Give me strength,' he moans into his dirty palms.

Predictably enough, the drain which couldn't cope with a normal dry day in Nagpur gives out completely about two minutes into the rain. The gurgle soon becomes a continuous bubbling until, with a sound of faint panic, the grille disappears into a surging flood of brown water that splashes up onto our floor, and does not recede. We set about hoisting everything of importance onto the (already damp) charpoys.

At first light – as soon as my eyes open – a copy of the

Nagpur Times is squelched under our ill-fitting door into the flood, presently a couple of inches deep. This weighty broadsheet is well on the way to papier-mâché by the time I've paddled to the door to rescue it. This morning, the lead story is on the continuing drought in eastern Maharashtra. Closely followed in the wake of the paper is the chai-wallah who can be heard for some distance splashing his way down the corridor before he raps smartly on our door. It's comforting to know that the whole place seems to be flooded and not just our bunker after all.

Without hesitation in paces the chai-wallah. As a breed such people are strictly opportunist, darting out to vend high-speed chai at any opportunity and without exception congenially incapable of hesitating. He smacks his sandle squarely into the gooey disintegrating mess that was part of the *Nagpur Times* not five minutes ago, serves up two cups of chai, beams, spins and whacks out again sloshing filthy water everywhere. As I sip and wait for Rossiter to surface I find myself wondering how many papers he will tread in this morning, or any morning; indeed how many does he wreck in a week's plodding, in a month – OK, per year then? This is the kind of train of thought you should get locked into only whilst cycling and here I am, not even out of the charpoy. It is clearly high time I got up.

Down the road from the concrete mess in which we are staying, the cricket stadium in Nagpur is getting a good deal of painting and rebuilding in time for the one-day Test Match due in a week or two. The stadium does not actually exist all the way round the barren brown pitch, but we are assured by club officials that all will be in order in time for the big day.

After we have been here for two days, there is no sign whatever of our wheel. Rossiter passes a good deal of the time in the kitchen. The kitchen is a small black and smoke-filled outhouse next to our room and from the moment when Rossiter returns from the bazaar bearing his huge tin of 'Champion Oats' it is clear that he will have to cook them himself. First of all, one of the several hundred cooks who seem to disappear into the smoke of the kitchen wants to plant them beneath the banana tree in the hotel garden. Subsequent explanations about porridge meet either with blankness or heaving laughter from whoever happens to be emerging or entering the smoke-zone. Only after one of the cooks bravely attempts to deep-fry a bowl of oats does it finally dawn on us that Rossiter will have to boil his own porridge, and he sets to it at once, ignoring the general hilarity of the battalions of cooks and under-managers who waft around the precincts of the hotel.

After two days of waiting around I can stand waiting for our spare parts no longer and set about calling Indian Airlines in Delhi from the telephone exchange whilst Rossiter tries him from the hopeless-looking hotel phone. As I stand in the queue there, clutching my ticket for the STD Booth, I notice, to my amazement, Rossiter riding pillion on the back of someone's Enfield. He rushes in. 'Forget it – the wheel's here. It's been airfreighted. I got through from the hotel and the manager offered me a lift down here,' says Rossiter, nodding knowingly at the manager who smiles broadly back at me, twirling the ends of his bushy moustache. I've a feeling the two of them know something I don't.

'Well don't just stand there, let's get going. You're the one who keeps on saying how much you want to start riding again.' And with that Rossiter thanks the manager who wishes us luck and insists on shaking our hands as we pass out of the exchange and straight into the nearest Ambassador parked outside. 'Er – Indian Airlines Office, please,' says Rossiter.

The driver looks at us, his face frozen in complete amazement. 'I am waiting for my brother, please,' says the man, no less astonished when he finally finds his voice.

'Ah,' I say, 'this isn't a taxi – is it?' and without waiting for a reply we both hurtle out of the other rear door and stand blinking in the sunshine with no available taxi to spirit us away from the scene of our embarrassment.

Eventually we do find a rickshaw, pedalled by a boy so lethargic that we end up taking over the pedalling ourselves

Welcoming party, Lower Sindh

hikhara boy, Nagin lake, Srinagar, Kashmir   Farmer taking lunch, Banihal, Kashmir

Holy man carrying the Kavadi, Thaipossum festival,
Tamil Nadu

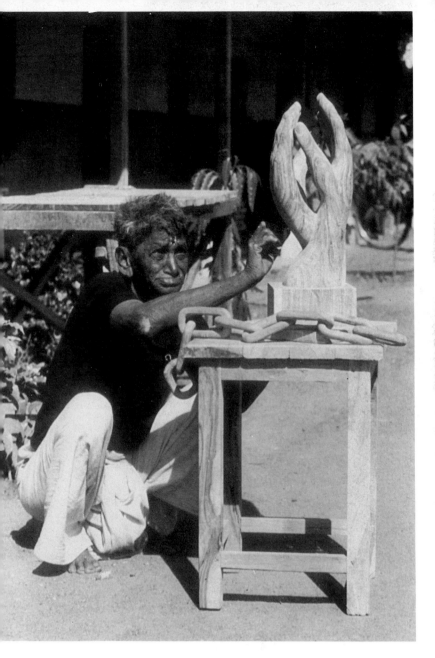

Sculptor, Anandwan, Maharashtra

Rolling Sadhu, Madya Pradesh

Forty winks on the sugar cane, Karnataka

Messenger, Khana National Park

Bathtime in a tank, Haryana

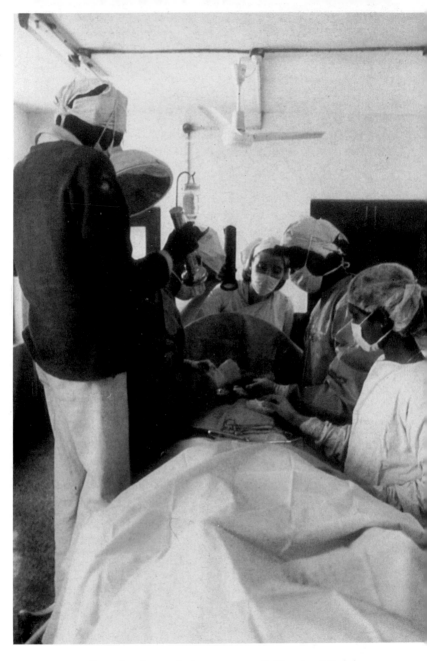

Operating theatre during power cut, Lakhnadon Mission
Hospital, Madya Pradesh

Eswaram (fourth from bottom) and the kabaddi men,
Velur, Tamil Nadu

Ploughing beneath the Western Ghats, Tamil Nadu

Sikh widows after the riots, Soltanpuri, Delhi

whilst the kid lords it in the back, avails himself generously of our supply of spiced cashews and then charges us way over the rate outside the Indian Airlines Office, by which time we are in such a tearing hurry to seize the new wheel we pay him without thinking.

Inside the office there is a rather statesmanlike exchanging of mutual forms, receipt dockets, cash and rubber stamps – well before anyone even thinks about looking for the wheel. I maintain that a bicycle wheel is a fairly distinctive shape – even when wrapped up in hessian for air-freighting and I am sure I can see our wheel at once when we go with the Receipting Officer (who for some reason is dressed up like an airline pilot) into the arrivals bay. It is now patently obvious to me which parcel is our wheel but Captain Airfreight insists portentously on going over the documentation hanging like rosettes from every parcel in the room. There are portable generators, books, cabinets, a garden roller and about five hundred other parcels none of which could possibly be a bicycle wheel. Within minutes this behaviour has got me to screaming pitch as the Captain totally ignores my pointing and pleading in the direction of the wheel. Rossiter is immensely amused at this, liking few things more than seeing me coming up full force against the nerve-destroying imperviousness of Indian officialdom.

In the Captain's own time our wheel is handed to us; we complete further documentary procedure and return to the bunker, put on the new wheels and find, to our horror, that it is even more warped than the one which insists on shedding spokes. This is one of those times when Kannyakumari seems to be a very far off place, not the kind of place you ever actually get to.

Once again our new-found manager comes to the rescue. 'My friends,' he smiles calmly, twirling in quiet concern, 'there is no despair in this thing – '

'No?' I say to him, looking up in total despair from the ruins of the wheel, so badly bent it will not turn fully in the frame.

'No despairing at all,' continues the manager, 'I am telephoning to my friend Mr S. M. Pardhi and he is coming very soon. He will be able to advise us. Please,' he touches my shoulder as I squat by the wheel with Rossiter stroking its injured arm, 'your wheel is not remaining permanently bifurcated.'

Mr S. M. Pardhi is absolutely as good as his reputation and soon has us cycling behind him down to the magnificent bicycle emporium owned by the brothers Sengupta. By dint of unspoken forces coming to our aid, the shop is being opened up specially (today being a Sunday) by the younger of the brothers. Within minutes, their mechanic has been summoned and proceeds to dismantle the sick wheel spoke by spoke at quite unbelievable speed. Despite his activity, chai and samosas are effortlessly on hand by the time the cross-legged mechanic has tailored the wheel down to the hub.

At times like this we both feel real idiots trying to explain where we have cycled from, but the Senguptas express not the slightest doubts in either our mental stability or the possibility that we could get to the end of our journey. I don't share their confidence though the calmness of the Indians on occasions like this increases the irrational feeling we both have that ourselves and our incompetence notwithstanding, it will be all right in the end.

Of course there is no question of payment when the wheel's rim has been straightened and re-united with its spokes. Instead there is a long, lazy, hot afternoon sitting around in the dhaba across the bazaar from the Senguptas, eating dozens of sweet marzipan cakes and drinking sugar-saturated chai in what in almost any other circumstances would be an extremely uncomfortable and tooth-destroying experience.

The next day, after a leisurely breakfast in town of curried chickpeas – chana – and parathas, we say our goodbyes to the various levels of management who turn out in force to wish us well. Considering this nameless temporary hotel has only about eight occupied rooms, the staffing levels do seem a little excessive even by the standards of labour-intensive India – though quite what goes on in the dingy depths of the kitchen not even Rossiter has been able to discover. Even as we leave, new and unfamiliar faces are entering the dark of this kitchen to cries of greeting from even further in. When we leave we are delicately asked not to go through the dining room, as there are ladies present and we are, as usual, wearing shorts. We ride off down the drive to a cheer and waving from the staff while their boss looks on twirling for all he's worth in the emotion of the moment.

We push south, past the Public Open Space where I'm sure the spicy flavour of the mass wedding feast still lingers in the air, though the shamiana has now been pulled down. On, through the military cantonment – often the dominant part of an Indian town, with its well-planned buildings and the working example of 'space' which the rest of a town hardly ever cares to take up – and past the radio beacons at the extreme edge of the city. The traffic falls away, cars disappear and only lorries on a long haul and bullock carts on a major plod now share the road with us. Nervously, we stop and spin the rear wheel on Rossiter's bicycle to check it has stood up to the suburbs. Then off into the parched yellowy land of Maharashtra, enjoying again the slight stinging of dust-filled air against our faces.

By the middle of the day it is hotter than we have yet known it and there is absolutely no wind. The air seems beaten into still submission beneath the flaring dust-sky: that unforgiving dead silver into which you can't look much higher than the shimmering horizon itself. When we stop we are, again, caked in sweat and dust, baptized once more into the way of life along the Indian roads.

It is so good to be under way again, especially after the wheel troubles, that we both almost enjoy the inevitable swatting and flicking at the flies we have to compete with all the time when we stop to eat. I suppose these flies are the same as house-flies at home except lighter brown, smaller and swifter a million times. They contrive to crawl all over whatever you eat even as you lift it to your mouth with your fingers and on more than one occasion I've been stopped in mid-mouth by the ticklish sensation of a live fly mixed up with my mouthful of banana, dal or whatever. The done thing seems to be to spit the lot out at once into the dust, whereupon the intruder, family and friends tuck into the steamy mouthful in the dust.

At about four o'clock we come to Hinganghat, which is not so much a ghat as a raised plateau of higher land up to which we have climbed most of the day over an endless expanse of jumbled, shattered rocks and thorn bushes, with very little happening in the way of cultivation. There is a small filling station on the left-hand side of the road just before the whitewashed town comes into sight half a mile or so to the right of the road. In the forecourt a man with the look of a proprietor about him grimaces from the sides of his spectacularly ill-fitting false teeth. He sits on a huge old pumpkin which will continue to be his chair until the dry air finally crumbles it into dust. Without a word he nods to a boy who collects two bottles of Campa Cola from the well where they have been keeping cool. The boy walks up nervously and thrusts the bottles forward, leering like his father.

Although I'm grateful for the drink as we've been unable to refill our water bottles for the last ten miles or so, the Campa does not agree with me and I sidle the forecourt and vomit into the dust. Curiously, this seems to produce much satisfaction on the face of the pump-proprietor.

'Feel better then?' asks Rossiter, revolted.

'Not much,' I tell him, sitting in the dust, thinking about how thirsty I now feel. There is a moment of silence before the proprietor speaks to us in Marathi. We nod. Rossiter smiles. The man disappears from his pumpkin into the shack at the back of the petrol pump and returns a moment later with a copy of the *Nagpur Times*. He points lavishly at our photograph and the story of our ride underneath it which appeared in today's edition of the paper. He sits himself once more on the pumpkin and stretches out his hand to shake ours. So we shake vigorously together, in the hot late afternoon sun in this lonely petrol station, nodding, smiling, laughing and marvelling at the false teeth grinning out automatically from the man's weathered face.

The ludicrousness of all this is well and truly dawning on me when another man approaches and smiles (with his own teeth) as he bounds towards us in an immense pair of brilliant white, flapping pyjama pants. 'Welcome, welcome to Hinganghat,' says he, pulling from his black waistcoat his copy of the *Nagpur Times*. 'What do you require from this place for your well beings? Your good names please? I am knowing this from my newspaper but I am enjoying conversing with you both.'

Such questions have echoed across the country of course but it is disarming to see how the article by Mr Aloysius Lobo of the *Nagpur Times* seems to convey the right upon us to demand anything of Hinganghat that we may need. At the moment, in fact, our needs would be pretty well catered for by finding the P.W.D. resthouse which we were told was here, when we were back at Nagpur. As soon as we suggest this to Pyjamas, he tells us to follow him on his bicycle and leads us to the edge of the town, where the huge concrete water tower that dominates Hinganghat seems to grow out of the P.W.D. office. Quite why we have to register in the office before going to the resthouse never really becomes clear and it may be the rule throughout the state – which could be a problem. Either way, the formalities are really quite painless and we are soon going through the town behind Pyjamas who yells unstintingly at the boys who gather to run behind us, counting to ten in English by way of welcome.

Unfortunately, the chowkidar of the Hinganghat resthouse is no reader of the *Nagpur Times*. 'Take that room,' he tells us in Hindi without looking in our direction and apparently indicating a stable across the yard. Pushing open the door we discover one rotting charpoy with a bird's nest in it on a floor covered in dung and old bits of straw. The disturbance of opening the door is just too much for the roof, which instantly sheds one of its huge heavy clay pantiles, shattering on a stone outside the doorway.

'No', says Rossiter, eyeing me nervously in case I show symptoms of moving in.

Outside, some ten or so of the boys are still with us, several of them stoically hanging on in there with the counting, 'Wan Dow Dree Far ... '

'Yes – that's really very good,' I seem to find myself saying, more in admiration of their stamina than their pronunciation. As the chowkidar doesn't seem to recognize our existence further and Pyjamas has disappeared, there seems nothing for it but to start playing cricket with the boys who have a ball and a piece of roughly bat-like wood. When it becomes too dark to see the ball – and they're all clearly far better at cricket than either of us two are – we decide to make a sudden bid for the resthouse proper and wheel all the gear into one of the two rooms whilst the chowkidar is out of sight. Our inward progress is momentarily halted by a large sandy-coloured scorpion. Rossiter stands aside to let it pass out before saying, 'Good God – what the hell's that?'

'Remember Seoni Chapara?'

'Another scorpion? Really?'

The chowkidar does not take it amiss in the slightest that we should have moved in precisely where he told us not to. Indeed, he seems to perk up no end seeing us ensconced there. After dark he suddenly appears with a huge mountain of rice and sabze – curried marrows, potatoes and chick peas in this instance – and launches into a major explanation of how he studied catering in Bombay for a month several years ago. To this news, we make loudly appreciative noises about the food which, though gritty, is nonetheless delicious.

Rossiter however, decides to eat only a small amount tonight, not because he's feeling ill but, 'It's no good – I'm bloody well going to lose some weight on this journey so I may as well start right now.'

'You already have lost weight – I'm sure of it,' I tell him, in a rare burst of supportive comfort. 'But isn't it getting a bit late for starting this kind of thing? I mean, we're well over half way now – you should've started this sort of kick way up north.'

'I agree, but it's easy for you to go around in your usual way telling every one else how they should run their lives.'

'I don't tell everyone else – just you.'

'In any case, you can go around eating what the flies have rejected by the metric tonne and still look like a bloody rake.'

'That annoys you, doesn't it?'

'No, I just wish you'd get sick once in a while. You know, nothing serious, but something naggingly unpleasant – a bowel job perhaps for a week or so – just so you'd have some concept of what it feels like to be a human being.'

'Cheers,' I say, looking wistfully at Rossiter's half-eaten meal.

'Oh go on then –' he shoves the plate across to my waiting right hand, 'clean it up.'

An hour or so after we have eaten, as we lie on our bed trying to work out what our respective friends and families are doing at home, the chowkidar comes back in with his huge, ancient oil-lamp. He beckons urgently from the doorway. We get up and follow him out across the courtyard to a tiny stable (smaller even than the one he originally put us both in) next to his house. In the soft glow of the lamp he shows us the new-born calf which his water-buffalo was carrying round ponderously as we cycled in earlier this evening. 'It is good. It is good,' he murmurs to himself repeatedly in the steamy warm comfort of the tiny mud-walled stable.

A molten-red sun is lighting the yard horizontally from the east as we leave early the next morning, as the cow buffalo turns her jaws on sugar-cane tops while feeding her calf from her rich udder. Although it is hard to understand all of what the chowkidar says to us, it is clear that he associates our unexpected arrival with the birth of the calf, which seems to us a very high compliment and one that we remember for the rest of the journey. He stands at the edge of his yard in his dhoti and Bombay-tailored printed shirt watching us leave until we have pushed our bicycles through thick dust to the tarmac of the road half a mile away.

This morning there comes another of those small but wonderfully significant and exciting indicators that we really are making progress across this country. It is coffee. One of the banes of Rossiter's life has become the sickliness of heavily-sugared chai together with buffalo milk which is much richer in taste than cow milk. For Rossiter particularly – as for most of western humanity – the change from chai to coffee is a one hundred per cent improvement. Around mid-morning the aroma of ground coffee comes strongly from a roadside dhaba nowhere in particular and sucks us both straight from the road. The coffee-wallah does good business. But now coffee looks as if it could bring a whole new dimension into our life. Above all else, coffee in India means the South.

On the subject of food and eating, our light-hearted argument last night about our differing weights, metabolisms and standards of hygiene erupts into something a bit more serious when we stop in a village to eat during the heat of the day. I am a little ahead and decide to pull off at the first dhaba I come to which I suppose really isn't up to the average standard. By the time Rossiter pulls up I am already well into a cold chapatti taken from a pile on which flies have been meeting for several hours, days perhaps.

'Why are we eating here? I mean why are you eating here?' Rossiter demands, still panting from the ride.

'Dunno really, I suppose it just happened to be the first place I came to.'

'That's typical. Absolutely typical. You just don't even look, do you? You don't bloody care where or what you eat, do you? God – you really are an animal. Look at that – did you see that? The guy cooking those chapattis keeps gobbing in the fat. Don't you care about that?'

'He's testing out the heat of it – heat's got to be right you know, or they won't cook.'

'Well, that's just brilliant when you're eating one that's stone cold and about a week old by the look of it. I've *trod* in better things than that.'

'Ssssssshhhhhhh! You'll upset the management.'

'You seek out these places deliberately. You'll end up killing yourself. You think it's very cred to swan into places like this, mingle in with the rats and push fistfuls of crap down your gullet. Well, I'm going to take you to my club in London when I get you back to England – assuming you're still with us. That'll teach you a thing or two about style and civilization. You're a pervert when it comes to eating.'

'I'm hungry – didn't have any breakfast.'

'Well – just don't come running to me complaining when you're lying on the slab in some godforsaken morgue, that's all.'

And with that difficult request Rossiter grabs his bicycle and pushes it firmly down the road. I watch him go until his bare torso mingles into the same brown colour as the countryside. Just as he is about to disappear I can see him pull in to what is no doubt a more upmarket place to eat, a place with a roof and proper walls. I glance at the dung-walled shack I have been eating from, watch the one-toothed old cook spit again into the sizzling fat and decide that Rossiter may have a point. Not that I'd admit it to him.

He has, in fact, found one of those excellent Sikh dhabas which crop up from time to time even this far south. From a battery of three hefty forge-like clay ovens comes a range of curried cauliflowers, aubergines, mutton, dal and delicious kheer, all to be consumed on well-slung charpoys under the spreading shade of mature sal trees that line the road. True to form, Rossiter has decided to round off the modest amount he's eating with some ice-cold Punjabi Kingfisher Lager. 'You've been seduced away from the Hilton, have you?' he says, smiling again.

'No, not really. I was feeling like seeing how the other half live so I came on over. Do you really belong to a club in London?' I ask Rossiter, shocked by this little revelation.

'Ha! I knew that would freak you – just knew it. I do, actually, as a matter of fact. But I was lying about the civilization bit – there's not much of that about there, I'm afraid.'

In front of us at the roadside, rows of trucks are pulled up while their drivers stop and eat, and from the road you can see a series of gaudily hand-painted 'Horn Please' signs on the back of these sturdy, but mirrorless, vehicles. The drivers sit about dozing, chewing pan or shovelling fingerfuls of sabze or byngum into their mouths faster and more deftly than we'll ever be able to manage. The sizzle of hot fat and the soft patting sound of chapattis and parathas being flapped from hand to hand before cooking mingles with the slap of fingers on mouths. In the quiet, hot hour of eating few vehicles pass on the unshaded road.

After dozing for some time on the charpoys between the dhaba ovens and the roadside, we eventually wander over to the bicycles and those drivers not sleeping off their lunch wish us a softly-spoken 'Ram Ram' as we freewheel away. Just beyond the row of dhabas, a river is still just about flowing, edging its way without eddy from one low, sun-sucked mud-pool to the next. In one of the pools three women have been fishing right through the hot part of the day with small hand-held nets, yet they seem barely to disturb the thick syrupy water. They swing the nets in regular rhythmic sweeps, sarees pulled up tight and tied between their legs like dhotis. Steady footprints lead down over the mud from the fringe of a paddy to the lip of the pool where the water sinks lower by the day, tracing the place where the women went and now one small brown heron probes for whatever the passing feet may have disturbed from the dark river mud.

Having just decided to get going again, we find ourselves drawn into the rhythm and pull of the nets. So we sit and watch for a long time, undisturbed by anybody, in the unexplained way that sometimes happens. They catch no fish while we watch, but in their movement it seems there is no particular hope of catching any, just a kind of absorption in the act, the movement of fishing.

Then, suddenly catching each other's eyes we're off again, noticing at once that the sky has clouded up since we ate and the air is heavy and humid. The vast, undulating land of the Deccan further north has changed today into sharp hillocks and gullies which send the road into an endless series of tortured twists. These gullies must get ripped deeper with every monsoon, or indeed forced into different shapes and courses altogether. The country for some miles to the state frontier is rather like the Chambal on a smaller scale – though thankfully the few people we do see this afternoon are not carrying firearms. Here the dust is very bad and we have to hold tee-shirts over our mouths for peculiar stretches where it blows around in thick, angry clouds. What is so odd is the fact that there seems to be hardly any wind on this close afternoon to stir up anything, let alone thick clouds of dust.

After two hours of cycling we are both feeling exhausted. In this kind of weather the dust cakes even thicker than is normal and the sweat runs off your body in maddening itchy streams. When we stop there's barely anything of the chirrup of grass-hoppers always audible when we stop for water-breaks. Ross-iter's face is criss-crossed with white lines where the sweat has evaporated into trails of salt. He tells me slowly and quietly that mine looks similar. Neither of us has any energy for the usual weighty and totally irrelevant political arguments with which we often pass our stops: today we just sit round in silence drinking and chewing a nog of raw sugar cane, donated by a passer-by a few miles back.

On the other hand, the change in being able to look right up into the sky is something quite new, unknown since the cold days of Kashmir. Overhead, billowing dark clouds are filling and spiralling over a land that no longer seems to cringe and harden beneath the rock-splitting sun. Instead the gaunt rocky outcrops that come up every now and then at either side, now stand out in dramatic defiance against the boiling black sky. This surely means thunder.

As luck has it – as if to heighten our appreciation of the drama of rainfall here – the storm breaks exactly as we reach the Pranhita River that divides Maharashtra from Andhra Pradesh. We pass under the octroi post as the first huge drops plop onto the ground sending up minor explosions of dust. Down in the huge basin of the river, a cattle fair on the sandbanks is now in complete confusion. Umbrellas sprout amid the distant shouting and screams of excited people caught in something few of them must have expected. Impromptu awnings appear and are hastily set up while dogs are refreshed enough to start fighting each other and annoying the cows again. But it is the cattle and buffaloes – the justification for the whole fair – which come into their own by doing precisely nothing, apparently hardly even registering the storm that seems to throw all other forms of life into high excitement.

As with the storm on our first night in Nagpur, there is very little rain for half an hour or so but lavish amounts of spectacular forked lightning and only a clap of thunder for every fourth or fifth bolt. For a long time we stay on the bridge watching the cattle-fair collapse into anarchy and wait, wait, wait in the open for the delicious cool of the rain as a small group of amazed little boys stare at us from a safe distance, unsure whether to run or laugh.

We set off again when the rain finally lets loose. This turns out to be a very bad idea indeed since the road disappears after twenty heroic yards of Andhra Pradesh. Theoretically it is under repair but you can tell by the give-away plants growing in the piles of sand at the roadside that this is going to be a long and extremely slow job. No workmen and no contractors are to be seen for the next long twelve-mile push to Adilabad. Of course, the rain throws everything into muddy confusion, but it is all utterly delicious and by the time we come upon dry ground we are beginning to feel almost cold – an unexpected treat.

The corollary of all this, of course, is that when you come out onto dry and dusty ground again, being squelching wet, the dust-cover settles into its film of mud almost at once; and Adilabad is indeed one of the dustiest towns I have ever seen.

Perhaps this is due in some way to the large cement works, set some way from the town across a dry plain on which nothing grows because it is covered in cement dust. Dust is everywhere, and on or in everything in Adilabad. In a fishtank in the entrance of a small Lodging (hotel) a dead carp floats fins up, bloated and rotten, killed no doubt by the thick film of dust covering the surface of its water. Things are not helped, as we sit drinking warm and stale Limca from a street-stall, by the fact that Adilabad apparently employs more than its fair share of sweepers whose sole function seems to be to get as much dust as possible airborne at any one time – on so windless a day as this they seem to be going about it with suicidal relish. The stall-holder brings us two more bottles and wipes the dust from the tops with an expansive and much-practised gesture.

As we come down the one main street of the town, we can see through the haze that all hotels here – all two of them – are called 'Lodges' – a characteristic of southern India.

'I'd prefer getting into a P.W.D. and finding a well to wash all this crap off myself,' says Rossiter flatly.

'Aren't you interested in this north–south business then?'

'Well, I'm pretty sure about how things are really – I mean look at it in England – because I live in the south I know that somewhere like Birmingham is up north, isn't it?'

'No it isn't, it's in the Midlands.'

'It's not. It's northern, obviously, all that industry – got to be northern, hasn't it?' says Rossiter, deliberately winding me up.

'Well that's a pretty warped way of looking at it,' I tell him, gazing hotly at him through the haze of dust. 'Personally, I reckon they ought to sort it out with large signposts, except nobody could agree. You see, when you go up, say, the M1, you get these bloody great signs saying 'The North' when you're in the south but they never have a 'This is the North' when you get there, do they? Can you imagine the stink it would cause if they tried it – hordes of Geordies defacing anything south of the Tyne Tunnel ... '

So go the irrelevant arguments that spring up out of nowhere and are, I suppose, a subconscious way of trying to stay in touch with the familiar in the face of so much that is constantly new as we push south.

We resolve to test our theories out on people here, beginning with a small group of officials from the local District Collector's office who call us over further down the road. As soon as we ask them whether they think Adilabad is in the south or not, we start to think better of the idea. It turns the group into hot debate at once, for to be in the south is to conjure up associations with different languages, festivals, food, Tamil problems – you name it – and yet these men seem equally unwilling to be associated with the north with its different set of idiosyncrasies. By the time we leave in search of the rest-house it is all they can do to agree that Adilabad is in Andhra Pradesh.

For the rest of the day Rossiter – now thoroughly enthused by the idea – keeps dredging up intermittent morsels of information about Somerset until you'd think the people there were some species of earth-eating pygmies, a civilization sundered from the rest of England by the raw powers of ethnic tradition.

With no apparent alternative forthcoming, we are directed to the Police Club where itinerant officers of the law stay in dark, drab rooms, parking their lathis in the lathi-stack on one wall of the entrance hall of the bungalow. A pile of them indicates there are plenty of officers staying tonight. The chowkidar of the Police Club does not seem to mind our arrival, but shows us to a tiny room with evil-smelling green shine oozing from the walls, assuming perhaps that we will leave. As soon as we find out that the simple shower in the stinking bathroom works, we're sold on the place, even if one of the two plastic charpoys has been set on fire in the middle of the room creating a large hole and a solidified pool of plastic on the floor. The other has only two legs and has been rammed onto a shelf by way of the other two.

'I'll take the shelf,' says Rossiter, with one look at the burnt plastic catastrophe. We settle in to the speechless astonishment of the chowkidar, who simply watches us unpack and wash.

I am aware of a cock crowing. I'm not sure that either of us has had much sleep at all but the sound of the cock puts us in mind of an omelette – the best thing to have here for breakfast –

except that no eggs actually seem to be available in Adilabad. After trying to find some in the bazaar along the main road of the town it's clear that none of the local fowls does anything but crow. Failing omelettes we settle for chai and then pedal off down the road.

With the open country the tarmac appears again thankfully and so we make good time bowling along the smooth road in the cool of the morning, noting that the land has changed again subtly to become much more wooded. It continually surprises us the way that the landscape, vegetation, even the geology of the country alters nearly every day in some shape or degree and today it is trees, sal trees and scrubby forest rapidly losing its leaves in the short winter and occasionally giving off an almost autumnal whiff of leafy decay where enough moisture has gathered to produce it.

After an hour or so we happen upon a very ship-shape dhaba with thatched roof and whicker windbreaks to protect eaters and food. 'Breakfast,' yells Rossiter up ahead of me. 'I detect eggs.'

He isn't disappointed, for the Sikh who runs this place also runs a fleet of hens comparatively corpulent beside the half-starved things that peck the dirt in most places. These hens positively select what they'll deign to eat and give eggs which have at least vaguely yellow yolks instead of the usual grey mess that spills limply into the omelette pan on most occasions. The only problem for me is to try to have the omelette cooked without onions. All the way from Kashmir I have pleaded with street-sellers in Hindi, in English and in desperation not to put handfuls of powerful purple onions which I really cannot stand in their omelettes.

So, as I begin another tired explanation, Rossiter stares off down the road sighing very loudly with embarrassment. I point at the pile of chopped onion lurking maliciously near to the eggs. I make some very negative faces and gestures whereupon the Sikh launches into a defence of his onions, believing I am questioning their integrity.

'Oh can't you just eat them this once or put them to one side.

This is getting very tedious, you know,' says Rossiter, looking vaguely upon a scene he's watched too many times before. I'm too far into this now to retract and the cook is genuinely perplexed, only set at ease when I eventually convince him that the onions are OK by gnawing into a whole raw one, which rather defeats the whole point of things, as Rossiter wastes no time in telling me. The whole episode is entirely futile as, assured of the soundness of his ingredients, the cook duly throws in an extra helping of onions as well as the mandatory green chillis and I sit down, shut up and eat.

We spend most of the daylight hours climbing steadily in what turns out to be a very hot day with no sign of any of the humidity and storms that passed over us yesterday. The rise in the land takes us out beyond the thin forests we came through after Adilabad and into country where the soil often gives out into bare rock pavements, and small cacti cling to the cracks for life and lizards scuttle for cover, rasping the rock noisily with their bellies as we approach. What this area must be like during the hot season I dread to think – even today it is impossible to pull the bicycles off into the sandy verge since we're sure the heat of it would damage the tyres. By the time we reach Neredikonda, after thirty miles or so, my throat is sore with thirst.

Neredikonda is absolutely a one-street village of wood and dung houses, and tiny shops filled with ancient biscuits in glass cases being slowly eaten by large, lethargic flies. The roofs here are of sugar-cane tops dried brittle and yellow by the moisture-less winds. At the far end an old man is dolefully stirring a huge clay pot full of rice. A row of withered green chillis lies out purposefully in the sun, and next to them he dollops out the rice for passing travellers. We eat as best we can, throats shrivelled and knotted with dryness. The problem – as always in these situations – is that the only water available is from the village well, across a small field of withering millet. It is brown and opaque, which means an almost unbearable half-hour wait for the water tablets to work while we sit, chewing over the gritty rice, trying to find enough saliva to swallow.

We cross six ridges this afternoon, all of them spaced so evenly about three miles apart that it is like pedalling over some great, regular design laid out along the land. At the last and highest of these ridges the map is called for by Rossiter. This is the Satmala Range. Behind us, the series of huge brown furrows, dotted with sal forest, line out to the north into the haze, shimmering their way across the land. Overhead, several vultures circle, the feathers of their wings spread against the blazing sky, quartering the rock, dirt and crabby scrubland for anything that could succumb, ourselves included.

Ahead, the view is spectacular: a drop of several hundred feet into rich, green and brilliant country such as we have not seen for over a thousand miles. Several huge lakes lie out in the afternoon sun, silver and unreal, dotted with palm trees and past them, our snaking road, as empty as it has been all the day. Beyond the lakes is the mysterious image of a wide, slow river fusing everything around it in clear colour and banishing all to the south of it to a heat haze. We have arrived at the Godavari basin.

The satisfaction of the climb is forgotten, and it is enough squatting on a curious concrete tower that stands to one side of the road, to sit and watch all this spread before us. We are joined there by a man who has been gathering sticks in the wooded slopes. He drinks from our water bottle like people here drink from the wells, pouring the liquid straight down his throat, holding the bottle at some distance above his gaping mouth. He doesn't seem to mind – or even notice – chlorine, and we sit on together, gazing south.

Finally we just can't put it off any longer and roll down the steep scarp of the ridge, descending perhaps a thousand feet in a few short, wind-blasted moments. The road is kind to us but for one large pothole on a hairpin bend half-way down. It's good to let off the brakes and open up, with the excitement of green country up ahead. When the road finally flattens, it is fringed with high palms. 'This is the *south*,' I shout to Rossiter as he whirrs past.

The road continues dead straight and smooth for several

miles into Nirmal where the people are darker, their features flatter; their signs indicate that we've come into a Telegu-speaking area. Signs of our progress like these fill us with a rush of excitement, and looking back now, the Satmala is simply a low purple veil blocked intermittently by the palms of this new-found country. Perhaps because of the nearby lake, the air smells very different here, with a soft sweetness to it completely lacking in the high dry land to the north of the hills.

Election-time still marks the skyline of Nirmal, the northern entry to the town being dominated by a colossal hoarding eighty feet high in glorious gaudy colours depicting the political figurehead of A.P., Mr N. T. Rama Rao. His ample shape and shining face look out over his political estate, assured once again of a resounding victory for his party Telegu Desam. The hoarding style is deliberately that of the huge boards that depict the paunchy heroes and heroines of the screen outside cinemas across the country and indeed this is fitting for a man who made his name as a movie star. At the southern end of town Indira Gandhi, even more gaudy in colour but sterner in expression, looks out to the south. Her presence, and not that of her son, seems ample comment on the style and predictability of the election as a whole. Two Indian crows in their pale pink waistcoats sit jabbering just at the point where Mrs Gandhi's famous badger-stripe of grey hair reaches the crown of her head.

After stopping for a celebratory beer and some crisp samosas we press on to the Godavari, which we cross just before sunset. Although its course is cut by large sandbanks, much of the river flows fast, silent and deep even at this season. Large bats, with wing spans perhaps two feet or more mingle now with the day's last swallows. Five miles on it is quite dark and there is no sign of any town in the offing according to the regular kilometre posts which are usually very reliable. By this time the mosquitoes are out. We come to a halt, unsure what to do. 'Any ideas about sleeping then?' I ask Rossiter, who is rasping away at old mosquito bites in the darkness.

'Well I'm not going on in this. I can't see a thing. We might as well sleep around here. I'm pretty well done after this morning's climbing.'

'I'm not exactly fresh myself.'

We are feeling so elated by the change of scenery today and the amazing fact that there is actually tough, scrubby grass and not dust at the edge of the road here, that we really do not make much attempt to find out what may lie a few miles down the road. In fact, we don't make any effort at all, disregarding even two trucks that come lumbering by, lighting us up as we move off into the edge of a field of cane.

Soon we are both stretched out between the coarse grass and the tall canes, rustling in the cool night breeze. 'I don't think this is going to be too bad,' I say to Rossiter, stretched out in my cotton sheet sleeping-bag which was white a long time ago, with my small, filthy towel and a tee-shirt for a pillow.

'No,' comes the word of Rossiter a yard or two away, which could mean a number of different things, but I won't press him further.

The night indeed turns out to be not too bad. It is far worse than merely 'bad', it is an experience in how bad a night can be, how long and dismal, how like a nightmare from which you can't wake up and forget since you are hardly ever asleep in the first place. We should really have known from the experience of the past few nights in beds that mosquitoes would be a problem. They move into the attack as soon as we're lying even vaguely still. The tell-tale model-aeroplane whine assaults the ears at once and soon afterwards the biting begins in earnest. Mosquitoes have the facility to get inside whatever you're trying to sleep in; and they also have a particular liking for biting on your knuckles which become unspeakably irritating and itchy.

The first thing Rossiter says this morning is in reference to a conversation we had yesterday in which I held forth on the ecological dangers of using DDT to get rid of mosquitoes. 'Don't you ever, ever say anything against DDT again, OK?' he says quietly, almost menacingly, edging his unrested, bitten and filthy body from his sleeping-bag. 'I can tell you something else as well,' he confides as we pedal slowly off down the road. 'The guys who worked out how to make chloroquine had better know what they're at. If there's any hint of malaria going around here I reckon I'm a dead cert for it.'

After about ten miles we come to Armoor, a peculiarly well-kept neat place with a brand new painted stand in the middle of the crossroads in the town centre for policemen to stand on and direct traffic. As we cross, an old man carrying a large bundle of sticks on his back freezes in mid-carriageway and cries out in shock at seeing Rossiter approach, bitten face first. He stands open-mouthed, in gummy astonishment, as we pass by. Indeed, his reaction is not so singular as it first appears for we are soon stared at in varying degrees of distaste by the whole cross-section of Armoorians, fearing perhaps that we are carrying some major disease into town. Perhaps we are.

At the far end of the town there is a coffee stall, open even at this early hour and we walk in feeling as if we've come from a battlefield. Two children take one look and tear off behind the solid stone counter, leaving us to make off with their toys. 'You really don't look good after last night,' I whisper to Rossiter, seriously worried we might not get served for fear of contaminating something.

'You're not exactly smooth-skinned yourself, as it happens.'

But the dhaba-man does appear at last and he does serve us, though he looks long and hard at our faces and arms whilst doing so. The coffee, needless to say, is wonderful, its hot steam soothing the bites on our faces so that we sit there blowing into the rough clay cups, bathing our faces in it, which stops the dhaba-man in his tracks. Then a young man with a sprucely trimmed beard comes in, looks at us on his way to the counter, picks up his coffee and turns for another look. He takes a sip, sighs and approaches us, looks unembarrassedly at our faces again and announces roundly, 'My good friends, you are both needing coils please. I can see this very plain.'

'Eh?' says Rossiter, looking down at his crotch in horror, but the man is already leaving.

'Maybe it's time to leave town before we get each other into trouble,' I giggle, equally mystified by this sudden announcement – but the man has now returned with a small parcel in his hand.

'Will this hurt much?' asks Rossiter, trying to keep a straight face. The man proceeds to unwrap his parcel of newspaper – standard shop wrapping paper in India – and produces a pale yellow plastic bag. From this he pulls out a small green spiralled coil, places it on the stand provided in the bag and sets fire to one end.

'And that'll stop us getting pregnant?' I murmur in disbelief.

A small flame burns for several seconds before going out in the most appalling cloud of acrid smoke which quickly begins to fill up the coffee-stall. But the man is smiling, even as he begins to be obscured by the smoke. 'Ha!' he shouts, gesturing in triumph at the smoke, 'now you are seeing?'

But neither of us is really seeing, since the smoke makes our eyes run and starts us both coughing violently. Somehow, though, Rossiter has hidden reserves of enthusiasm for whatever really is happening to us. 'Yes … yes, I see. Very … very impressive. … Do you sell many of them then?' he splutters heroically.

'But you are seeing now, my friend, you are seeing ninety per cent solution of your problem with the coils,' says the man to Rossiter, abandoning me as an incoherent semi-asphyxiated waste of space.

'You are now seeing,' he continues, now invisible to me through tears and smoke, 'with these mosquito coils you are having no bitings and scratchings. There is no mischief with coils and mosquitoes are very bad in this place. What is the purpose of your journey?'

'A bicycle ride,' I hear Rossiter say, somewhere nearby. 'We are bicycling from Kashmir to Kannyakumari,' he adds helpfully.

'That is very far from this place,' comes the sound of the coil man.

'Which one … do … you mean?' wheezes Rossiter as I shut my streaming eyes on all this.

'Both of these places,' he laughs, 'both very far off from this place, you know.' He tells us this as if we didn't know. I think he thinks Rossiter is laughing. As I can't stand the smoke any longer I stagger out into the road, gulp some fresh air and look round in time to see the man exit as well, having given Rossiter the supply of coils: 'So, my friends, there is being no more biting on your programme for you. Ram Ram!'

With that, he turns and walks off as fast and purposefully as he suddenly appeared. Given that these coils overcome human lungs, they could quite easily be the answer for the mosquitoes that have troubled us more and more since Nagpur and which cannibalized us last night. Rossiter agrees with me having gone the full course in there, he may be a little red-eyed but he's sold on the idea of using the coil.

Ever since we left Gwalior when lines of carts blocked the road out of the town, the sugar-cane harvest has been with us intermittently, leaving us through the barren plateau of Madhya Pradesh and reappearing as we freewheeled down to lower and more fertile ground. Today, in Andhra Pradesh, it is getting underway with a vengeance. For a long way we can see the small sugar refineries coming up with their tell-tale plumes of thick black smoke and, when we get within a mile or so – a thick smell exactly like that of home-made strawberry jam.

These refineries are small places, each one servicing only the immediate area. There is always one main refining building with the chimney on a long low whitewashed building set inside a high whitewashed wall. Though the walls are always at least eight feet high, you can quite frequently see stockpiled cane drying out in huge heaps often more than twice its height. Always, from the gates of each refinery string out long queues of cane-laden bullock carts, immensely heavy contraptions with solid wooden wheels. Most of the carts sport sleeping drivers lying in the dimples their weights have worn into the top of the loads. They sleep on large cloths to prevent them from sticking to the syrupy sap of the canes, waiting out here under the sun for the gates to open. Sometimes only the blue plume of bidi-smoke gives away the presence of a driver resting high up on his load. The white bullocks stand between the shafts chewing their cud with unhurried rotating jaws, their patience as limitless as their drivers'.

Seeing these small refineries appear every few miles with their ancient-looking traffic queueing typifies those Indian meetings of the ancient weaving itself into the working fabric of the twentieth-century state. This is in the essence of India and yet here, it is the timeless old method that delivers too efficiently for the modern machines and jaggery vats.

For some days now, Rossiter has been complaining of a non-specific pain in the stomach, which will neither blow itself up into something more dramatic nor leave him in peace. Finally, he announces after we have eaten that he will, at last, have to deploy one of the extensive range of suppositories which he has insisted on bringing. The suppositories have become something of a standing joke between us in recent months, since I did not know what a suppository was until Rossiter took me on a guided tour through the colossal pharmacy he's brought with him, just before we left Heathrow. The word 'suppository' had simply been something vague, for me, something inadvisable to mention on the whole. As I didn't believe the explanation he gave me as to what one does with a suppository – and still don't – I'm heavily in favour of his deploying one – or two perhaps – and noting what will happen.

When a lonely bridge over a nullah comes in view, unaccompanied by any sign of humanity, Rossiter slows to a halt, dismounts and paces around in the road. This could be the big plunge. 'Go on – do it!' I urge him, without dismounting.

'Mmmm – I don't know. I'm not sure this really is the time,' murmurs Rossiter, staring at the broken up tarmac and stroking his unshaven chin.

''Course it is. Go on, you'll rue the day if you don't slip one in. You regret it for the rest of your life – that you failed to stand firm when the hour of insertion came upon you.'

'Stand firm – nothing's been bloody firm with me for two

thousand miles. Firmness, my boy, is precisely the problem. But I'm not sure if a suppository is the real answer.'

Rossiter disappears with the look of a man who might be gone for some time and is lost behind a clump of bamboo by the nullah bank. No sooner is he lost from sight than there comes an enraged squealing from beyond the thicket and out comes Rossiter again at high velocity followed by a disturbed sow and her eager litter. In his haste he drops his suppository and the sow snuffles it up with an eager grunt.

Back on the bridge, Rossiter takes several minutes to recover his breath before declaring that he has catered for a greater need. 'You should've seen the mess they'd been making behind there – I only hope that one stops the old girl up for a bit.'

From Kamareddy south to Ramayampet this afternoon is only about twenty miles along a good road. Unfortunately, at Ramayampet the locals display an uncharacteristic unwillingness to suggest anywhere we might be able to stay and though there is a resthouse, it seems to be full of very drunk officials, lolling about along the verandah, giggling hysterically at us when we suddenly appear. Finally, a likely-looking stallholder back in the small bazaar gives us the helpful information, 'Andhra Pradesh State Government Development Compound Sangareddi District is back along the road. You must be returning same way.'

'How far?' I ask.

'It is not far from this place. You go this way and then it is at rightside. Do not deviate,' warns the man, solemn-faced.

'Promise not to,' assures Rossiter, gnawing a lump of sugar cane.

This place is easy enough to find though we're not sure at all how it's going to help us find somewhere to sleep. However, our man in the bazaar evidently knows pretty well how the land lies around here and no sooner have we entered the wide and well-swept courtyard of the Development Compound than a smiling man, smartly dressed, walks up and greets us in perfect English:

'Good evening. My name's Francis – can I be of assistance to you?'

It is a wonderful feeling when people like Francis and his family arrive on the scene just when hope is fading with the light, and the imagination is fixing onto whining mosquitoes and a lying down by some godforsaken roadside in the small hours to be eaten slowly by insects. But none of this tonight: in a few minutes Francis has got us fixed up with one of the offices of the A.P.S.G.D.C.(S.D.) filled with officially registered office furniture.

As we unpack our few belongings, Francis introduces his two sons Rozario and Sanjay and explains they've come here to visit Medak Cathedral near here, which is having its Diamond Jubilee celebrations tomorrow. Francis' brother Xavier behaves all along as if he was expecting us to come for supper and delivers rice, four fried eggs (each), hotly spiced potato crisps, chapattis, dal, groundnuts and piles of delicious buttered spinach. Xavier is a man who believes in carbo-hydrates in a big way. 'So then – let's all take some tiffin together,' he smiles when everything is set down on the veran-dah. 'We must take all this quickly before the mosquitoes come – soon it will be quite dark and they will be with us.'

Over this 'tiffin' Xavier and Francis explain more about the cathedral at Medak and from the photographs they have the place looks huge – they insist it is the biggest Christian church in Asia, a massive chunk of buttressed and corniced England set down in the middle of a baked maidan in southern India. It looks too incongruous to miss and although I have an irra-tional urge not to deviate from our chosen route south, the combined force of Rossiter, Rozario, Francis and Xavier per-suades me eventually and we agree to go with Rozario to see the cathedral tomorrow. The decision taken, we make our goodbyes swiftly for the mosquitoes arrive in force as fast as day turns to night.

Back at the office I unroll my filthy sheet sleeping-bag into the knee-hole of an immense old desk, piled high with fingered ledgers and bearing a long registration number lovingly hand-painted above the right-hand flight of drawers. Before sleeping, though, it is necessary to clear the room of mosquitoes. In the unspoken way in which we demarcate who does what on this journey, it has become my job to go round wherever we happen to be sleeping swatting mosquitoes with our – by now bloodstained – notebooks. Rossiter has always lit the mosquito coils – at least ever since they have been with us. Again, habitually, I forget to go swatting until I've already got into bed and the first whine by my ear reminds me, whereupon Rossiter is entertained by the sight of me completely naked chasing elusive mosquitoes around the room, flailing a notebook in their general direction.

We're both woken, not by Rozario as we'd arranged, but by an early morning sweeper who doesn't let a small thing like two human bodies get in the way of getting airborne all the dust the office floor has collected overnight. As he makes no attempt to avoid raking us with his long and rough bristles, and as the atmosphere becomes impossibly dusty soon after he enters, we decide to get up and watch the local buffaloes mowing the compound lawn until Rozario turns up.

Rozario decides over puris and coffee in the local bus-stand dhaba (where everybody seems to have breakfast around here), that the best way to Medak is to hitch a ride in a truck for the fifteen-mile journey. 'It will be very easy to get a ride if the driver sees you two. You are not normal here,' Rozario tells us confidently as we eat. I wonder whether this is really an advantage in the long run, but Rozario is sure hitching is the way to go.

He's dead right. The first truck that comes along stops and we three get into the cab along with the driver, two co-drivers and three others getting a lift plus a duck with its wings trussed up which seems to belong to nobody in particular but staggers about, losing its balance amongst the jumble of straw ends and dust under the driver's legs. As usual in these situations in India, nobody is sure whether we should pay for the lift – you have the feeling the driver will ask for something from the moment you get in – but he doesn't actually get round to it until we get to Medak itself. Whatever the code of hitching practice here, our driver continues his way west five rupees the richer.

The cathedral lives up to expectations. Set some way off the road leading into Medak – a small and normally empty town in flat, poor countryside – it stands out on its dry grassy maidan, where sweet cakes, samosas, tea, and mementos of the Diamond Jubilee are being sold by smiling quiet-spoken women – the sareed equivalents of those who keep the church fêtes smoothly oiled through the sunny June days of an English summer. Rossiter and I sit supping tea with Rozario, trying to explain the incongruity of there being here a gigantic structure designed in Bolton, Lancashire.

This is, however, suddenly ruined by a chained gang of murder suspects who are led up the driveway to the cathedral door, as if they're on a mission of repentance. The clinking of chains becomes louder against the singing of the large children's choir coming from within the cathedral. The men – about twenty of them – are made to squat in the noon sun and are prodded by the guards who carry large sticks, swaggering about and smoking ostentatiously. If this is what happens to suspects then I dread to think what becomes of the convicted. Eventually, when the guards seem satisfied with the gratuitous display they've put on for nobody in particular, the depressing and sorry-looking gang shuffles and chinks its way back to the town.

Indian hymns ring out from the elaborate ghetto-blaster rigged up on one of the stalls here that await the crowds expected from the main celebration tomorrow. Inside the church, school choirs are parading up and down but the singing is thin and feeble and seems to get swallowed up in the huge height and empty space of the place. Indeed, apart from a few rows of variously sized chairs and a simple pulpit, the cathedral is virtually empty of furnishings. A small hand-cranked organ sits on the lap of the music teacher to provide an uncertain accompaniment to the parade. This is, of course, a rehearsal for the main celebration tomorrow but you can't help but feel the chasm between all this and the unrehearsed energy, exuberance and mayhem of a Hindu festival under full steam. The cathedral seems shell-like, sitting here on its dry mowed lawn, unmarked by the seasons, its square tower and belfry preserved in perfect condition, piercing into the deep blue sky. The building hasn't become sullied by the land it has been planted in: a monolith erected here in the English style, it remains after the English have gone home, a huge plant that has not quite taken root, but will not die.

There is a bus back to Ramayampet at two o'clock and when it leaves at three we are on it, having decided to try and reach Hyderabad tonight if possible. With the Rossiter rear wheel keeping a blessedly low profile and apparently a good road south of Ramayampet, we're both in the mood for a fast burst to the first big city we will have been through for hundreds of miles.

Having swapped addresses with Rozario we leave town in the hottest part of the day which confirms several theories Xavier has about Englishmen.

Smooth tarmac gives us the opportunity to get lost in what's happening away from the road, namely: grapes. Plentiful cool clusters of them – black and green – are quietly swelling away for miles on either side of National Highway 7, the vines strung out along taut wires sprung from concrete poles.

The effects of Hyderabad can be felt some miles before we enter the northern extremities of the city. The dhabas become increasingly sophisticated – some are even brick built. The tailors' shops grow in size while the fruit-sellers can offer papaya, jackfruit and pineapple alongside the everyday guavas and bananas. Newspapers reappear and the buses start to look less dust-caked. Twenty miles out the Campa Cola wallahs are doing business again and there is water on tap. Five miles out, there is the roar of an Indian Airlines 737 coming into the airport.

We get into the suburbs in great mood, which deflates rapidly when I lose all patience with Rossiter about staying in a particular hotel here. It's not really a particular hotel – it's more like the first hotel we come to and I'm feeling hungry. 'Looks OK really. It's certainly cheap,' I tell him, having checked out the hallway and tariff.

'It looks a right bloody hole to me. In any case, why are you so worried about money all of a sudden? We're not short, you know.'

'No, it's not that. It's just sort of convenient here. You know, there are places to eat right here, so we may as well – '

'I'm not eating in one of your dhabas tonight and that's that,' says Rossiter flatly.

'Well look – why don't you go in and give this place the once over. It looks fine to me,' I continue.

'Thank you, O Egon Ronay of the Subcontinent. I'll take that with a whole heap of salt,' says Rossiter, parking his bicycle and walking into the hotel.

All is unfortunately lost even before he reaches the doorway. On the way there he is suddenly and dramatically overtaken by a partially furred cat dangling a twitching rat from its yellow fangs. Rossiter stops, watches the cat enter the hotel stealthily and disappear. He turns, walks to his bicycle, gets on it and heads into the city centre without saying anything. I think he has just rested his case.

7

'Here we go. Here we go. Here we go.'

National Union of Mineworkers

Having put up for a night with the Hotel Kakatiya, it's important to get out of it quickly the next morning. This is principally because the piped music that comes insistently from a small grille in the wall above our bed cannot apparently be turned off. Having coped with it all night, we ask the character who sleeps at reception about it and he eventually produces the Manager himself, who then explains that you can only turn off the music by turning off the entire electrical supply to the whole hotel. 'And that, as you are appreciating at this moment, is not at all possible.'

You can't help wondering that a switch or two placed here and there might bring untold flexibility to this system – but it's pointless debating the never-never-land of electrical choice. At least it's a change from having batteries of switches that don't do anything.

In Hyderabad there are a number of Indian Coffee Houses which are one of the big rewards of moving south across India. There is a large chain of these places run by the South Indian Coffee Growers' Association, all with white-robed waiters with elaborate starched cotton headdresses like large cockatoos who charge about spilling your coffee as if according to some unseen regulation governing exact required spillage per person. Increasingly we find ourselves spending large amounts of time in these places where the coffee is always cheap, hot and excellent. 'That's how you know when you're in the south,' says Rossiter over breakfast in one such emporium.

'How – when people start selling coffee and puris like this?'

'Partly,' he muses, 'but really just the existence of these places. It's a sure sign we're getting somewhere,' he says in his typical way of reviving a previous long-forgotten conversation.

Last night, during our tour of the hotels and hovels of this windy and dusty state capital, we went past the Press Club and decided we'd call in this morning on anyone who might be interested in our trip. With that still in mind today we breeze over to the Club which seems to happen upstairs, over an enormous concrete garage kept under tight guard by several under-employed shifty-looking types who flap about nervously in enormous brightly printed lungis when we march in. Collectively, they conspire to give the powerful impression that something is clearly about to happen – but it never actually does.

Our inquiry here elicits not the slightest interest from the clerk by the door upstairs to which we are eventually allowed access. He does not, in fact, wake up. We leave a message that we'll come back at two o'clock and leave. We drift into another coffee house that runs according to the Slit School of Coffee Vending. In one corner a concrete slit, stained black with coffee, is the source of all the puris, idlis and coffees sold on the premises. A hairy arm shoves out the coffees and food regularly through the concrete slit, spilling them in mid-shove. Orders are shouted vaguely through the slit by waiters utterly blasé about the business of communicating through rough, black-stained concrete. Is the Unseen Provider behind the slit even human?

To our utter amazement, at two o'clock on the dot we are swept up past the shifty garage men at the Press Club into a large conference room upstairs in which thirty or more reporters are apparently waiting for us. The Andhra Pradesh daily papers are represented: English, Telegu and Urdu versions are all present. Reporters from the nationals like *The Express*, *The Times of India* and *The Hindu* have come along, as have the Press Trust of India, Reuters and All India Radio (AIR). This is rather daunting, really, but for at least ten minutes there's the business of sorting out how to spell our names. Rossiter – the name – has been causing all sorts of problems across the country and today is no different. It takes a long time to get all the letters mutually agreed upon and then put into an acceptable order and when that's done various scribes frown and squint at the final product on their pads with the greatest scepticism. Rossiter is slightly put out at the spectacle of the Press refusing to believe in his name – but we move on to the journey, with Rossiter holding forth with such gusto that it is impossible to slip in a word. After a while I just sit back and watch him in action, recounting the highlights of the journey to date. He seems not the slightest perturbed that only two of the thirty-two present are writing anything down. They interrupt him in mid-flow regularly and I can't help thinking they're getting the story in a truncated form as a result. Rossiter ploughs on.

Suddenly, apropos of absolutely nothing, he is pulled up by a tiny, wizened old man with huge black spectacles, from All India Radio. 'Please will you give your opinions on Mrs Thatcher and the miners who are striking in your country at this time?'

'Ah,' says Rossiter, momentarily caught beyond the crease. 'Well, I think my companion Mr Thomson would be very interested in answering your question.' I attempt to kick him under the table but can't reach. Anyway, this gives carte blanche to the scribes, who from now on turn their attention to the political situation in England with which neither of us has had the slightest contact for three months. We are busy trying to do what we can for them (still not taking the trouble to write anything on their pads) when the direction of things abruptly changes again. A man claiming to be from the *Indian Express* suddenly stands up and holds aloft a portfolio of photographs apparently of a series of sculptures. He jolts it and it concertinas down to the ground displaying lots of large black and white prints of huge stone sculptures. 'This is all work of a friend of mine from A.P. state. I am interested to know what you are thinking of his work.' As it's difficult to see either

Indian Express himself or the photos behind which he is balancing on a chair, we move closer to get a better view. As we stand, it's the signal for the whole conference to break up amidst wild thanks from the chairman and several of the reporters, most of whom drift away with little more than our names in their notebooks.

The whole portfolio which the reporter shows us contains immense sculptures inspired by the Andhra countryside south of Hyderabad. We promise to look out for the colossal boulders that must have inspired this work, when we head south again, still not sure quite why we are being shown these things in what was – until very recently – a press conference. 'They remind me very much of Henry Moore's work,' declares Rossiter, who is at once absorbed into artistic appreciation without being remotely worried by the incongruity of it all.

'Oh yes, Mr Henry Moore, Mr Henry Moore,' repeats the reporter. 'Mr Henry Moore is a very good sculptor but the fellow who is making these works is the first sculptor of all Andhra state. The best.' He raps his index finger pointedly at a particularly impressive sandstone block, smoothed and rounded into a huge bear-like shape. 'Now,' he continues to Rossiter, who has shown much more interest than myself, 'I am asking you please to arrange for an exhibition of this sculptural work in your National Gallery which is in Trafalgar Square in London. I am knowing this place very well.'

The reporter fixes his gaze upon Rossiter, who has gone very quiet indeed. It is difficult to tell whether he is subdued by this reporter's energy and artistic faith in his sculptor-friend or more likely overcome by the compliment that his standing is such in the international art world that he can, of course, swing an exhibition in the National Gallery any time at all. 'That might be a little difficult to arrange, you know,' he sighs at last, as if having weighed up all the logistical difficulties in a pause of ten seconds or so.

For some reason there is much activity the next morning which is not entirely due to the two minions and their three sub-minions who arrive and attempt – at a very early hour – to transport our panniers the thirty feet or so to the front door of the Kakatiya in exchange for immense amounts of backsheesh. They eventually leave when they realize the backsheesh will not be forthcoming except for one who carries a bag just for friendliness. When they've gone a man with an aerosol arrives. We caught him spraying our bicycle saddles last night with his can of air freshener and he is always to be seen or faintly heard in the precincts of the Kakatiya, spraying away at an odour somewhere. This morning he arrives with two sidekicks, each with smaller, less important-looking cans. He never knocks, just comes right in, can first, his youthful minions carrying the papers. 'So,' he says by way of greeting, 'you like my rose?' He gestures extravagantly at the huge red bloom stuffed into the breast pocket of his brilliant white kurta.

'We love it,' I tell him flatly.

'Ah,' he says, 'I see you are not so happy, so early in the morning it is for you – but see – I have brought you the papers, they are all telling of your bicycle programme of all India – see!'

And on cue the minions step forward and throw all the papers onto our bed. Seizing his opportunity, Aerosol begins blasting away with his can whilst we read about ourselves, 'Alex Thomson and Nikloos Rozister', in the English-language editions amongst the stack. 'You see – this is a new fragrance today – very special for you –' comes the voice of Aerosol echoing from the dark depths of our bathroom.

'Great, love it,' murmurs Rossiter, head buried in the *Indian Express*. Our plans for packing up to leave are aborted for a while, at least.

Clearly the reporters in Hyderabad work to the principle of memory-reportage – the idea being that if anything is worth reporting you'll remember it without the indignity of having to write it all down. Ironically, the hurdle of Rossiter's name was the most widely noted item of information, and this morning it's the most wildly inaccurate piece of the entire story. Nevertheless, all Rozister's highlights of the journey are faithfully set down here in clear computerized black and white type and when the atmosphere gets too much to bear because of Aerosol and his team's work, coupled with the remorseless piped ragas coming out of the wall, we all repair to the reception hall, pay the bill and have Aerosol and half the staff translate the Telegu, Hindi and Tamil versions of our story from this morning's hefty press-stand.

The effect of the written word is potent. Most of the Kakatiya's several million staff seem to be on hand to see us off – even though we're only going round the corner to the All India Radio station. As we pull off along the crumbling road outside the hotel, Aerosol leaps from the ranks to give our tyres a final blast of fragrance, 'Sweet smell all the way to Bangalore!'

At the studios of All India Radio things get off to a bad start when the studio producer meets us in reception. 'You are from BBC. Huh! This means you are working for the CIA. Huh! Very bad thing – very bad thing indeed.'

It's little better in the studio, where our interviewer Mr Purokayastha evidently finds interviewing the frontline of the CIA a little too much. For twenty long minutes he chain-smokes and writes out the questions he thinks he'll ask, hands trembling visibly. Unfortunately he has to ask our names and there's a great deal of arguing, gesticulation, role-playing and diagram-drawing before the central concept of 'Rossiter' is straightened out.

Finally, Mr Purokayastha is ready (he thinks) and gives a tentative signal to the producer, who leers menacingly at us from behind his glass panel. When we are poised to relate what's been happening to us en route, Mr P. begins. 'Now I am asking first of all Mr Niklis Rossissidars, what advice he is giving for the Indian youth of today?'

It is no better when it comes to me, next. 'Now I am asking second of all Mr Alegsi Tumbsin what is his solution for the problems of world unemployments in this present century?'

All India Radio have seen all the articles in the papers and want, understandably, to widen the debate a little, develop the story away from the context of the road perhaps. All in all, the interview takes nearly two hours partly because of the nature of the questions but more for the way in which Purokayastha operates as if some invisible man has a pistol pressed into his temple. The sweat pours from him, he cannot keep his large black glasses from slipping down his nose, the ends of his moustache tremble and before almost every question he has to pause for a cigarette, smoked in silence, avoiding our gaze.

Finally, though, it is all over. Mr P. relaxes at once and shows us around the building. He asks us if we would like to be paid for the interview but we tell him a tape of it all would be worth more than money. He nods quietly. The vintage tape, however, never arrived at the flat in Delhi where we asked him to send it.

Picking our way through the city, men repeatedly dash out of coffee stalls and bus queues or bazaar stalls, screaming creative versions of our names and waving copies of *The Deccan Herald*, the *Indian Express* or the *Telegu Eenadu* and pointing ourselves out in print or pictures. Very soon there is an escort party assembled to show us on to the right road without our even having to ask – the newspaper story is quite enough to tell the people that we want the Deccan Highway to Bangalore and beyond.

Besides the inevitable sugar-cane factories at the roadside, there are some interesting other businesses dotting the road for many miles outside of the city itself. Between Hyderabad and the middle of the day we pass two distilleries; a silkworm factory; a large (and very dusty) asbestos works; a dynamite company; and also a serum laboratory.

Along the way this morning and also in the afternoon, there are groups of migrant Rajasthanis, working in the sugar-cane and road-mending here as they were in Madhya Pradesh and as they work on the building sites of Delhi: a people in constant migration for what work can be had away from the arid poverty of their western semi-desert state. The women are very distinctive. In almost all rural areas they invest their income heavily in jewellery but the Rajasthanis really go for it. Huge silver earrings pull down their lobes perhaps an inch and a half with several matching necklaces, nose studs and thick rings through the middle of the ear. Their arms are encased in white bangles above and below the elbow giving them the appearance of having armoured limbs, while the tinkling sound of a group walking along the road comes from their intricate ankle bracelets. As if that's not enough, their skirts or sarees are brilliantly coloured and studded with tiny mirrors for the full decorative effect. All in all, you can hear and see a group of Rajasthani women coming towards you from a long way off.

We decide to stop for the night at Jadcherla, about fifty miles south of Hyderabad, the most likely place there'll be anywhere to stay that we shall pass through today.

In the town the police chief is unable to help us. This is partly because there are no hotels or lodges in the small town, but it has more to do with the fact that he has been drinking toddy for some time.

After a good deal of fruitless 'discussion', we leave him slumped over his desk and head for the row of dhabas by the crossroads on the highway and sit down to eat and take stock. On the way there Rossiter hits a boulder in the road because it is dark by now and we still have no lights. This leaves him much shaken and grazed quite nastily. Just as we reach the first of the hotels, however, a farmer collars us both and shrieks, 'Friends, friends! I have a vision! On my way here tonight I had a vision that I should be meeting two friends. Please – you are my guests. Let us eat together and you may be sleeping in my house. It is quite near. Please!' He motions off into the darkness the other side of the road, 'You come – ha!' With that we are off with him – with Mirahmed Arif to be precise – and his chicken farm is at the end of a dusty track off the road to the other side of the hotels. He warns us to walk slowly and noisily down the sand of the track, 'for my friends, many serpents are living at our feet!'

Mirahmed speaks in exclamations the entire time, with

fanatical excitement in his eyes. As soon as we are sitting comfortably in the small verandah of his house, he notices Rossiter's grazes. 'But you are hurt! How? I shall bring medicines at once.'

He reappears in a few minutes with a large jar of what looks like tar. On the label there is a notice in bold type that reads FOR USE ON BULLOCKS ONLY.

I glance at Rossiter, glad I'm not in any way grazed just now. 'Go on then – dab it on good and thick – do you good,' I tell him. Mirahmed looks on all the while, manically, with his glazed expression of violent generosity against which we're both pretty well powerless. Rossiter dabs – and winces instantly with the evident pain.

After we've eaten, Mirahmed suddenly introduces his son Mohammed, whom he has systematically ignored until now. He then continues, as if Mohammed had never happened, and comes straight to the point: 'We may now speak of religion? Yes!' he answers himself. 'My religion ha!' and he roars with laughter, though without amusement.

From then on for nearly four hours he forces a discourse on us concerning his religious beliefs which seem to evolve from the principle of 'Double Christianity'. This postulates – amongst other things – that Christ came down from the Cross and gamely made a pilgrimage east, rather a long way east, and ended up dying in Srinagar in Kashmir at the grand age of one hundred and twenty years old.

Mirahmed is, in fact, an Ahmadiya Moslem. The sect all began in 1879 when Mirza Ghuram Ahmad began preaching in Quadian in the Punjab. Being of a confident disposition, Mirza informed people that he was the long-awaited Mahdi – as well as being the Messiah.

It was he who came up with the theory of Christ's eastward procession for eventual burial in Srinagar – and Mirahmed has the photographs of the grave to prove it. Mirza backed up his ideas with the theory of Jihad, or war against non-believers, until his death in 1908. No doubt with this impetus, the sect is highly propagandist. Rossiter is beginning to feel ill and exhausted. As he succumbs to sleep, Mirahmed starts playing speeches by the Caliph at high and distorted volume on his ghetto-blaster. You might think this would shut Mirahmed up, but no: he simply goes on talking at me in his fast, cascading English, over and above the shrieking Caliph-cassettes.

Finally, way after midnight, Rossiter suddenly sits upright, then bolts into the bushes by the house to be violently sick. Mirahmed continues his involved tale of how he met the Caliph in Lahore with not so much as a hesitation. At this point, I take the bull by the horns and suggest that in view of Rossiter's imminent physical collapse bed might not be such a bad idea, might it?

It is actually a deeply peaceful night's sleep – for both of us, lying out against the cool stone floor of the verandah on thin cotton mattresses stuffed with soft grasses. Rossiter celebrates the next morning with a grandiose emptying of his stomach in the bushes, whilst the Caliph comes on good and loud out of the blaster before the sun has risen. I'm glad everyone is behaving according to habit this morning, at any rate.

The escape from the Caliph (who has latterly exceeded even Mirahmed as a threat to one's sanity) comes when we both cross the fields in the thin, clinging dawn mist to wash at a huge stone trough two paddies to the far side of our road south. Warm water, by some complete miracle, bubbles vigorously up from the bottom of the trough three feet down. We both agree it's like a jacuzzi – but since neither of us has ever been in one, we have to take each other's word for it. Rossiter is feeling much better as the sun dries him off. Across the paddies egrets flap, white and ghostlike in the vague mist. A hoopoe arrives at the edge of a paddy, gliding in silently.

Caught in a difficult tactical situation, we decide to leave Mirahmed as soon as possible even though Rossiter is not sure how far he'll be able to cycle. He's adamant about escaping, however. Yet at the same time Mirahmed has been very good to us, fed us and put us up for the night. Yet because of the conversation we know so little of him, beyond the perplexing claim that he sells chickens and their eggs entirely to customers in Saudi Arabia, which seems a little far-fetched when we are sitting on a small farm to the south of Hyderabad hundreds of miles from the nearest port on the Arabian sea. But Mirahmed is insistent about this, as he is about everything else. By eight-thirty in the morning we would welcome a little bit of doubt.

As the Caliph plays on we edge our bicycles through the dust of the track on to the road. Women from the town are coming slowly and with steady poise from the trough where we washed, the huge pitchers on their heads filled with water. I hope our being there didn't delay them with the morning's work.

For the first hour or so, we take things very gently and Rossiter is soon talking once again. When he falls silent for long periods it is a sure indication that things are not too well within. It is along the road today that we see dramatically how the sculptor in Hyderabad could be inspired by the local landscape here. On either side, for miles around, weird boulders rear up from the red, sandy soil eroded by the endless Deccan winds into natural dumbells standing upon their own rounded pedestals sometimes twenty or thirty feet high. These remarkable formations are rather like some exaggerated tor, or the Bridestones of North Yorkshire, except they seem to be of granite. Sometimes they appear to grow right out of a field and the millet (which is common in this part of the state) stands in disorderly rows ploughed around their bases. They are with us for several miles before the road crosses a small and apparently insignificant nullah and the soil turns to sand. At this point the stones are lost in an ancient geological divide, replaced by low cacti-studded hills.

A mile or so past the nullah we pull in for a drink of water from the bottles – one of which is now leaking steadily, a casualty of the constant vibration. As usual I'm impatient to get going again. 'Go on then, I'm going to need a lot of rest today,' says Rossiter, pulling out a cigarette, 'I'll catch you up.'

And so I leave him, cycling off slowly in the heat so that he will catch up with me. After about an hour he comes up alongside and for some reason I'm prompted to ask him how much money he's got. He suddenly looks at me, brakes hard and pulls up, a look of panic on his face. 'Oh shit –' he breathes.

'You've left it back where you stopped?' He nods, wiping the sweat from his forehead. 'Check the panniers – just in case,' I say, noticing how thin and husky my own voice sounds.

'I know I left it there – took it out to find my cigs – it's got to be back there,' says Rossiter, already turning his bicycle to retrace our route north again.

The wallet, needless to say, has everything in it and my mind races, as we both pedal furiously, on how to replace travellers' cheques, visas, passport . . . you name it.

Then, not ten minutes back up the road, two young men on a scooter flag us down and there, in an outstretched hand, is the familiar black wallet. Both of them seem bemused by our show of thanks which must look a little theatrical, but they are glad enough of the money we give them. After this, everything seems terribly relaxed, and although there is a long way to go today to get anywhere to stay, there can be no earnestness in our ride after this little emergency. Besides, Rossiter is simply not well enough to force things.

Several miles further south we suddenly come up alongside one of a party of Railway Scouts, a kind of Indian offshoot of the mainstream but still very much in the Baden-Powell tradition. The one we meet first, Edward William, tells us he and seven others are on a bicycle tour from Jabalpur to a jamboree at Tirucharappalli. They are not travelling the seven hundred miles very lightly, judging by Edward William's gear, which includes a heavy rucksack and thick canvas tent, enormous black leather boots and another heavy-duty canvas bag slung over the handlebars of his bicycle containing, amongst other things, a ledger about an inch thick in which we sign our names. Thinking about it, we're rather taken with the idea of having a visitors' book for a bicycle – but it's a little late to start that kind of thing now.

We exchange notes about the bicycles and both try out his heavy and gearless 'Hero'. When we pull away from Edward after riding with him for a couple of miles, we feel he could do with some of the lightweight technology that goes into our touring bicycles.

'The point is,' Rossiter explains, having as usual found the point in it all, 'he reckons he's doing over a hundred miles a day on that bike. Do you realize what that means? If he had one of these he'd probably do about two thousand – it's frightening.'

'I don't know, he seems to be really into it the way it is – besides, I bet they don't have any mechanical problems.'

I should, by now, have known better than to tempt fate by saying unsolicited things like that. As if acting upon the instructions of some sinister force bent upon holding us up, Rossiter's back wheel breaks a spoke just after we pass the time of day with the rest of Edward's party. We crunch to a halt in the dust and the main group of Railway Scouts cruise by in a few minutes. This faces us with a dilemma: either this is simply a casualty of the roads since Nagpur, and there have been some pretty bad stretches, or this wheel is going to do exactly what the last one did and we'll either be shedding spokes all the way to the Cape (if we have enough spares, which is unlikely) or we'll be finishing the journey on a couple of Heroes.

It does not look good right now. Up the road, in the direction from which Edward should be appearing soon, a couple of vultures land. For some reason this drives me mad. I run at them screaming obscenities and throw stones at them, insulted by their presumption of infirmity. Turning back to Rossiter, I see he's retching heavily again at the side of the road. It is very hot, we have passed nowhere with water since he last vomited and our bottles ran dry several hours ago. He emerges after a while, while I flick the broken spoke and wonder what happens next.

'I've got to get some water, you know. Soon,' he says in an odd, distant voice.

What does happen next, of course, is Edward and being a scout he is prepared and has a little water – at least enough to wet Rossiter's dehydrated mouth and cracked lips. According to Edward there is a village five miles south of here. Because of the water situation and the fact that it is treeless country just here with no shade, Rossiter goes off with Edward on my bicycle while I set off, pushing the Rossiter machine, accompanied by the vultures above me. We dare not risk riding the bicycle – even unladen – in case the wheel warps even more.

It is actually not that bad walking for a change and when my own thirst gets bad after an hour or so, I stop the first passing truck driver who is delighted to offer a drink of water and offers to take me to Kottakota – the next village south – even though he is heading north!

At least things are getting organized by the time I arrive in Kottakota's one small street – for a start, Rossiter is talking again. 'OK?' he says, when I turn up. Not much, I admit, but at least it's a start – and soon there's more. 'You can get a thali opposite – try out the lassi. Anyway, I'm feeling a bit steadier inside so I'll get started with the bike while you eat. Oh – this is Mr K. Muner Ahmed, he knows what's what at the bicycle shop up the road.' Mr K. Muner Ahmed smiles broadly from his dazzling white kurta, with crisp, disciplined creases. It amazes me how people like this seem to be able to wander about their business in the dust and smoke and dung of the bazaars and still look gleaming white and pristinely creased at the end of the day. It also explains why Indian ponds, tanks and rivers are lined with women bashing the living daylights out of white pieces of cloth for many hours of the day, all over the country's dhobi ghats.

By the time I've put a large thali inside me with several refills and washed my hands and face, the wheel has a new spoke and is well on its way back to the rest of Rossiter's bicycle. All that remains for me is to visit the imposing well at the north end of the town and fill up the water bottles.

Soon after leaving Kottakota the road climbs up on to higher ground, turning as it does so due south, whereas we had been going south-east all the morning from Jadcherla. Large areas of rock-pavements stretch out before us with small parties of grouse-like birds running, sometimes flying, rapidly across them. Once again those odd, wind-worn rocks stand out like stark Henry Moores placed at random into this barren land. For miles there is nothing in the way of farming beyond odd groups of disgruntled brown and black goats.

My attention is suddenly caught from this unforgiving rock-scape by what seems to be a dead animal at the side of the road. It's not in the slightest unusual to see dead animals – but it's very odd if they're not being eaten by vultures, crows or jackals. I slow as I get near and what I thought was a carcass rears up at the front, turns and the foaming pant of a dog in the final stages of rabies begins to hobble towards me, its back legs paralysed, bald patches of purple, bloody skin showing through on its rib-furrowed flanks. There seems to be enough room for me to get past along the road before it can reach me and I go for it without stopping.

This leaves Rossiter, several hundred yards behind. The dog slumps in the middle of the road exhausted and if there were any boulders around I'd put it out of its torment, but there's nothing to hand. Rossiter comes into sight the other side of it. When he gets within shouting distance I yell to him, 'Stop!' He doesn't hear and continues to look at the country around the deserted road. 'Rabies!' I scream as he halts by the dog. He retreats extremely fast for thirty yards or so, turns and looks again at the dog in disbelief. The only alternative is to take a wide detour across country to avoid the animal. Because of the cacti and thorn bushes that dot the land, this means two trips: one to carry the gear and another to carry the bicycle which would otherwise puncture on thorns lying about everywhere.

Both on the south side of the dog, we are re-strapping the panniers when a lorry approaches from the south. When it's nearing the dog we point it out to the driver, wondering if he's seen a rabid animal before. Fortunately he seems familiar with them. He starts up in reverse, and backs about fifty yards while we clear off the road. He then begins to shift forward, revving through the gears, gathering speed and lining up the right-hand wheels with the ravaged body.

Over the last fifteen miles into the town of Kurnool, Rossiter's bowels come right out in sympathy with his stomach and we have to stop frequently in the darkness. At one such stop, for some reason I start singing, perhaps because I often play records in my head when I'm cycling anyway.

'Please –,' says Rossiter suddenly, 'just keep on singing when we get going . . . I think I'll be OK . . . it's just really nice to hear singing for some reason – even yours – so keep on doing it . . . Let's go.'

And so we set off with me trying to sing as hard as possible next to Rossiter who is trying as hard as possible to cycle, or breathe, or even both of them at once. Well, somehow we reach Kurnool despite thick, moonless darkness and random samples of Indian cows taking their kip in the middle of a road that turns increasingly rutted as the light fails. By the time we get into the town I'm running short of numbers to warble at my ailing companion.

It takes a couple of days for Rossiter to recover, but then we choose the wrong morning to leave town. 'Christianity it is!!' insists the groundnut-seller, and persistently ignores my attempts to pay for the freshly roasted nuts he's ostensibly selling. 'Look! It is Christian peoples here –' and he waves in the direction of the Kurnool high school who are ploughing down the road towards us and screaming hymns with much gusto but much less finesse.

For some time now we are prevented from cycling out of Kurnool by the procession led by gourd and serpent players and a man bearing an enormous, battered sousaphone. Quite why the local school is on manoeuvres in this fashion, nobody seems able to tell us, least of all the groundnut-vendor, who has now removed his false teeth, believing he will thus impress his message the better on us. 'Christianity people – like your good Queen Mother!'

This, evidently, seems to be enough to give the school carte blanche to create screaming mayhem around town and further snarl up its deep traffic problems. Meanwhile the straggling columns of schoolboys and girls (separate ranks, thank you) wail and stop every three or four paces because the entire procession is now stuck, creating a headache for non-existent traffic police.

So there's a good deal of pushing the bicycles and steering them gingerly through the choked-up streets of the old part of Kurnool before we arrive in more open thoroughfares towards the large bridge over what could possibly be a river given the right part of the year. To the left, eastern side of our sturdy bridge, an ancient crumbling brick version shambles half-way across the swampy depression before crumpling into a heap festooned with creepers and mosses – Kurnool's answer to Avignon.

Having met the Press up in Hyderabad, we are assailed by people of all ages who seem already to know our names. Because newspapers are widely read, and widely read aloud in areas where literacy is not widespread, news travels and people have made the connection that we shall be travelling their way – though this is hardly surprising since there is only one road of any size at all south through this part of Andhra Pradesh.

By the late afternoon the slopes of the Erramalla Hills, covered in their bumpy coat of thick knotty grasses with curious, bare, pebbly patches in between, have drawn themselves up steeply against the road until the valley we are going through begins to verge on being a gorge. At this point the Hyderabad to Bangalore Railway comes up alongside and our small single-track tarmac road, as if for comfort, hugging it against these hills glowering on either side in the fast-fading light.

A sign appears at the roadside – one of the marvellous, stalwart, stonebuilt signs that look so much a part of the landscape. It indicates in Telegu (the language most widely spoken in this part of the state) that we shall soon be in Gooty. Below that comes the Hindi version and finally comes the English – just as every fifth way-marker or so is in English along the main roads in India – still one of the most widely spoken languages across the country as a whole.

Before we come to the town itself we can just make out the immense ramparts of its huge old fort spreading along the ridge of the hills rising to our left. According to how the pendulum of power was swinging at any given point, the fort has been used across the centuries by Moghul, Hindu and latterly British rulers to control this much-disputed region – a lonely and hostile posting the British soldiers must have found it too, stuck up there in the blistering heat on those bare, bleached hills.

Now the ramparts stand there enclosing the invisible, deserted fort. Like so many such places in the countryside it comes up into view unencumbered by signposts, warnings, marks upon maps and so on – there is nothing to tell you the fort exists here until its high, gaunt ramparts arrest the eye in pure surprise, powerful and ghostlike, striking up out of the lunar Deccan wastes.

The town is another world, a place of life, feeding off the trade the modern road brings in: donkey carts, camel carts, bullock carts, trucks and buses with more paint and colour than a fairground stall, the roofs piled high with bundles of goods.

At the coffee-stall the man serves the beverage with true southern style, pouring the creamy brown liquid from one small steel beaker to another. He holds one high over his head while the other catches the foaming coffee held as low as possible, a golden steaming jet forming a momentary column between the two. This cools the coffee, puts a fine head on it and advertises the drink all in one flourish.

Whilst we're sitting here drinking our coffee on a stone bench next to a stone table, an earnest young man approaches through the mandatory small crowd of gawping boys. For a moment he seems rather at a loss, but then he smoothes back his gleaming black hair and begins: 'My name is Rakesh Chandra and I am reporter for a Bangalore newspaper. I am wishing to do interviewing with you concerning your bicycle programme of all India about which my colleague in Hyderabad is telling me very much indeed. Our meeting in this place is fortunate thing for us all. Let us thank God for this.'

'Very fortunate I'm sure,' I say.

'Pardon me?' replies Rakesh, evidently not understanding.

'He says he's very glad to see you,' adds Rossiter helpfully.

Seizing the opportunity of an English speaker in Gooty I decide to press it for maximum advantage. 'Can you tell us anywhere where we could stay the night – then we could do the interviews – yes?'

'Pardon me?' says Rakesh again, totally blank.

'He suggests that. . .' chimes in Rossiter, pleased by the fact that I'm evidently incomprehensible to this man.

By the time the interview actually begins we are in the R&B resthouse (Roads and Bridges, not, sadly, rhythm and blues). By now, Rakesh has made his mind up about me and the peculiar incomprehensible noise that comes out of my mouth and addresses all questions to Rossiter as if I simply don't exist. 'Please, tell me highlights from your long bicycle programme,' he begins.

'Well,' I answer, settling back into my large wickerwork chair to begin the grand speculation the question seems to merit.

'Please –' says Rakesh, waving me away as if I'm some deeply distracting spectre, 'please – I shall speak to your friend here. You are not making sense to me.'

I retire hurt at this point and decide to go and wash myself at the well outside, even though it's dark. Meanwhile young Rossiter sits there being genial and having his cosy little tête-à-tête with Rakesh, while I wonder if I really am incomprehensible and if people have not simply been humouring me these last few months to keep me happy.

Returning after some time, feeling refreshed and much less

irked, I find both of them still at it, nattering away and evidently getting on very well. 'Mmmmmmmmmmmm,' I sigh theatrically and very loudly, 'absolutely delightful water out there – really cold. I feel so refreshed.'

This excites no reaction in Rossiter or Rakesh beyond silent staring at me, dripping and half-naked, as if I'm some kind of weird monster. 'Pardon me?' says Rossiter with a glint in his eye.

The road south of Gooty is excellent and there is a strong hot wind blowing from the north-east and fairly bowling us along this morning. The only problem with a wind, of course, is the amount of dust it blows up, and there are periods of cycling with tee-shirts over our noses and mouths, eyes squinting in a vague and ineffective attempt to make out where we are going.

This slows our progress somewhat, but towards the middle of the day we come upon a row of trucks parked up at one side of the road with no dhaba in sight. As there is about one truck along this road every twenty minutes or so, it's worth stopping to see what the fuss is about. On the other side of them, a sturdy concrete channel flows past with brilliant blue water and hundreds of tiny fishes. The truckers are standing, sitting, splashing about in it all, soaping themselves or their clothes which festoon all the thorn bushes on either side of the channel, drying in the hot sun in minutes. Unravelled brilliant purple and red lungis lie in long strips along the concrete coping of the channel.

We are welcomed into all of this, of course, and a lengthy water-fight inevitably ensues with much laughter and gurgling until we eventually haul ourselves out to sit on the hot rim of the channel eating bananas and smoking bidis under the blinding white light of midday.

In the past weeks when the countryside has been arid and the only vegetation rough grasses, thorn bushes and cacti, we've been in the habit of always lifting the bicycles off the road whenever we stop and placing them carefully on ground not covered with the vicious thorns that everything which grows around here seems to produce. They lurk like scorpions in the dust, retaining their piercing hardness long after they have died.

Well, perhaps it's just the urge to get out of the heat and dust today – at any rate I simply freewheel off the road and within seconds have punctured both tyres. I console myself by thinking how neither of us by now has to think where anything is in either of our panniers, so well imprinted on our brains is its place. I'm well involved with fixing the punctures by the time Rossiter catches up and comes off the road. He dismounts but with a heavily laden bicycle he still picks up another puncture by the time he's covered the ten yards from the road's edge to my patch of windless shade. 'Puncture? says he in a flash of inspiration.

We're just about ready to *lift* the bicycles back onto the road again when, stroking his tyres either for emotional solace or to check for thorns, Rossiter suddenly breathes, 'Shit.'

I try, just for the mental exercise, to imagine that Rossiter has not found a large thorn sticking into one of his tyres. 'I've got a huge bloody thorn in my tyre – look at that.'

I look somewhere more soothing, like straight into the sun.

For some reason neither of us can be bothered to do anything about the offending thorn so we cycle on with it fitting snugly into the tyre and tube – and there it stays innocently enough until the evening when we have enough energy and commitment to pull it out, bear the soul-destroying hiss and put it right.

The opportunity to do this only comes after much trouble in the dirt streets of Penukonda. By the time we get there the Indian landscape has pulled off another of its quick and unexpected changes. For the last twenty miles or so we are led by our smooth and empty road into greener, more cultivated land and gentler hills after the bare ridges and rock-piled hills we have been past in the last couple of days.

Rossiter does not seem to feel hungry – although his stomach and bowels have resumed normal service, so far as

I'm willing to investigate. So he abstains from eating anything of the huge thali which I locate in the first dhaba we come to. I plunge the oily fingers of my right hand into a greyish mound of rice. 'You really are an animal, you know that?' inquires Rossiter, watching my oil-blotched digits work a dark chilli sauce into the rice. 'I mean – you could've at least washed your hands after mending the punctures. You never had any standards before we even came here but you managed to let even them drop, you know that?'

'That doesn't make sense – you're tired.'

'Anyway, that rice is as dirty as your hands.'

'You know what, you should've been an environmental health officer. You'd love that. You could spend all your time trucking around people's houses complaining about the state of their kitchen or their bloody table manners. Snooping on rats and so on – that'd really be your kind of scene. I'll see if I can't fix you up with some council when I get back. Anyway, aren't you hungry?'

'No. Not for that crap. I'm sick, sick, sick to death of eating rice. I'm going off to find someone in possession of an egg. I'll see you at the bus-stand if you can still stand up after *that* lot.'

Rossiter takes his leave, passing one more withering look at my fingers working away to feed me. I have to admit there is a distinct taint of bicycle oil in all this food, detectable even above the searing heat of the green-chilli sauce.

At the bus-stand the 'small hotel' we were told was there is indeed small – two rooms so far as we can make out and both of them full. The bus-stand itself is devoid of buses but full of Penukonda's cow-quota one of which, like us, is trying to gain access to the hotel rooms for the night. Ignoring the amiable attempts of the receptionist to thwart it, the cow moves in through the half-open door of one room only to be violently repulsed by the occupant whom, I can only presume, is Moslem. 'Come on,' says the egg-less Rossiter, 'this is quite hopeless.'

We leave with the cow, who has placidly decided to return to her sisters, who are sitting around with expressions of mild, chewing wonder at us from those huge pool-like eyes, their front legs delicately tucked up beneath their soft white flanks.

Over at the Government Inspection House the chowkidar is not so much sneering or overbearing, he simply refuses to acknowledge that we exist, looking straight through us to talk to a group of monkeys invading the courtyard whilst we ask him if we can stay there. 'It's caste,' Rossiter roundly declares as we retrace our pedals back out into the bazaar. It is typical of Rossiter to overlook the possibility that the chowkidar may be a supercilious idiot in favour of the grand social context of things. 'You see,' he goes on, 'we're outcastes. That's the real problem. I'm sure that's why he was like that with us, just ignoring us like that. We just didn't exist for him, did we?'

'He could just be a miserable bastard,' I suggest.

'No. No way. I'm sure that was simply caste – if anything can be "simply" caste. Anyway, I think this is the point where we go for the District Magistrate – if there is one that is.'

This line of approach has worked well enough in the past and soon two men on a motor scooter and three starving dogs have formed an escort to take us to the 'Crown Court Judge' which they insist is the best method of procuring somewhere to spend the night. It occurs to me that we could be under some gentle and obscure form of arrest, but it's too late to worry about such details now.

Sure enough, we are taken through the old winding streets of this hilly town to the Judge's house and there, before our eyes is Mr Justice Kumar, in bed with his white, Russian fur hat with his wife next to him. It is not every day that one is shown straight into a judge's boudoir but in the case of Mr Justice Kumar there really is no other way of approaching since his bedroom opens straight off the street through a thin wooden door. There is no hallway to the house: you simply walk in and you are at his bedside.

He appears to be charmed by our sudden entry although all I can think of is the relief that he wasn't asleep – or worse. Mrs Kumar smiles in a vague kind of way and the group of geckoes hunting flies along the walls scurry about in sucker-footed excitement at us breezing in unannounced. Or perhaps not so unannounced, for Mr Justice Kumar's opening question suggests some prior warning. 'So, you are requiring accommodation in my town?'

'Oh yes please,' says Rossiter, 'and we're very sorry to ... er ... disturb you like this,' he continues, deeply troubled by the un-Englishness of going straight into someone's bedroom.

'You shall stay in my court tonight then. It will be quite comfortable for you both. There is plenty of space.'

Unfortunately I do not hear this quite correctly. People here habitually refer to their beds as 'my cot' and in an Indian accent the difference between 'cot' and 'court' is hard for an English ear to detect. I do not detect it at all. 'Oh no. No, really, you mustn't give up your bed for us. Please, there must be somewhere else where we could go – '

'Court – you fool. Court, not cot,' hisses Rossiter, rigid with embarrassment.

Judge Kumar looks levelly at me and continues, 'You may be sleeping in the witness box or the benches for the advocates – there will be plenty of space for you both.'

'Ah,' I smile as winningly as possible, 'Yes of course – I thought you'd said cot. Ha! Ha! Funny eh? Still, it's been a long day for us ...'

I see that neither Rossiter nor the Judge is in the slightest amused at this. For a moment there is an uneasy sort of silence. Then the Judge thankfully breaks it. 'My man will show you the way – good evening to you both.'

With that we turn back out onto the street where an ancient type in long white flowing kurta and matching beard appears. 'I am Judge's Man. Come.'

He sets off at an immense pace completely out of place with his thin and decrepit appearance, striding off down the narrow streets lit by oil lamps from the few street stalls still trading this late.

The court stands back from the nearest road, separated by neatly cropped box hedges and what would be lawns if it was damp enough for the grass to grow here. That makes the large, whitewashed colonial building unique – for no other building here except the Mosque stands back from anything at all. Indeed, the Judge's house epitomizes the out-front spirit of this tightly packed little town.

In court – Crown Court to be exact – it's a pleasant enough night since the British laid out the entire place on the evident assumption that mass trial could be needed at any time – there are acres of space across the various benches and in the very large dock where I eventually bed down. Judging by the sounds in the dark courtroom, a large number of mice inhabit the place and several times during my sleep I'm stirred by the patter of tiny rodent feet over my frail, filthy and generally abused sleeping-sheet.

Judge's Man comes early in the morning bearing chai for us both – a drink we are no longer at all sick of in the coffee-dominated south and we gratefully slurp away whilst trying to fathom out where on earth all the mice could be holed up by day.

We then follow Judge's Man off on a lightning tour of the town which his boss has evidently ordered. Judge's Man is keen enough and striding even faster this morning than he did last night. He takes us first of all into the old semi-derelict mosque tucked in at the base of the hills that rise steeply out from the west of the town. Inside, flakes of peeled paint lie about in piles just as they have fallen from the walls and ceilings, yet despite its air of neglect the mosque is still used daily for worship, and lights and incense burn in the inner holiest parts of the building to which we are not admitted.

At the very edge of town, beyond the mosque, is an extensive network of ruins, pits, wells and overgrown towers of what used to be the palace for the ancient rulers of the town and much of the surrounding land. Nowadays the whole palace is a large unkempt ruin simply left at present to rot away, in the meantime providing a haven for snakes and scorpions to bask and hide in its crannies. Deep, dark green vines and creepers with large and brilliant yellow flowers are imperceptibly crumbling what remains, and the two huge old trees that rise out of the debris must have seen the place if not in its heyday about four hundred years ago, then certainly in better days than this. Some of the masonry is very curious here, being simply huge blocks of stone fitted together by their shape, without mortar, to form those walls that are best preserved. This style of building reminds me of the architecture of the Incas in the perfect way in which these huge stone blocks are fitted to each other. In one of the few complete rooms still standing the corners of the ceiling are dominated by the biggest cobwebs I've ever seen, some seven or eight feet across. I should not like to meet the spiders capable of spinning these great dingy sheets.

Back at the Court, Judge Kumar has arrived in his office (which sports five geckoes this morning) and is preparing to mete out the day's justice, exchanging his white fur hat for a wig. Clearly, with today's winter temperatures edging as low as 85°F, Judge Kumar is taking no chances of catching a chill by going about with an ill-clad head. Quite what he must make of our plimsolls-shorts-and-nothing-else approach to things I cannot imagine.

Anyway, it would be an easy day's ride today down to Chik Ballapur about fifty miles south and in striking distance of Bangalore. During the rest of the morning the road continues smooth, winding its way through the greener hills that began to appear late yesterday. Today many of these slopes are being assiduously quarried for the good building stone that lies just below the thin topsoil. Rossiter has been going on for the last two thousand miles about the wonders of stone as *The Superior Building Material*. He was a happy man in the Himalaya. He grew melancholic in the brickfields of Haryana but now with the sight of whole hillsides being chipped away by individual hard sweat he can settle to one of his favourite themes. 'Mmmmmmm – granite!' he sighs looking deep into the first quarry the road passes.

'Can you smell it then?' I ask.

'You wouldn't understand. It's the ... the feel of the stuff.

Such a pure material ... solid ... I mean to say, just look at Aberdeen,' he says, staring suddenly at a far point at the top of the quarry.

'I can't quite make it out – is it where that group of guys are near the top, the ones with the barrows?'

'No, I knew you wouldn't understand,' smiles Rossiter, mildly enjoying the evidently manly pleasure the sight of a granite quarry brings to his soul.

Today we get served our first thali on a banana leaf which, for me, is final confirmation of The South. A large slice of the leaf sprinkled with water is slapped down onto the (granite) table and the many and varied elements of the thali are subsequently dolloped on top. At the end of the meal anything left including the leaf is simply thrown to the nearest passing goat/pig/chicken/dog/cow/buffalo/human, making a few rupees from collecting up banana leaves and selling them off as animal feed. For some reason this sets me off on one of my favourite themes, with which I've been haranguing Rossiter on and off for rather a lot of miles: the benefits of re-cycling waste.

'Well, that's all very well but I bet you wouldn't say no to a nice cheese-burger à la plastic carton as soon as you get back to England, would you?'

'That's hardly the point, is it?'

'Honestly, you really do get so pious when you're on your hobby-horse you know. You'd be the first one into the nearest McDonald's,' says Rossiter trying to wind me up – and succeeding.

'Me? McDonald's? No way. No way at all,' I tell him flatly.

'I'll hold you to that.'

Later in the afternoon another rare chance of a swim presents itself when a large village tank on the left-hand side of the road seems to be full enough for a dip. Wheeling the bicycles across the delicious lush grass near to the tank and past a small but thriving banana plantation, we then strip off and plunge into the clear and surprisingly cool water. Immediately, three old men from the nearby village come down to the water's edge to stare at us frolicking about in our soaking wet underpants. They remain there till we come out and for a long time it is good just sitting with them largely in silence, sharing the few glucose biscuits that we'd bought in Penukonda and staring out at the wide expanse of water, watching the mud where we were swimming slowly sinking and settling once more. These three old men have a very knowing way of smiling at us – though what it is they know, we have no idea, which perhaps, we feel, is just as well.

As we cycle on it does occur to us that the entire tank may well have been happy home to untold disease and pestilence – it certainly was the latrine for the village as we both well know but seemed big enough to absorb any such minor organic effluent. But there was something in the way those old men kept smiling at us ...

It takes the state frontier with Karnataka to break us out of the silence such thoughts impose, as we go along side by side after the swim, for there is no feeling like that of entering a new state to give you the sensation of progress. Rossiter chooses this moment to suggest that we should have had photographs of every frontier but I am adamant about not going all the way back to get them. We make off down the road after a quick drink of sterilized water sitting atop the large stone sign spelling out the fact that Karnataka welcomes you, heartily.

Chik Ballapur is a place of plenty after the towns and villages we have been through since Hyderabad. Near enough to the markets of Bangalore the fruit is piled in high stacks at every street stall. You can have a choice of coffees – a choice of rices even – in the spotless dhabas and 'hotels'. The shops are full of electrical goods and the streets are swept. I cannot for the life of me find anyone begging here, from the top end of the town right through to the bus-stand and telephone exchange which are inevitably the standard places for begging, but no, no beggars here.

It is outside the telephone exchange that we are accosted by a manic type without teeth: 'Please – I am retired bus driver and it is my full duty to show you to the house of Doctor Robinson with whom you will be very happy to stay within his house and you will assuredly be given full welcome by his wife Mrs Robinson please – ' and he gestures down the road. It's odd how you just follow in these situations after a while, I suppose he must know what he's talking about.

The retired bus driver takes us out through the main street of Chik Ballapur, then off west along a wide road lined with mature spreading trees. Just off this road he strides confidently up to the door of a large bungalow. An oil lamp is burning on the wooden verandah attracting a great cluster of nocturnal insects which, in their confusion, bounce against it with a regular twanging sound. But the retired bus driver ignores all this, makes straight for the door, raps upon it smartly and then, in a flash disappears leaving us standing one side of the door and a smiling woman the other side of it whom I presume to be Mrs Robinson. She quickly brushes aside any possible embarrassment in the situation by making it plain that this kind of thing happens regularly enough across every year and that the bus driver is something of an old 'friend' when it comes to the deliverance of strays and waifs to the Robinson bungalow.

A cosy evening ensues talking with Mrs Robinson who, with her husband, runs a 160-bed hospital here financed by the Church of South India. Yvonne, a medical student from Aberdeen – the granite city – is here doing her elective and not once during the entire evening does Rossiter get the chance to compare notes with her on one of his favourite topics of conversation about which enough has probably been said already. He seems but slightly perturbed by this since the whole tenor of our evening here is so relaxed. The Robinsons do not believe in last-minute hurry so next year's home-made Christmas cards are being folded individually by all of us tonight, in late January. There is something very soothing in doing some simple manual task in a group whilst the conversation flows over the top of it.

Outside, as we sit talking, large purple and black Boring

Beetles are slowly and determinedly destroying the wooden pillars that support the entire verandah. As their name suggests, the beetles tunnel perfectly carved tubes about an inch in diameter through the hard teak timbers. There doesn't seem any way to get rid of Boring Beetles once they decide they've acquired a taste for your timber and they whine and bore on, pausing every few moments, perhaps to question their motives – but more likely to catch their breath.

Thanks to the Robinsons, we also get a splendid night's sleep, not having to inhale, for once, the thick odour and smoke of the mosquito coils. The Robinsons have excellent mosquito nets over the beds – devices I always expect to see frequently in India but in fact very seldom do.

In the morning, we all go off for a tour of the hospital just opposite the bungalow. Although the hospital is obviously much less of a front-line establishment than somewhere like Lakhnadon, it nonetheless has a considerable number of different tribal peoples from a wide area to serve. The Robinsons accept only nominal payment for any treatment. It is a soothing place to be treated in too. White bungalow wards stand surrounded by mature pipal trees, dwarf palms and banyans. The maternity ward is set apart from the rest of the hospital in its own bungalow, and the old iron beds have been adapted to take tiny swinging cots for the babies at the foot of them. This morning, as the sun streams in, it is a soothing place of soft breathing and gurgling from the row of gently rocking cots.

After a lovely, languorous breakfast involving heavy amounts of toast, English style, we eventually pack up the panniers and pedal off towards National Highway 7, turning right onto the deserted single track road, for Bangalore.

We are in the city early in the afternoon, and it is easy to see just why Indians are so very proud of their 'garden city'. As we come in from the north, we look down upon what seems simply a series of partially built-up parks stretching across several low hills. Somewhere towards the middle of the greenery arises a small, out-of-place area of high-rise buildings but beyond it and to either side leafy Bangalore goes on. Remarkably, there are areas of open ground in this city which actually seem to stay as such instead of being quickly condemned into shanty towns such as spring up elsewhere. Bangalore actually 'begins', instead of sprawling into the countryside and yet when you're in it there's an uncluttered feeling of space, quite uncharacteristic of most towns and cities.

At a little after two in the afternoon we are sitting drinking coffee in Benson Town, a typically tree-lined and well planned northern suburb of the city. Only a few hundred miles separate us from the Cape now. But for the moment there's time for a much-needed wash and for the one-day Test Match at the municipal stadium – India v the MCC.

8

'You cannot be serious.'

J. P. McEnroe

If any Indian city is on the make, it's Bangalore – people have been telling us that all the way from Delhi. They say it's the place where the future is being made in India after it was found that Bombay was too infernally congested. So those making it happen in the commercial world moved south. Certainly, the city has escaped the worst excesses of most cities we have come through by being planned, rather than simply happening in a gigantic sprawl. Wide avenues lined with mature trees filter gracefully from the central parks, traffic bowling along the smooth tarmac, directed by immaculate traffic-cops who pirouette on their podiums in the centres of the main junctions, looking like large cockatoos in their elaborate crested headgear. The high-rise city centre is orderly, the suburbs settled – it's the yuppy capital of south India, giving you the odd feeling of knowing where it's going.

Unfortunately, where it seems to be going is West. In Brigade Road – very much the place to hang out in the cool of the evening – we sit in a café (very definitely not a dhaba) where everything is plastic and Abba plays incessantly. Rossiter eats a large steak (presumably buffalo but here you can't be sure) as we sit watching young men – and women – in jeans, strolling by, their heads strapped into their Sony Walkmans. The sledgehammer heat of the Deccan in summer is something Bangalore escapes, being rather higher, and the World Empire of Denim has come and has conquered all the year round. It is like coming half-way home again to a street of smart boutiques, hi-fi stores and garish hoardings advertising digital watches. But it has all come so suddenly, there's a feeling of pressure and anxiety about keeping abreast of the trends that you do not find elsewhere. Bangalore – the fastest growing city in India – has also the highest suicide rate.

In contrast to Brigade Road, we are staying at the Indian Social Institute – a haven of undisturbed tranquillity run on monastic lines by a small group of Marxist Jesuit monks. We stay in one simply furnished whitewashed room, part of a courtyard overhung by mature banyan trees. In the middle of the yard sits the monks' large Friesian cow, a beast of total placidity which every day consumes a vast pile of succulent green sugar-cane leaves and tops, slowly, steadily and completely. In return for this she gives the richest milk I have ever tasted and donates her dung to provide gas from the small conversion unit tended assiduously by one of the Brothers. The Institute acts as a co-ordinating centre for studying development across the country and there's a Documentation Centre with shelves piled high with Marxist magazines, books and papers.

Our main priority, however, is to try and get tickets for the One-Day Test Match happening on our third day in town. This leads us – Rossiter more than keen – to the West End Hotel where the MCC and their entourage of wives, girlfriends and Press are sunning themselves by the luxurious swimming pool.

Only when we're into the splendour of the West End and seeing other westerners does it dawn on us that the combination of endless dust and sun has made us go a rather odd colour. Added to that, the shortcomings of our clothes do stand out somewhat when everyone else seems to be cruising about in Gucci shoes, safari suits or minimalist G-string bikinis – and that's only the waiters. We're distinctly ill at ease.

'Let's get something to eat and drink – it'll be OK,'' says Rossiter, sizing up a motorized trolley purring across the velvet lawn by the pool. He flaps off in cheap flip-flops and oil-caked shirt.

I look around, trying to work out whom to ask about where the BBC man could be lurking. Rossiter returns in a moment with two bottles of Campa Cola, two lumps of ice in each and three crisps on a serviette embossed with the hotel logo. He looks a broken man. 'Twenty rupees,' he breathes, aghast. He lifts up one of the crisps, looks at it as if it were made of gold, then bites a corner off it. 'Twenty bloody rupees – that's more than we spend in a week! We're bankrupted.'

He bites again and chews more thoughtfully. 'Superb crisps though – try one,' he moans, suddenly content, his stomach as ever overcoming any economic concerns.

Eventually a waiter who doesn't completely despise or ignore us tells us where to find Peter Baxter, the BBC's man with the MCC. Baxter appears at his door after some considerable delay, with nothing except a towel round his middle. He doesn't bat an eyelid when the door pulls back to reveal us standing there, looking sweaty, uncomfortable and generally unpleasant.

'Er – hi!' I say finally, suddenly realizing it's hard to know where to begin this conversation. 'Really sorry to interrupt your bath – but we've just cycled here from Kashmir ...'

Somehow the ridiculousness of all this is got over by just ploughing straight ahead with how we come to be at his door in the middle of his bath, spoiling a rest-day by asking for tickets for a Test Match.

Once more, Baxter takes everything coolly in his stride. 'Come along first thing tomorrow when I've seen the lads and I'll see what I can do – there's a pretty good chance there'll be tickets for you,' and with that we leave him to the unseen, unimaginable luxury of his bathroom.

We are delayed on the way out of the hotel by a small crowd of boys out autograph hunting, doorstepping any white face entering or leaving the main entrance on the basis that they must play cricket for England if they're male and vaguely adult. Despite telling them repeatedly that neither Rossiter nor myself plays cricket for anybody, they *will* have our autographs and besiege us for half an hour whilst your real live team members swish by in taxis, unnoticed.

*

We are in luck next morning – two tickets are waiting at the hotel reception where the staff who looked at us yesterday with utter contempt are now all smiles, cordiality itself, opening doors and making a way for us both through non-existent crowds. As Rossiter picks up the tickets from the counter the Receptionist-in-Chief places his hand gently on Rossiter's wrist, stretches his smile still wider and says, 'Perhaps I am thinking you are in need of money, yes? I am giving very good prices for your tickets, Sahib.'

I may as well come clean at this point by saying that the reason we want to go to the match is really to sample the atmosphere of Test cricket in India, where the game has much wider appeal than even in Britain. We have been 'following' the current series of Test Matches intermittently, welcomed to groups of villagers massed around the odd transistor radio thousands of miles from the grounds, intent on the action and every stroke of play. This has given me the impression that the atmosphere within the large Indian stadiums must be worth being a part of.

We are not disappointed. Once admitted to the ground, we're able to divide our time between sitting up in the tiny commentary box slung high over the packed South Stand, wandering amongst the crowd, and sitting with the players. Up in the box, Peter Baxter relays meaty thirty-second summaries for Radio 2 listeners in Britain waking up to what's evidently a freezing and snow-covered Sunday.

Outside the ground, policemen carrying heavy lathis turn upon certain stall-holders without warning, threatening or actually hitting them by way of extracting paltry backsheesh. The stallholders seem willing enough on the whole – perhaps they know that the threat of physical violence will be readily backed up by the ill-paid policemen. In any case, there's good money to be made today selling bidis, samosas and chapattis to those coming to the match without the benefits of wives to fill the tiffin-tins.

About forty-five thousand people are crammed into the huge concrete bowl for today's match. Across the yellow pitch the brand new electronic scoreboard flashes up various figures which by mid-afternoon are beginning to mean something even to me. The atmosphere of the place is quite startling, the great grey cauldron of a stadium falling to complete silence as every ball is bowled, then breaking into expansive rolling applause when something significant is done by the MCC and a huge cheer when something pleasing comes from the Indians – like Sunny Gavaskar coming in to bat.

All this breaks down when it becomes clear late in the afternoon that the Indian team is not going to win. The Bangalore crowd, or large sections of it, have not paid good money to stand out on hot terracing and see this kind of thing happen. They decide to take matters into their own hands and begin showering their own fielders with a hail of half-full tiffin tins, bottles, scorecards and newspapers. Stale chapattis waft down onto the outfield harmlessly, whilst iddlies and rice squeezed into balls are thrown with considerable accuracy. Mangoes explode like splattered eggs on impact with the rock-hard earth. After one of these connects with Kapil Dev's backside, Captain Gavaskar decides to lead his team off.

The response from the crowd is to try to burn the stadium down – a hard thing to do as it's all concrete. Nonetheless, some promising fires are soon dotting the terracing away to the right of where we're standing. At this point the policemen are let off the leash, rushing, lathis first, round the edge of the field and up the terracing to tackle the fires and beat up anybody within range. It is quite remarkable how apparently jam-packed terraces so suddenly produce large spaces. All this is much more agreeable to watch than the cricket.

After forty minutes' play have been lost and Peter Baxter has had no new numbers to add to his reports to London, calm is restored more by mutual will than by the efforts of the police who now seem intent on weeding out harmless-looking individuals miles away from any trouble and frog-marching them from the ground for predictable treatment. Meanwhile in the centre of the field – where the grass is green – Paul Downton and Alan Lamb complete the MCC's victory to all-round applause so polite you would never have guessed there had been any interruption.

There is another reason which holds us here longer than we'd expected. It is Rossiter who comes upon it early in one sleepy morning at the Institute, cocooned behind his mosquito net in bed. 'Oh, my god,' he murmurs, 'do you realize what the date is today?' I do not, principally because I am still asleep (though were I awake I doubt if it would make much odds). 'Alex – wake up,' says Rossiter, now right out of bed and shaking me awake.

'What the hell are you doing?'

'Shut up and listen,' he hisses at me. 'Listen, we've got to get our visas renewed if we're going to continue south. I've just remembered they expire in under a week.'

'How long did the High Commission reckon it took to get it done?'

'Three weeks,' says Rossiter.

'I'm going back to sleep.'

The idea of a massive bureaucratic wrangle at this hour is altogether too much. But Rossiter will not let it (or me) rest. He's clearly in one of his rhinoceros moods and will not let the matter go until he's charged it down and nailed it.

'We could always truck on down to the Cape regardless,' I offer lamely, 'I mean – who on earth would notice? Who's checked our visas since we've been here? How would they find out? In any case, the worst they could do would be to send us home and so long as we've got to the Cape that doesn't matter does it?'

'Will you stop asking such bloody silly questions,' snorts Rossiter importantly, very much the rhino-in-charge. 'You know that wouldn't work. We'd be two miles out of Bangalore and some fanatic Intelligence Supremo or other would cruise up asking to see our papers and bang! Next stop Bombay airport.'

'Well – can't we just have a coffee or two before trying to get this sorted out?' Rossiter frowns darkly, relishing the skirmishes ahead. 'OK – just one then? Jesus Christ – we've got all day you know,' I beg.

'I know – not long enough, is it? Let's go. We've got to see Mr Gaudachar.'

'Mr Which?' I ask as he barges his way out of the door.

'The Commissioner of Police,' replies the long-suffering Rossiter, as if to a tiresome child. 'Mr Gaudachar is the Commissioner of Police, OK?' He spells things out for me, wasting valuable time.

I'm deeply indebted, but still confused. 'How can he help us then?'

'Look,' says Rossiter, 'How long have you been in this country, eh? This guy's the Commissioner of bloody Police, OK? You understand that? He's a big cheese around here so he can fix visas, he can fix passports, he could probably fix you a bloody peerage if you paid him enough, so if you've quite finished let's get on down and visit him.'

Nothing for it then, but to sit back and watch how Rossiter's new-found intimacy with the local law can help us out this morning.

The answer to that seems to be the door of the police headquarters where they aren't used to having visitors dropping in for a chat, and an armed guard leaps into the doorway blocking our path. He tells us Mr Gaudachar is away and won't be back for two weeks. Rossiter doesn't hesitate for a moment at the news, he goes straight for his pocket to produce our official-type papers. Unfortunately, the guard gets the wrong idea and, thinking he's about to be jumped, slams Rossiter against the wall and pins him there with his pistol. 'I was getting my papers,' he explains in a strangled voice, looking at the guard as if he were some minor irritation. Foolishly, the guard accepts this and lets Rossiter pull out our bundle of papers, making lavish claims about our significance to the BBC and the British Government. The guard wilts at the sight of all the headed notepaper and we're through to the reception desk where Rossiter is back on the front burner.

He leans well out onto the counter, lowering his voice, 'It is imperative that we speak to Mr Gaudachar's second-in-command here,' he says firmly and quietly. He then delivers himself of an extraordinary sentence in which 'official', 'BBC', and 'government' crop up repeatedly to ram home the intergalactic importance of who we are. 'And between you and me,' he adds, beckoning the desk sergeant down to his level over the counter and glancing around to check nobody else can hear, 'We are *officially sponsored by Air India*. That's right, *Air India*. The *National Airline*.' He nods, then, for full effect, exposes the poor man to his (filthy) *Official Air India Tee-shirt*.

'Please – you wait here, Sahib,' gasps the sergeant and disappears, mopping his brow. He's back in two minutes. 'Please, you are seeing very soon Deputy Inspector-General of Police Intelligence Mr Maluka. You please go out of this building, turn rightside, then leftside and enter opposite building to third floor leftside corridor third door thank you and good morning.'

Well, we find him in the end. He sits the other side of the biggest knee-hole desk I will ever see, simultaneously answering selections from his six different coloured telephones. From a distance as we approach across his wide, open office, this gives the impression of his being some kind of large beached octopus, flailing tentacles of arms and flexes to regain the open sea. Mr Maluka, we conclude, is very important. There is plenty of time to reach this conclusion since he is quite unable to talk to us for almost ten minutes. Indeed, I don't think he even sees us for five, as he sweats and grapples with different conversations on different lines.

Rossiter is triumphant at getting this far. He keeps nodding at me in a peculiar way, no doubt knowing something I don't. Nice office though.

Suddenly one of Mr Maluka's hands becomes unaccountably detached from a telephone, and Rossiter grabs it, shaking while Mr Maluka's mouth shouts down the red telephone, whilst the other hand cradles the white phone. That accomplished, the hand moves at once to the orange one, lifts the receiver and the Maluka mouth barks down it, 'Registration? Twobritishnationals ... exceptional circumstances ... requiringimmediateaction ... Isendthemovertoyouthisafternoon ... expedite!'

Slam goes the receiver.

A Maluka hand extends a finger towards the door. We take the hint and leave, reluctantly drawing the easy banter between us all to a premature halt.

By four in the afternoon we are both in a photographer's studio on Brigade Road having the final touches put to the photos that will go on the visa extension forms which run to four sides. It is a triumph over the legendary Indian bureaucracy and an illustration of what happens when Rossiter gets the bit between his teeth. I've said very little somehow, all day.

'Coffee?' says Rossiter.

On the morning we leave Bangalore, Rossiter's bicycle decides this is the moment to throw its front cog-changer right out of line for no apparent reason. I have often observed that bicycles, left unridden for a spell after regular use, have the malevolent habit of producing some absurd mechanical complaint as if in protest at resumed use. As we draw the mandatory crowd whilst we both fumble around with this, Rossiter sees with utter disbelief that the whole of his back wheel is out of line.

'Why – why does this happen to me all the time?' he mutters. 'You can carve it up any way you bloody well like but something, someone has got it in for my bicycle – or maybe my bike's got it in for me. You get on your bike after a week here: no noise, no rubbing – nothing. I get on mine and it sounds like a bloody car-wrecker's yard. Why?'

Rossiter looks up from the machine at the crowd of gawping and silent men and boys. No answer there.

Thirty miles or so south-east of Bangalore, the road pitches steeply down ahead of us. It dips to set us freewheeling at first round smooth grassy hills then on, down, lurching faster into ravines with craggy rock-faces at either side. We accelerate past troops of monkeys; parrots flash past vivid green. For perhaps four or five miles this continues – the road dropping all the time and good enough to let us speed forward. We haven't had this since we reached the Godavari.

Eventually the road widens out and flattens into much more fertile, lower country with neat fields of maize, millet and cane properly fenced in, interspersed with paddy. By the time our freewheeling speed is lost we are nearly in Krishnagiri so I pull up at the roadside. Rossiter soon appears behind me, eager as ever for the chance to have a drink of water and a gnaw of some cane. 'You know what this is all about don't you – this hill I mean?'

'What?' pants Rossiter exhilarated by the rapid last few miles, 'You mean the hill?'

'Yes – just you look at the map – it's brilliant,' I tell him, spreading the sheet over his handlebars. Through the coffee stains, dirt, smears of oil and unaccountable bloodstains a large black line crosses the country: The Route, faithfully pencilled in most nights. Rossiter gets to the end of it and tracks down our exact location. He begins to smile.

'Shit,' he breathes, 'we're off the Deccan. *We are off the Deccan.*' When we get going again, the Deccan, the great table land of the Indian interior rises up behind us, solid hazy-blue in the distance of the darkening north horizon. Sticking out from it are small rounded satellite hillocks on the lower land like huge light brown molehills, sentinels warning the north-bound traveller of what's coming up ahead.

Progress at this stage, however, is increasingly a mixed emotion and we cycle into Krishnagiri – glad and excited as ever to be in a completely new place, another stage along the snaking line on the map – and yet ... and yet there's now a twinge as there was when we left the mountains in the far north, the twinge of loss of the barren grandeur we have grown accustomed to.

Thinking over the day from my bed in Krishnagiri's small hotel, I feel it's much happier and simpler passing the man-made boundaries on this journey. Today we passed the state frontier, celebrated by the sign saying,

HEARTY WELCOME TO TAMIL NADU

I was so pleased to have reached the southernmost state I insisted on climbing it to be photographed by Rossiter. I fell on the way down and grazed my leg which is now throbbing painfully, lying here with the fan swishing lazily in the cool evening. But the fan cannot combat the smell of my leg; for as I slipped a man who owns a curd-stall on the border rushed out and insisted on rubbing fresh curds into the graze before I could stop him. For a while it did soothe the pain but now it's back with the stench of stale curd for company.

Only as we start out the next morning is the full impact of coming off the Deccan obvious. The road today is made into a tunnel by the rich palm trees entwined above us. Paddies run for miles on both sides making the road like a causeway. At this season many are being replanted and teams of heavy white bulls slosh through the rich chocolate mud, churning it for the replanting. Behind them darting herons step in, mud-coloured, semi-visible, spearing with deadly precision anything worth taking, before flapping up to rest and preen in the highest palms. Pass through any village here and the heavy smell of muddy growth from the paddies mixes with wood smoke, spice and rich fresh southern coffee – always on the boil somewhere. It can be hard to stay on the bicycles at times like this.

In many villages, coir is being processed into ropes. Whole settlements become festooned with piles of the raw coir (which the children use as trampolines) and the open spaces are soon covered by long thirty-yard strands of it being spun slowly into thin string. These in turn are twisted and bound into thicker ropes according to the orders from the merchants who export from Madras and Cochin.

In contrast to all this, we find ourselves eating today in a small town called Dharmapuri. We have often wondered where on earth you get engine spares in India, where garages are a distinct rarity and spares-shops apparently non-existent. Well, Dharmapuri is the answer. The entire town seems to be composed of tiny stalls – one has nothing but sparking-plugs all lined up. Tyre-sellers ply their trade behind giant castellations of retreads (and quite a few no-treads-at-all) with no room for storage.

There is nonetheless a fine dhaba vending large-scale thalis liberally dumped onto a generous slice of banana leaf – the days of plates, knives and spoons have long since disappeared now and it's only when you see the frightening density of a banana plantation that you realize how they can keep up with the demand for one-use-only banana leaves.

An hour's riding south of Dharmapuri a roadsign lies in store for us. A slight rise in the country into drier, rockier land for a few miles was all the excuse needed for the Tamil Nadu road-gangers. They knew when they had a 'ghat section' on their hands and made the most of it. As we approach the summit of the ever-so-slight ridge a large sign at our left reads:

GO FIND A ROAD THAT RUNS OUT TO THE SKY
GO FIND A HILL WHERE THE BIG WINDS SWEEP BY
GO SEEK A PLACE WHERE KINGFISHERS SWOOP
IN THE GREEN SILENCES LIFE SEEMS SO GOOD

TIRED OF JOURNEY? BREAK HERE!
REST SHED AHEAD! NATIONAL HIGHWAYS!

We take our break just to wonder at the exuberance of all this – which is just as well since the 'REST SHED AHEAD' does not actually seem to exist.

As we let go down the other side of the ridge I find myself wondering how long so smooth a surface as this can go on for. After so long on so many varied roads and tracks I admit to being a bit obsessed with the condition of tarmac – which is no way to see a country. By the time I get to the bottom I'm cursing such thoughts which come into my head, apropos of nothing whatever and seem so often to predict disaster.

Rossiter does not appear round the corner of the last bend so I start plodding my way back up in top gear, and find him back near the top where his (new) back wheel has broken a spoke. We are a long way from anywhere as it happens and cannot face going north so there's nothing for it but to begin walking south. For nearly three hours push, passing through two villages neither of which has anybody with a wheel jig. That's unusual since bicycles are so ubiquitous, but after a while we're both quite enjoying the change to walking.

With about an hour to darkness (there being very little twilight this far south of the tropic) we locate an ancient and crabby old man who won't look at his wheel-jig for less than twenty rupees. We agree the price and then proceed to do most of the work ourselves since all he seems to want to do subsequently is examine our water bottles. We get to work. Across the course of the journey even we have picked up a tidy amount of knowledge as to how to straighten out warped wheels and thread new spokes. A far cry now from the very first time a spoke went, up at Panipat in Haryana where it seemed like the journey had hit a major disaster.

Rossiter gets on with the job which means there's time for me to cross the road and do business with the coconut-sellers on the other side. Such men dot the road south from this point on, suspending large bunches of thirty or forty nuts on a long coir rope from a coconut palm. The nuts do not have the brown husk they have when imported to Britain – when fresh they have a smooth golden skin. Having selected my nut from the bunch one of the sellers steps forward, cups the pod in his hand then lops off the top of it with one swipe of his machete. This leaves a neat hole through which I drink the delicious sweet milk, and there is surely nothing so refreshing; but it's also so rich you're soon stopped from going through the whole bunch. Once the milk has gone I hand back the pod and the man places it squarely in his hand. Then, with an action so practised he can look right away when he's doing it, he brings the machete down vertically through the pod with a force that it stops in there, just short of continuing right through his hand. The first few times this happens I find the sheer nonchalance rather alarming, wondering what happens en route to becoming an expert coconut-splitter.

With the pod split the man then hacks off a wedge of pod-skin to make a scoop, then I get to work on shovelling out the delicious, creamy meat from the soft hollow of the nut within the pod. Coconuts are very much the staple of life in the south, the meat and milk finding its way into all kinds of food; the coir used in ropes, buildings and furniture; toddy gleaned from the sap of the trees to get drunk on and timbers and leaves for roofing. Small wonder that they say here a good healthy coconut tree is worth more than a son, providing an income for seventy years or more. Perhaps this is why a laden palm will be closely guarded, its trunk carefully studded with rusty razor blades and rings of vicious thorns to dissuade would-be climbers.

By the time I've finished eating it's nearly dark – completely so a few minutes later when Rossiter finishes with the bicycle, having at last enlisted the help of the old man we are paying for the job. As cycling at night is no fun at all and there's no moon tonight, we decide to move off down the road until a likely spot presents itself for a night out. Everywhere where there are not paddies on both sides of the road, herds of goats scatter in panic as we approach. After a mile or so of this, enough is more than enough and we stop, put the bicycles against the nearest palm, lock them together and spread out our dismal sheets in the dust.

Although it's pleasantly warm this far south all through the night, there's not a lot of sleep to be had. For one thing the noise of crickets and insects is too loud. Then there's Rossiter's happy thought that these palms (which are ringed with thorns) could shed sundry nuts during the night with grave consequences for our prone bodies. Then there are the ants, not too obvious at first but which after some hours, when we're both too weary to be bothered to move, really discover us. They don't bite, mercifully, they don't sting, and they don't squirt anything unpleasant in our direction – but they do incessantly scamper all over us perverting the course of natural sleep and, as the hours go by, sanity itself. After what seems like a lifetime of rustling and scratching in the dirt Rossiter heaves a particularly grave sigh. 'You awake?' he breathes.

'No,' I tell him.

'This is awful – bloody awful.'

'Oh really? I was just thinking it's years since I've been so comfortable.'

'Look,' Rossiter goes on, 'next time we get stuck out at night we stay somewhere in a village, and that's that.'

'OK – but you saw where we were tonight – nowhere at all to sleep.'

'Anything's better than being tortured by these bloody ants. I can't stand it.' He sits up and lights a cigarette.

I can't be sure, but maybe I fall asleep at this point. Whatever, when I next look over at Rossiter he seems to be in exactly the same position.

'You been sitting like that all night?' I suddenly ask him.

'Oh no. I nipped out for a swift gin and tonic, played a little snooker and then put in a few hours on the waterbed. Refreshing just isn't the word ... Let's get out of here, shall we?'

And with that, darkness or no, we pack up and dribble slowly down the road scaring goats again, letting the breeze work some of the dust from our faces and hair. Our water ran out at about midnight last night and now the only welcoming thought is a cup of coffee at some unknown, unidentified point we hope is somewhere up ahead.

Coffee comes after several hours at Salem and is soon accompanied by large quantities of puris and a dozen or so eggs cooked for us by a surprised boy who opens up specially and certainly knows his way around a fried egg.

Much refreshed by this we tip him, leaving him standing next to his large frying pan in his small white dhoti, as openmouthed when we go as when we came in. Getting through Salem proves more difficult than getting into it and the road soon dissolves into a maze of tiny streets going nowhere and blocked with Salemites rising with the dawn. After insisting I know the route through these ginnels for too long I'm forced to admit we are completely lost. There are still times when the noise and congestion in such streets as these just gets too much. Auto-rickshaws block each other's way and stand there, horns screaming whilst people, goats and pigs squeeze past. On each side of all these streets are open sewers which are the norm but at times like this when all you want to do is to get out, their smell gets particularly oppressive.

The only way out seems to be to hire another small (but much less bewildered) boy who is illegally driving an auto-rickshaw. By following close behind him we eventually worm our way out of old Salem to the by-pass – utterly deserted and apparently unused, if the town is anything to go by. We pay the boy the absurdly high fee of ten rupees – he'd demanded fifty with a straight face – and turn our bicycles south once more onto the empty concrete road.

We decide to take things easy after the night's lack of sleep. Rossiter is not very well and we come to a prolonged lunch-stop in Namakkal, thirty miles south of Salem. Without knowing whether he'll be able to continue or not I begin making vague inquiries about which road to take south of here – there are two alternatives, neither of which looks particularly promising. I get talking to two very dapper types who roll up to the 'hotel' we are eating in on their shiny new India Enfields. They say if we continue on the road going south we'll come to the Cauvery River. 'This will be best for you – for there is a very good pursil there?' says the older one, taking a large pull on his drink of banana lassi.

'What's a pursil?' I ask.

'It is the ferry boat. It is a very difficult thing to steer – completely round and made all of bamboo and buffalo hides – you will be enjoying the pursil ride very much.' This sounds really too good to miss and, cooled considerably by several lassis, Rossiter feels ready to move after another hour or so.

It takes us all afternoon to get anywhere near the Cauvery because the two Enfielders didn't mention, of course, that the road is either bad or non-existent for much of the way and there's a good deal of walking to do. Rossiter, complaining of a pain in some recess of his insides, doesn't take particularly kindly to all this and we have to rest as much as walk — with occasional bursts of unexpected cycling in between. It is a lonely road, the only sign of life being odd groups of bird-scarers shouting and whistling hysterically next to small patches of maize. The birds seem quite untroubled.

By late afternoon we're in a place called Omalur, well down into the lush flood plain of the Cauvery and entirely hemmed in by thick banana and tobacco plantations. It takes us a long time to ascertain that the river is nearby — let alone locate the pursil of which nobody at all seems to have heard. 'Shit,' sighs Rossiter (he's said that a lot today) and sits down on some rice sacks at the edge of the road. There seems nothing for it but to follow the road which now veers west, since there's only one road. At least it becomes tarmac-ed all the way instead of being a freelance track when the mood takes it, as it was earlier on. The consolation of having to detour along the river, though, is the sheer fecund growth of everything around us. Dense banana groves loom up on either side against the fading day, interrupted by little patches — almost gardens — of melons, marrows, lettuces and succulent tomatoes. Mango and jackfruit trees stand out higher every now and then but higher still are the coconut palms — sixty, seventy feet high perhaps with great branches of twenty feet or more and clusters of golden-ripe nuts. This, we later learn, is some of the most valuable and fertile land on the entire sub-continent and cycling slowly through it all, you get the feeling you can almost hear things growing. The smell of growth certainly hangs heavily in the air as it did just after Krishnagiri, a richy earthy scent coming off everything around us.

The excitement of going through country like this is, however, dulled by the thought of avoiding another night outside. Our maps shows several roads over the river which do not exist and I'm beginning to wonder if the town of Velur exists either, when we ride into it, just after dark.

Velur may exist but there is nothing in the way of places to stay in – no lodges at all, nothing. Stuck for any plan of action and feeling fairly sorry for ourselves, Rossiter decides that bottles of Kingfisher Lager will do his stomach a lot of good. Seeing the beer stall, he buys eight, stashes them in the panniers and pedals off along the almost dark streets, guided only by the light of the oil-lamps in the shops. This allows us to dodge sleeping cows in the street and also to see a resthouse out of the blue just off the road where it joins again with the National Highway.

Its doors are padlocked.

So, taking it as read that we're just on a thin streak of luck at the moment, we pull out the beer bottles on the verandah of the resthouse, yell 'Chow ... ki ... dar' every now and then and prepare to spend the night drunk on the cool, beaten earth floor of the verandah.

Suddenly, a couple of bottles later, there comes a voice from the darkness, warm and deep, fluent English. 'Hello there? Are you asleep? Look – if you want somewhere to stay for the night, you'd be welcome on my farm. Why don't you come along with me?'

'Just coming,' Rossiter shouts back, this being no time to consider any hidden dangers in going off with a voice from the darkness. Tonight the offer of a bed is enough to swing us both instantly.

The voice, it turns out, belongs to Eswaram, one of the most important farmers in Velur. 'Call me Sandy,' he tells us, as we pedal alongside his Enfield down the track to the farmhouse.

The house is one large, cool room open to a central court-yard and partitioned off into separate bedrooms at night by reed screens dropped from the bamboo rafters of the roof. The courtyard allows the night's breeze to filter through the screens as you sleep on thick rush mats rolled out along the stone-flagged floor. It is the optimum design for keeping cool in the tropical climate of Tamil Nadu. The mud walls are at least a foot thick, and smoothed off with plenty of whitewash. At one end of the one cloister-like room there's the tiny kitchen from which Sandy's wife Nisha produces enormous dishes of freshly caught fish from the river.

The Cauvery itself flows sluggishly, a quarter of a mile wide, at the end of the track passing Sandy's house. Carp seem to appear mysteriously for Nisha most days – though you never see anybody fishing here. By the back door of the house there's a large stone trough from which water is taken for cooking and eating, fed directly from the same spring that fills the large well in the yard behind the house, deliciously cold even in the middle of the day. Beyond the well in the flagged courtyard at the back of the house sits Sandy's prize Brahminy bull, one blue horn, one red, munching away in complete, contented indolence on whatever is thrown in his direction.

What starts as an overnight invitation ends up being a stay of several days in Velur and the next morning we are given a taste of what farming in the Cauvery valley seems to be about. For a start there's none of this early-rising business. We all get up two, maybe three hours after dawn to begin the day with a delicious breakfast of coffee grown in the Nilgiri hills, to the south-west. Then come the puris, delia – a mixture of jaggery and rice – with buffalo milk and baked, spicy carp caught yesterday down the track in the river. Even at this hour it's uncomfortably hot to be eating out in the sun but the courtyard is protected by another large screen and is cool all day.

The actual work in the fields is done mostly by labourers who come in from the villages to make a little extra money at the busy times of the year. They work – women and men – from soon after dawn till about midday when it gets too hot to continue, earning about five rupees (roughly thirty pence) a day. It's pretty well the going rate for such work, poorly paid the world over. At least it does tend to be guaranteed across the busy times of the year, particularly for some families several generations of whom have been working on this loose basis for Sandy's family.

The whole system of agriculture around here works along a tightly controlled system of canals and irrigation dykes which extend the fertile land far beyond its natural limits on the

Cauvery floodplain itself. The system is controlled by enormous oil pumps manufactured in Peterborough in 1910 and set into rather terrible pits from which they belch steam and smoke all the hot day long, their fly-wheels, fifteen feet across, whirring in endless, blurring toil. The pumps are used because the State Government will not let the farmers use grid electricity and so, for the time being, the peaceful fertility of the cane, betelnut and banana groves relies on these regularly spaced engine-pits.

Our stay here also gives us ample opportunity for messing about in pursils which I'd begun to think were simply a figment of the imagination. But they are indeed here, fifteen or twenty feet across, buffalo hide stretched over a bamboo frame – like an outsized coracle. They are only watertight in a loose sense of the word – waterloose perhaps – but that hardly matters when river water in the Cauvery is like a warm bath anyway. Out in the middle the current is quite strong even though the water is only two feet deep or so; nevertheless, the pursil man manages somehow to keep the whole thing dead straight by paddling with only a short piece of slightly flattened bamboo. I try this and send us all into a rapid spin. If paddling a Kashmiri shikhara is difficult, then paddling a Tamil pursil is an art form to be acquired over many years.

In a pursil or out of one, the river here is magical with its fast-flowing stretches, and its languid lagoons, where the water is positively hot. The banks, drooped over with creepers and overhanging palms, are havens where brilliant kingfishers nest and hunt in the shallows.

Sandy's family are Brahmins, and the track that passes Sandy's house reaches the river next to his family's temple. The temple is over six hundred years old and now quite overgrown with creepers. It has a huge wild banana plant sprouting from its small crumbling gopuram, whose huge leaves obscure the old statues encrusting its walls.

On the third day of our stay here Ravi, Sandy's eldest son, tells us that a cobra has been seen in the temple. This, together with the rumours at large about a panther being seen at night in these parts, are taken by most people as bad omens – though Sandy himself seems perfectly sanguine about it all. Even so, there's a good deal of edginess when we decide to go for a swim at night in the river. A boy from Velur drowned yesterday in one of the whirlpools near the roadbridge – as we edge into the warm water tonight his funeral pyre still smoulders on the bank. But the Cauvery at night is a magical place to swim – many of the fish are phosphorescent, clearly visible from a long way off and much tamer than they are in the daytime; even the bigger ones will let you come quite close. Overhead, huge bats with the wingspans of seagulls flap lazily about, hawking the thousands of insects that gather near the banks, leaving the open water clear.

Sandy has only one real design upon us whilst we're here, which is to introduce us to the game of kabaddi. 'India's national sport,' he says, proudly.

The first step is to introduce us both to officials of the All-India Kabaddi Federation. This is very simple since they are Sandy's best friends whom he meets every night at the petrol station on the edge of Velur. Few customers ever call for petrol, since there's very little traffic and, to be brutally honest, very little petrol either. But it's the place to go of an evening, every evening in fact. Deckchairs are produced, set out on the dirt forecourt and friends drop by – or not, as they feel inclined. Sometimes there is chat, sometimes not. The whole situation is nothing if not deeply relaxed. We sit here for several hours most evenings watching what happens and as nothing very much ever happens you don't have to put in too much effort.

Sandy's old friend Praveen runs the petrol station and is, amongst other things, the local doctor, lawyer and official for the All-India Kabaddi Federation. Tonight, he takes us into the 'office' to explain the rules. The office is also the surgery and farm office as well as kabaddi office and is decorated with a huge, inaccurate portrait of Edward Kennedy complete with large red tikka-mark in his forehead to add a little Hindu respectability. It seems the Senator visited these parts some years ago, showed more than passing interest in the game and became an honorary member of the Federation. Praveen comes straight to the point having outlined the game to us. 'What we need is your support for our game at international level. We wish for kabaddi in the next Olympics. We will be winning many gold medals for India in this sport. But I am thinking we must have full advantage system for Indian players who are smaller than other nations' players.'

'But other nations don't even play kabaddi,' I point out.

'That is not the point,' continues Praveen. 'We must have full advantage for winning of Olympic gold medals at kabaddi. We are hoping you can help us with this.'

Faced with this level of honesty it seems rather churlish to point out that this might not be entirely fair – even if Rossiter and myself did have any influence with the International Olympic Committee.

The next afternoon a game of kabaddi is specially laid on for us at the local school – and it's quickly apparent why size is an important factor. The game appears to involve two teams of seven on a pitch about the size of a badminton court. A player leaps from one end shouting, 'Kabaddi kabaddi kabaddi kabaddi kabaddi kabaddi kabaddi ...' non-stop while trying to touch as many of the opposition as is possible in one breath. Meanwhile the opposition have to prevent him returning back to his half, though they can't cross a line on the court – as far as they are able they also try to pick up the chanting player. Bodily contact, as you can imagine, plays a very big part in the game as does the size of one's lungs. 'This team is very good,' says Ravi as another chanter gets smeared into the hard-baked dust. 'But,' he goes on, 'Tamil Nadu people are really too small for this game. Northern people are best. Sikhs – they are very tough kabaddi players.'

Any plans we have for leaving the next day are completely thwarted by the Thaipossum Hindu festival which breaks into full swing from dawn onwards. Sandy and Ravi have knowing smiles on their faces, pleased as punch that propriety now obliges us to stay on to see this festival happen.

Across the morning a series of processions troop past the house in celebration of the recent cane harvest and on their way to the temple. Although it is ruined, the temple is still very much a holy place and the priest comes by carrying a golden shoulder chariot known as a Kavadi, yoked across his shoulders. This will be anointed with milk in the temple, an offering to the local god Murugan who will (it is hoped) protect the town from this harvest to the next. Ravi says they're putting a good deal of extra effort into things since the appearance of the cobra in the temple some days ago.

Drummers pass us playing Thavauls – deep bass drums played with a short curved stick – at extraordinary speed. Orumis – hand-drums – are played by twenty or so temple boys, some only six or seven years old but playing in crisp unison. The melody over the drumming comes from several long pipes called Nagawarams giving a nasal, wavering sound. The entire band is in no hurry whatever to get to the temple and stops for our benefit to play us three or four different numbers each lasting the best part of half an hour. There's a good deal of competition between different elements of the musicians when Rossiter suddenly appears with his small tape-recorder.

Not until early afternoon do we decide to leave and as we do so, Sandy has something else in store. He takes us out to the back of his house to a small plot of ground he has prepared without us knowing. There, two tiny seedlings are waiting to be planted. Rossiter has a betelnut seedling; myself, a mango. For some reason, the way in which we are led here perhaps, the small act of planting the trees is deeply moving.

By the time I stand up, dusting the thick, stoneless soil from my hands, there are tears streaming down Sandy's face and Ravi can't look up from the ground. The welcome here has been uncomplicated and complete and we say our simple goodbyes in like manner, leaving them standing at the front of the house.

We move off down the track, turning once to see them standing still, watching but not waving, off down past the still padlocked resthouse, onto the National Highway, past the petrol station, deckchairs dotting the forecourt in readiness for the evening and onto the long bridge taking us south over the yawning reach of the Cauvery.

By dusk we're in Dindigul nearly sixty miles south. Most of the ride has been in silence, with the two of us often far apart, pondering on the stay in Velur, rapidly becoming another memory. In such a state the unspoken urge seems to be to go as fast as possible, and on a good road the distance to Dindigul comes easy.

Over the last few miles into the town itself the welcome from people walking or driving along the road in carts is quite unprecedented. Almost everyone we see yells the Tamil greeting 'Vanekum' and many have time for a quick, 'Native place?' or simply 'Where?' if the shock of seeing us both suddenly gets too much.

During the evening we spend in the town we're given a brutal reminder of something Mrs Robinson said to us way back in Chik Ballapur – 'In India animals get a pretty hard time of it.'

It's a simple enough thing to say but it's something that will sooner or later be borne out by anyone's experience in the country. As we come out of a coffee shop tonight there, in front of us is a cart loaded with sacks being pulled by the sickest pony I've ever seen or ever hope to see. Exhausted, its back legs have crumpled leaving its front half held up by the shafts of the cart it's no longer capable of pulling. Its ribs press out against the skin of its flanks, furrowing them deeply. Open sores run trails of pus down its sides and legs, fluid streams from its anus and foam from its mouth, the lips pulled right back in a grimace of agony. On top of the cart sits the driver who brings down a heavy whip repeatedly on the animal's back, driving it further to the ground as it snorts flecks of foamy saliva onto the ground.

236

All around nobody stops to wonder, a lorry hoots at the hold-up and nobody is concerned in the slightest that the animal is being beaten to death. Perhaps because of this, both Rossiter and I are held back from doing anything, from intervening – even if there is anything constructive to be done short of buying the pony from the man there and then – and then what to do with it? Questions flash by as we stand in horror at what's going on, all of them edged with the feeling of shame at not doing anything about it. It is the total acceptance which shocks; it is this acceptance that stops us doing anything, from wading into a foreign place and telling people how they shouldn't be doing what they are doing. So, we turn away, go back to the small hotel we're staying in feeling bitter, shameful that we would turn away when next faced with something like this again.

The Thaipossum festival continues to raise its noisy carnival atmosphere, particularly south of Dindigul where the road the following day is clogged with pilgrims wearing saffron colours. For thirty miles or so the roadsides are crowded with families trudging up to Palmi. There, a huge golden chariot will be carried in procession up to the temple as part of the annual festival. Again the Orumis and Thavauls are much in evidence, some bands of musicians stopping to give impromptu concerts from the back of trucks or on the roadside to speed the pilgrims northwards. Some groups dance wildly to the drumming, spilling into the edges of the paddies and getting covered in mud. Others sit in small family groups, carrying their bedding rolls and sipping coffee from tiffin-tins.

Over all of this, today, hangs a heavy pall of low cloud, hiding the top half of the mountains that have appeared to our eastern side. I am once more startled by the sudden changes in what people grow in different areas. Just as we would suddenly find ourselves surrounded by fields of onions in Madhya Pradesh, or dots of celery in Karnataka, now, for some reason, we are among sunflower fields that last for perhaps five miles on and off and are then gone for ever.

*

There is no previous point of comparison, though, for the gigantic gopurams that dominate the skyline at Madurai – one sight of them from the flat, straight road into the town from the north, and we have no inclination to continue further south today. The gopurams are to south India what the Taj Mahal is to the north, the symbol of tradition, which here is Dravidian, Hindu, in the way that the Taj symbolizes the splendours of Moghul India; except that the Taj is now something of a shell but these gopurams – colossal sacred pyramids – are still very much the hub of the living modern city. There are four of them, rising up on the four points of the compass from the complex of the Shree Meenakshi Temple.

At a little after one o'clock we find ourselves peering up at the foot of the western gopuram, two hundred feet high and encrusted from top to bottom in a riot of gods, demons, messengers and misfits, likely looking and distinctly farfetched monsters. Because of these encrustations, the gopurams are also home for a variety of starlings, Indian crows and parakeets which somehow nest and are more or less left in peace by the troops of macaques also living there. So kind is the climate here to the stone, it's hard to believe the temple is well over three hundred years old.

No way of knowledge has its feet more firmly on the ground – and in the bazaar – than Hinduism, and so inside the gates of the Meenakshi there are rows of spices and bangle-sellers setting up shop for the afternoon's trading. No chance of anyone coming along and upsetting the trestle tables in Madurai, it seems.

Also, because of Thaipossum, the temple is absolutely crammed with pilgrims, many of whom are none too pleased to find that the sacred bathing tanks have been emptied because of some organizational gaffe. No matter; within the darkened halls and catacombs of the temple complex various sadhus have arrived on elephants holding large sticks of burning incense in their trunks and are being pursued around the pillared hallways by crowds of pilgrims. The atmosphere in here is deafening because every shout and cry reverberates along the dark chambers lit only by the occasional oil-lamp.

All the processions seem to centre on one enormous elephant which has several huge incense sticks fixed to the top of his head, columns of bluish smoke spiralling thickly upwards. Now and then he turns unpredictably sending people falling over each other in an effort to get clear. Meanwhile all along the halls and stone corridors pilgrims anoint themselves with ash before the various representations of the gods, many of which are solid gold.

In the paved walkways and on the steps by the empty pool, lassi-sellers and inevitable Campa-Cola wallahs are on hand to cater for the thirst that soon builds up in the covered parts of the temple. Outside the throbbing of drums and the wail of the serpents being played below comes reverberating across to us and the others sitting here; it comes steadily, unceasing, like a vast underground mantra punctuated by occasional screams when the elephants make too sudden a move for those crammed around them.

We are inside the place for several hours having intended making it a quick visit. Once out and away from the temples it is pleasing to see the way in which the gopurams rise up, dominating the city which today has more than half a million people living in it, exactly as they must have overlooked it when they were built.

Leaving Madurai next morning Rossiter, for some bizarre reason, completely changes his style of riding. For two thousand miles or so he's been totally at home riding anything up to a mile or so behind me, only choosing to catch up to insist on stopping to drink, rest or eat.

Maybe he's got sick of seeing the back of me. He goes off through the southern streets of Madurai like the entire trip is a time-trial, leaving me floundering around amongst the street-elephants which are hanging about on the off-chance that the banana-sellers will start looking the other way.

I spend much of the day wondering how one can suddenly alter one's cycling style. It is really no less momentous than deciding to walk differently. Rossiter, meantime, is a small skin-coloured blur hunched on the road in the far distance up ahead. Closer inspection is only possible when I can catch up with him at the roadside with his beloved bottle of warm chlorinated water clutched to his large stomach, Charminar in mouth. I stop, panting. I wipe away some of the sweat from my eyes. Rossiter drags deeply, looks vaguely up the road and turns to me. 'OK,' he says, as I dismount and reach for my water bottle, 'let's get going.' The squeal of an un-oiled pedal, a whiff of Charminar Kingsize and the man is off again, eyes set on the Indian Ocean, apparently just out of sight.

The road is good, flat and remarkably straight all day, with nowhere to stop and eat on either side. As a consequence I see very little of Rossiter. One of our few encounters with anybody on this lonely day is at a place called Kovilpatti which we get to shortly before dusk. I am feeling completely done in by this stage: the day has been hotter than usual and sweat has incessantly run into my eyes until they're both bloodshot, feeling as if somebody's sanded them down. My legs ache – a result of a hard ride after resting in Madurai for two days, annoying me intensely as I have the idea (not unreasonably) that I ought to be fit by now.

Anyway, there's a man in Kovilpatti who sells an unnamed spirit in small green bottles with no labels from a shop with no name and no roof. Predictably perhaps, Rossiter is to be found here, bottle in hand. 'What kept you?' he says, smiling viciously.

I say nothing. Rossiter, however, goes on. 'I've been thinking ...'

'Oh shit,' I mutter.

'No – listen. See that?' Rossiter points into the sky at the moon. I snatch a mouthful of the spirit he has been drinking. A fuel of some sort, but it's all there is. Even after that the sky looks the same pallid, whitey-blue dome as it did before.

'What am I supposed to see?' I ask Rossiter in the end, just falling apart with suspense.

'Don't you see? The moon. The moon's full, see? Now I've

been thinking, it'd be good to go on by the light of the full moon – don't you reckon?'

'You *what*? Look, I don't know what's the matter with you but I'm shagged out. No way am I going anywhere by the light of any moon – except to a dhaba around here and a bed somewhere.' 'Oh.' Rossiter looks down, a little crestfallen. He looks at his little bottle of spirit and finds it empty. 'Another?'

By the time we attempt to cycle the two hundred yards to where the Anand Hotel is alleged to be, several more bottles of fuel have been emptied. Either me or the road is all out of line once I get into the saddle.

Then, somehow I'm off, no idea where Rossiter is – behind I think. It's dark now – fires lit near the stalls at the side of the road. I see a man slowly strangling a chicken; the noise is piercing. Suddenly I am pedalling very fast; everything simply begins to fly by and then, up on my right there's the sign saying 'Anand'.

Trouble is, by the time I can grasp this it's slipped alongside me. I lurch the handlebars hard over to where the sign was and the bicycle skids away off from under me, leaving me in the air for a moment then lying cut, grazed and giggling in the dust. I sit up and there's Rossiter. Nice to see him. He seems to be trying to pick me up. No. He's fallen over too. The ground is still moving although I'm sure I've come to a standstill. My arm is bleeding from a hole in the elbow. I look at Rossiter, smirking. 'Oh dear,' he says.

Fortunately for us our ill-executed attempts to cycle into the hotel entrance have been seen by a group of devastatingly sober gents whiling away the evening at the pan shop opposite. They come to our rescue smiling and laughing, with leering red mouths like a bevy of off-duty vampires. Thanks to them we are somehow got into a room in the hotel, with our bicycles, and spend the next couple of hours lying on two charpoys trying to get the earth to stop spinning and lurching to one side – or at least to do so more gently. This gets much easier when the lights go off without warning and, after some time, the manager of the hotel comes knocking on the door to explain. 'The electricity is vanished – good evening.'

Just before we left Sandy up in Velur, he wrote out an address on a scrap of paper and gave it to me, saying, 'This is the name and address of Mr Pandian, Superintendent of Police in Tirunelveli.' He squashed the paper deep into my palm. 'Call on him when you pass that way – you will be able to enjoy his fullest hospitality.'

The next day we need most of the forty miles to Tirunelveli to clear the fugginess of our hang-overs, as a good strong wind on our backs blows us down the road south.

Tirunelveli itself sports a cement works of such pure gaunt ugliness that it matches the monstrosity just north of Adilabad. But the full significance of this place is not apparent until we have made ourselves known to Mr Pandian himself.

When we first see him he's presiding over a meeting of local and regional police chiefs up at the local nick, a spacious and palatial colonial-style bungalow with immaculate box-hedges guiding you up to the deep cool verandah dotted with enormous wicker chairs, which we are not permitted to sit on.

Most of Pandian can be seen through the front door which is two feet ajar. He is, however, more than two feet wide even when squeezed into his chair at the head of the table and the remoter swathes of his belly are out of view. Sweat trickles down from his pate, staining his collar which is buried in there, under immense pressure, around his neck. Cascades of flesh and chins wobble and bulge over it, glistening with rivulets. Mr Pandian's second-in-command clocks in around the eighteen- or twenty-stone mark; but Pandian himself is right out ahead, in supreme command, spreading along the head of the table, pushing thirty stone.

Rossiter simply cannot believe the size of the man. 'Holy shit …' he breathes, nudging the door a little to give the full view of Pandian, side-on. 'He makes me feel positively gaunt.'

Eventually, everyone files out of the meeting room, strapping on their pistol-belts (Pandian's must be about eight feet long), which it turns out are very much the reason for their meeting. They have just been assessing the success of a week-long training course designed to make the local police shoot less but shoot more accurately at the right people. Having de-briefed each other thoroughly, it's time to pile into the jeeps and head off into the scrublands east of the town where a shamiana has been erected for the end-of-course feast and displays. 'You will come,' Pandian tells us.

'Thank you very much indeed Superintendent Pandian, that really is most extraordinarily kind of you to invite us,' says Rossiter, pressing the charm button. Pandian totally ignores him, preferring to talk to somebody else. Then he waddles away to insert his immense girth into a jeep that lists danger-ously once he's aboard.

Out at the site, a motley brass band has been hastily assem-bled, heavy on the cymbals and sousaphones, light on the trumpets and the ability to play in time. They are there to welcome, first Pandian and later the guest of honour, the owner of the cement works, whose arrival is marked with a truly mal-co-ordinated stab at 'For He's a Jolly Good Fellow'. The 'music' ends too early since it takes Cement and his son a long time to emerge from their Ambassador. Cement I is almost the same shape as Pandian himself and Cement II – whining and eight years old – is looking promising enough to exceed both men in later years.

Various subsequent assaults on 'For He's a Jolly Good Fellow' herald the arrival of lesser (thinner) local dignitaries – but they're all so late Pandian and the Cements can't hold back and begin crunching their way through plates of lamb and vegetable dishes served up with fistfuls of rice. The smaller dignitaries join the queue for what's left over.

Very abruptly, food is finished and whisked away by the police catering corps. It is display time, though not, as we'd foolishly assumed, displays of firearms. Far from it. First onto the large rug serving as a stage comes a young sergeant dressed in French beret, stripey shirt and bell-bottomed flares:

'He is disco-dancer,' explains an earnest young Sikh from the local force, 'the very best.' Unfortunately he keeps tripping today on the thick carpet unwisely provided for his display, on top of which the music keeps cutting out leaving him thrusting and pouting and ripping up the deep-pile with no beat to make any sense of. We all applaud wildly.

This is followed by several long bouts of stave-flailing involving men from the local constabulary who seem to have come into this world twirling stout mahogany staves around their heads. If they can shoot like they can handle a stave then law and order must be a simple matter of liquidation as and when necessary.

In fact things do not quite work out so simply, as we find out later in the afternoon when Pandian's second-in-command takes us off to visit the police station in town and the cells, which we're keen to see. In the main office of the station there's a large-scale map of the city covered with different-coloured pins. 'What do they all mean?' asks Rossiter at the different concentrations of colours at various parts of town.

'Well,' says the Inspector of the station, 'green is for adulterating cow's milk, white is for buffalo milk. Black is for immodesty with ladies. Blue is for dacoits, robbery, theft, murder, public nuisance, misdemeanour, beggary, driving misbehaviours – there are many things that are blue in this town.'

'I dread to think,' says Rossiter.

'There is no need of dread, Sahib,' the Inspector goes on, 'the town is totally under control.'

'But you seem to have blue pins stuck in all over the place – doesn't look under control to me,' he replies.

'It is so difficult, so difficult, in some parts there are many mischief-makers, but if there is a chance of trouble we can stop it – '

'How?'

'We send men into these areas, we arrest potential mischief-makers. We put them over there for some time, till the time of trouble has passed by.' He gestures across the office to the far wall, entirely occupied by the bars of a mass cell of the type one sees in westerns.

Definitely a bad idea to get known around here as a 'mischief-maker' – one's freedom of action could be suddenly curtailed at any time by being unexpectedly run in on the supposition that there might, at some point, at some time, in some place, be public mischief in the making. Given the size of the lock-ups, this style of pre-emptive policing and the apparently intimate knowledge of who could be up to no good – it's a wonder that the citizens of Tirunelveli manage to achieve any pins at all, let alone festooning the wall-map with unsolved atrocities.

Neither of us can sleep very well in the hotel to which the police have billeted us. This is partly because of the electricity generator next to our window, partly because of the enormous bright green praying mantis that discovers Rossiter in the cold shower and pursues him remorselessly out of the tiny shower-room, through the room and out through the open door across the yard – both Rossiter and the mechanical-looking mantis (all eight inches of it) entirely naked.

Partly, though, the reason it's hard to sleep is the very real possibility that we will both be in the Cape tomorrow, having run out of India to cycle over.

'We could always turn round and head for Calcutta?' I suggest to Rossiter when he has returned to the room and his voluminous pants.

'Er … no,' he answers me, having thought the whole thing through in less than a second, 'I'm fed up with insects eating me.'

On cue, Rossiter shows me his mosquito bites for the thirty-thousandth time, up one leg, down the other, back then front, then arms with any remaining areas of him mercifully omitted. I wonder if this beats counting sheep as a means of dropping off.

At first light we are stunned to hear the chunter of the police jeep approaching the hotel. They said they'd pick us up at dawn yesterday to take us to the police station to collect our bikes – but here they are, on time. This really is out of order and we get up in time to see the jeep swing into the yard. 'Somewhere out there there's that flying piranha,' is Rossiter's opening appraisal of the day – a reference to the praying mantis.

Up at the station all is activity on the verandah and behind it, our bicycles are presented to us having been polished by the conscientious Sikh we met at yesterday's festivities. The men under his command bustle around taking lots of time and effort to locate their rifles and affix bayonets to them whilst we attach panniers to the bicycles. The point of all the activity comes home to us as we're about to thank him and his men and take our leave (there being, of course, not a sign of Pandian at this hour – or indeed anybody else important enough to tip the twelve-stone mark). With an uplifted finger the Sikh stills our thanks. 'Please – one photograph,' he says softly.

That done, we are given a charming escort out of town by a jeep crammed full of policemen with rifles and bayonets bristling out in all directions in a terrifying manner. They blast the horn continuously, and the first few miles after they leave us are ominously quiet.

To our right, the mountains are coming up close to us this morning. India is so narrow at this far southerly point that you can always see them, blue and hazy in the morning light. Around us is open grass stretching away on either side, unenclosed of course and dotted with occasional stands of high palmeria palms, their tightly knit leaves pulling and falling like ears in the salty breeze.

Suddenly, a lonely elephant comes up on our western side, his blue-grey hide barely indistinguishable from the mountains rising behind him in the haze. He walks along a track as if to join our road, unhurried, unattended. Rossiter, being inordinately fond of elephants, takes this as a very good omen. 'No question about it – we'll hit the Cape today all right,' he declares as we sit watching the lonely plodder coming towards us.

By the middle of the morning the temperature is, as usual now, well up in the nineties. We're riding with a mile of the mountain wall going three or four thousand feet up bare and gaunt off the yellowing plain. As we ride side by side, trying to work out precisely how high we think it is and disagreeing completely, we're amazed to see a European man walking slowly up the road, wearing shorts and carrying a rucksack. Two more are coming along behind.

We pull over and say hello to the Trans-Globe Expedition – three young men from England attempting to run round the world.

'Well,' says Robin, 'we're not really running any more – as you can see. We had problems in the Gulf with visas so we had to change the route – so it's not really Trans-Global any more either, I suppose,' he says dolefully, 'unless you count planes – and we can't afford any more of them.'

All things considered, it's not going too well for the three of them and money shortages mean they're down to a budget of ten rupees a day. 'We're hoping there'll be more money for us in Madras – we've a friend in London who said he'd send it all out there – but we haven't heard anything for ages.'

'Oh – it'll be there – no sweat and Madras isn't far from here –'

'Maybe not on a bike – but it's a bloody long way from here to Tirunelveli on foot. I'm pissed off with it to be honest.'

For a while we sit chatting with them. Rossiter and myself irrepressible today, thinking how near we are to our goal, the Trans-Globals in very different mood with serious doubts and problems looming up ahead. Maybe we're not the right sort of people to run into with such a chasm between our moods.

Unfortunately, the Globals do not seem aware of the temperature changes in India. Even now the heat is daily climbing steadily this far south and the idea of merely walking (let alone running) in India after mid-April is hard to imagine. In the end we decide they might as well not know about this kind of thing – at least until after the money has come from Madras.

If Rossiter has his good omen early this morning with the

elephant, mine surely arrives about five miles south of where we'd met the Globals. After stopping for fresh coconuts I happen to notice the name of the dhaba from which the coconut woman is operating,

HOTEL WELCOME ALEX

which is not a name I can remember seeing before in this country. Perhaps there has indeed been some benign Intelligence up there after all, watching us wheel along this endless, thin, meandering road. Then, as this thought takes hold, as I ponder the apparently limitless feeling which the road has rolled into us both, there comes a perceptibly bigger bend in it. The main part swings round, suddenly veering west. There is a small side-road and with it a sign:

KANNYAKUMARI 8 KMS
CAPE COMORIN 8 KMS

As this road leaves the highway (as deserted now as it was when we joined it eight hundred miles back) it dips slightly and we freewheel without hands, sitting as erect as possible to try and catch a first glance of the sea. Eight kilometres – five miles, five bloody miles!

But the road has another surprise for us, when three of the five miles must surely have passed (and still not a sign of the ocean) we come upon a lorry loaded partly with biscuits. Only partly though: it sits lurched into a ditch with half the load shed along the grassy edges of the road. The driver is partying it up, radio blaring, stopping anything that moves along here to weigh it down with free biccies and, smiling, send it on its way. 'Aaaaaaeeeeeeeee!! Vanekum! Van ... e ... kuuuuuum!' he yells, catching sight of us. He sits atop a heap of biscuit packets, gradually crumbling under his weight to create a perfectly moulded seat. We take about twelve packets and head off. Three miles ...

Then, just before the two-kilometre post the road again drops suddenly and there, away to our left, is the shimmering of the sea — and unbelievably *blue*. 'The Bay of Bengal!' Rossiter shouts back to me.

As we go on it spreads around the horizon until there's sea dead ahead of us too – due south. 'Indian Ocean!' I shout up to Rossiter.

The first houses of Kannyakumari come and pass us in a haze. There's only one point to be made for, the end of the village. Black triangles dot the sea – the sails of the fishermen in their tiny dug-outs, some of them miles out on the glittering sea and there, glimpsed between palms and brilliant white houses to our right, to the west, is the sea again. For the first and last time in my life I give Rossiter a glance that means only 'Arabian Sea'.

Now – in the instant the three seas meet the houses, the palms fall away showing the road up ahead, the last yards, giving out onto black storm-flattened rock. A woman selling sea-shells stops me and puts a necklace of tiny shells round my neck. Maybe she wants money, I can't tell, but am off, dismounted, wheeling the bicycle out over the hot sun-soaked rocks to the edge of the ocean's lash.

Dimly, we're aware of a small crowd following, but can only look out to sea, out beyond the farthest southernmost rock, the fingertip of the country, ringed with foam. A crowd gathers. Nobody speaks. Their dhoties can be heard flapping in the stiff, hot wind. Rossiter moves from where we're standing. Vaguely, I hear him rummage in his pannier. He pulls out two spokes – all we have left now. He gives me one, smiling quietly. 'Go on,' he says, 'throw it in.'

Epilogue

Rossiter is not, by nature, an explorer. He did not say, 'Because it's there', when I asked him why he'd wanted to do this journey. In fact he said, 'Well – maybe it'll make me give up smoking or lose weight or something.'

It seemed, even before we left England, that the mood of things out on the road was not, somehow, going to be one of lofty speculation. So – as you see – it proved to be. If either of us contemplated our navels it was for hygiene, not philosophy.

It was in the same mood that we decided to raise money for Oxfam by doing the journey. As it turned out, money was successfully raised to be used in India. Also, Rossiter did cut down the fags – finding Charminar filters not quite to his refined taste – and discovered he was smaller at the bottom of India than when he trudged out through the snow to get on his bike at the top.

Something else happened too.

There were times I haven't talked about, when we were taken right out of our world on the road, to be shown something of the work Oxfam does in the country. Our stops at Oxfam offices in Delhi, Nagpur and Bangalore were much more than opportunities to delve into our air-freighted crate of bicycle spares, as things turned out.

The work Oxfam does here is utterly, completely removed from the brisk grey ladies in Britain's high-street Oxfam shops. It fast hit us both that it was also utterly removed from our peculiar little world of travelling south on bicycles. On two particular occasions we were shown into larger, terrifying worlds of grief, agony, exploitation. To us, it seemed we were taken into this by people who had made it their job to do something about it. That's how simply it strikes you, as an outsider.

Sultanpuri is a mixed Hindu-Sikh 'colony' on the outskirts of Delhi. When Mrs Gandhi was shot dead, they came to places like Sultanpuri to teach the Sikhs a lesson once and for all: bent policemen, small time politicos, shop-keepers – anyone with a grudge. The killing lasted for two nights there and only ended when the army was finally mobilized to restore order and set up the curfew we flew into at the airport.

Some weeks later Oxfam took us both to Sultanpuri. Out of the Landrover and into the bright sunlight, we stood for some time, dazed. A large crowd of Sikh women surrounded the vehicle, fighting for whatever the volunteers had brought out on their latest trip to the township. Long, low lines of rough brick and dung jhuggy shacks stand either side of the dirt roads. The gutters were open sewers, blackened with ash from burnt-down hovels. You could tell the Sikh 'homes' – they were gaunt burnt-out shells. Those that could afford expensive metal window frames saw them now tortured and twisted with heat. But most of the occupants had been killed or had fled. Mostly, the Sikh men here worked as sikligars – small-scale forgers and farriers using tiny makeshift furnaces with bellows powered by a modified bicycle wheel. The wheels now too lie contorted and charred.

In Sultanpuri about two hundred people were killed as the mobs went through the area with lists of Sikh houses thoughtfully provided by corrupt police. Most of those killed were men and boys, ritually scalped of their uncut hair, then burnt or beaten to death. Many of the women were then raped, some of them to death.

Across the dirt road the shacks were untouched. From chinks in bamboo walls bright eyes of Hindu women and children took us in, from a safe distance. When their children got more used to us being there, we saw they were thin and dressed in filthy bits of old cloth. At least some of the Sikh huts were built out of bricks, after a fashion, some had television sets – burnt before they could be looted. There were divisions of poverty even here, from one side of the street to the other.

As we stood around in the wreckage, a group of Sikh widows suddenly met us, pointed at our cameras and demanded photographs. Pawing the cameras, crying, beckoning, pleading at us, in the hope that such a photo might somehow bring back a lost husband or son. It was hopeless. All at once we found a gripping sense of panic taking us over, having no point of comparison, being surrounded that day by people who had lost so much, people bawling at us to take pointless photographs, or staring in mad daze at the ground or into the flaring sun, still unable to master the shock of what had happened.

We took some photos.

Ganesh, one of the volunteers, pointed out a small, thin girl crouching under two large sheets of asbestos leaning against the wall of a jhuggy. She was wearing a mauve shalwar-kameez, faded with sun and dust. She stared at the ground, still deep in shock, rocking slightly from side to side. Cradled in her arms was her tiny, silent baby. Her name was Praba and it emerged that the sheets of asbestos were all she could salvage from her home in which her three brothers, her father and her husband were burnt to death. Like many, she was too bewildered to even claim the meagre compensation the government eventually made available for such refugees. She didn't know, Ganesh said, where her other relatives had fled to. She was fifteen years old.

Even now, there were groups of Hindu women roving around Sultanpuri jeering at the Sikh women, who seemed impervious to it all. I felt, horribly, that our presence perhaps inspired this, but Ganesh, Nilanjin and other Oxfam volunteers assured me they jeered anyway – a favourite trick was to encourage the pariah dogs to shit on the ruined houses of the Sikhs.

Yet every day, twice a day, the Oxfam Landrover would turn up with food, blankets, candles and medicines, not just here but in twelve other such areas of Delhi. Long patient meetings were happening in the huddled shacks, trying, and trying yet again to bring both sides of the religious divide together. Elsewhere in more affluent parts, plans were being discussed, schemes put forward, as to how the women could now be helped when the time for simple donations had passed. These women had no idea how to make any money for themselves – that had been for the men to do. It was clear it was now going to change.

On the way back from Sultanpuri through the tangle of Old Delhi, you couldn't help seeing the posters for the general election. It was as if there were only one party in it: Mrs Gandhi's Congress (I). It was as if she were standing to be re-elected, dead or not. The hollow message of unity shouted out from every billboard:

INDIRA IS INDIA. INDIA IS INDIRA

Hundreds of miles further south, and a thousand arguments later, Rossiter and I were shown another situation where Oxfam was working against almost impossible political odds.

The Godavari jungle spreads over several vast river basins, south-east of Nagpur. When we got to Nagpur, Swamy, Oxfam's Director there, explained his plans for us. 'I am very anxious that you are seeing Hemalkhasa. There are so many health problems for the Gonds – malaria, TB – and they will be wiped out completely by the government dams which is why there are Naxalites, guerrillas.' Swamy took one of his rare pauses and leant forward to us, sipping his coffee, very much the conspirator, 'you are wanting to go – yes?'

'Er, yes. But I don't quite follow what you said about ... ?' said Rossiter.

'All will be clear,' replied Swamy with finality.

Hemalkhasa can't be reached at all in monsoon when the jungle roads are washed away. Even in the dry winter it took us thirteen hours by jeep. In a jungle clearing, Oxfam helps fund the Hemalkhasa hospital for the Gonds. With their pierced noses, their armour-plating of necklaces and bangles and their flattened aboriginal features, the Gond tribals still hunt and forage nomadically in the Godavari, as they always have done, bartering their bows and slings for silver and brass with traders now and then at the fringes of the jungle.

Vikas, the barefoot doctor at Hemalkhasa, welcomed us into the compound, glad at last to get the small generator we were bringing in with us. Round the fire after sunset he told us the entire tribe – fifty thousand or more – was threatened now by the government's plan to flood huge areas of forest to provide hydroelectric power. When the stream near the hospital flowed in season, he'd made a small dam in order to show the Gond headmen what a dam was.

'You see,' he told us, stoking up the tiny fire, 'the state government and the forest contractors are cutting down the forests so fast already. There is not much replanting. Every year it goes on and we can do nothing.'

'But the dams will destroy the forest,' I said.

'Yes – but only after everything has been cut – they will put roads into these areas to do it. I know it.'

It very quickly turned out that Vikas and his helpers here were trying to alert the Gonds to the fact that they were in danger from the outside world, to the fact that they qualified for rights as human beings. That, as well as coping with all their health problems.

The next day we saw what lay behind Vikas's phrase 'primary health care'. 'Come,' he said striding over to us, 'It is time you saw what we are trying to do here.'

He took us across the compound from his house, past the low whitewash-and-tiled hospital building and on, apparently into the forest. There, at the edge of the huge teak trees, plumes of smoke rose from several campfires. The Gonds were cooking, naked except for tiny loin-cloths. All the women were heavily laden down with silver jewellery, enormous earrings dragging their lobes almost to their shoulders over the years. If you're nomadic, you have to carry your wealth around with you.

Grasses recently cut for bedding lay strewn about, two semi-tame buffalo grazed behind them. They stared up vaguely at us when we came near.

'Welcome to my hospital ward,' said Vikas.

'But the hospital's over there,' I said, pointing behind.

'Yes – but these people are not ever being enclosed by walls. They will only enter if they are really sick – '

'But they are, surely?' I asked. I'd just caught sight of a small boy with a huge abscess the colour and size of a cricket ball on his anus. His mother sat near, swatting tiredly at the worst of the flies.

'Much better,' Vikas said quietly, 'that he is staying with his family. He is not so sick.'

Inside the hospital, there were about thirty beds, and an old tribesman – he was thirty-two – who had a small room of his own. He had fallen into a campfire during a fit brought on by cerebral malaria. The stench of burnt and rotting flesh was overpowering. Softly, Vikas pulled back the dressing, apparently without pain. The man had lost most of the flesh from his thighs and buttocks, and lips of yellow and black tissue glistened back at us.

'These people,' whispered Vikas, 'are so strong, they are responding so quickly to drugs because of their lives here, in the forests.' I held my nose to stop myself retching. Rossiter said:

'He's dying, isn't he?'

'No,' said Vikas, smiling incredulously. 'He will walk away from this place. I know it.'

But there were, of course, exceptions. Elsewhere, a little boy lay dying of tuberculosis. 'We don't even have the bloody disease at home,' said a voice in my head. I felt outraged, with nowhere to direct my anger against all this. In front of me he lay, his back caved in, his stomach pushed right out in the contortions of TB, preventing his withering stick legs from lying comfortably. I tried to imagine the insanity of never even being able to lie down in comfort. Apart from his mother, the family had now abandoned him here and the mother would

255

now shortly be going back to the forest too. Mercifully, the boy had lost consciousness.

Such cases were getting less and less frequent, Vikas told us during our stay there. When he had built the hospital fifteen years or so ago, the Gonds would have sacrificed children to ward off illness; now, at least, they came – and came many miles – to get treatment. In spite of the appalling cases, Vikas and his staff not only kept their sanity and compassion, but let it thrive in the most unlikely ways. When we came out again we sat in the sun. The grip of nausea passed away, the terror at what we'd just seen evaporated, largely I think, because Vikas calmly came back out with us, talking, steadily, about the future of the hospital.

The Gonds repaid Vikas and his team by presenting them, over those years, with a zoo. Next to the room we slept in there was a huge diesel fridge filled with dead squirrels and ground-rats. 'For the leopards,' Vikas announced. 'They live next to the hyenas behind the garage – they're all presents. They were found by the Gonds, always they are injured when they bring them to me. I think I am a vet as well.' He showed us the hyenas, large and menacing. 'They are vegetarian,' he said, dead pan.

'Eh?'

'Rice and milk – they have all they need. You are seeing – they are well, no?'

'A bit too well I'd say,' I told him, as one lunged against the bars of its enclosure.

Nearby, a sloth bear and two porcupines were tucking into, yes, rice and milk. 'Really, it is quite sufficient for them,' repeated Vikas.

'OK. What about *him* then?' asked Rossiter with tones of growing amazement – he'd just seen two large alligators in the same pond as some ducks who seemed under stress.

'Sometimes we are giving them a lizard, sometimes squirrel – but for the most part they are quite sufficient with … '

'No, no – don't tell me,' said Rossiter, holding onto a mango tree for support.

'But getting enough rice is a very big problem, especially during the monsoon times,' continued Vikas.

'Well er ... yes ... I imagine it must be ... terrible problem,' Rossiter murmured to himself, trying to make some sense at the scene unfolding before him.

Swamy had mentioned the Naxalites to us before we came here – it was not something people at Hemalkhasa talked about very much, but on the last night we were there the conversation came round to them and we saw another completely new dimension to the struggle the hospital was involved with.

The Naxalite guerrillas – Maoists – had found a cause in the Gonds, seeing how they were being exploited by the contractors who cut into the forest daily. They operated crudely but effectively, getting food and shelter from the Gonds, whilst waging a guerrilla war against the contractors. Anyone who helped the contractors or worked for them in any way was likely to find himself having his hand hacked off in some remote clearing.

We sat talking of this around the fire and it became clear that the Gonds didn't perceive themselves in terms of this conflict. The hospital staff doubted if they perceived themselves in comparison to outside people at all, as yet, though the dams were going to change that quickly. Of course, the Naxalites were not beyond terrorizing those at Hemalkhasa. 'And that,' said Raghubir, one of the doctors, 'is a thing we accept. It is part of our struggle here.'

'What happens then, if one of the Naxalites comes into the hospital injured or something? It must happen occasionally.'

'What happens,' he said to us quietly and without hesitation, 'is that we treat them.'

On our way out of the jungle Oxfam had something else to show us. 'The land goes green at Anandwan,' said Hiralal, who drove us there. And so it did. When Baba Amte and his wife Sadhanatai came here in 1950 with a few buffalo, fourteen rupees and six lepers, it was just another part of the barren, martian plain south of Nagpur. Amte – then a promising young lawyer from the city – had left his career, finding in the sick, the wrecked and the rejected something that could satisfy his energy.

'Men find inspiration in the ruins of temples and churches, but not in the ruins of men,' he told us squarely, welcoming us into what is now a town of five thousand people – the world's largest community of leprosy victims.

He was perhaps an unlikely figure to have built up the green lawns, gleaming white buildings, schools and workshops of Anandwan from the harsh scrubland of Maharashtra. Much given to speaking in aphorisms and sparkling with energy for the people there, he was incapable of sitting down. That's no figure of speech – a spinal injury meant he had to wear a large truss and could only lie flat on his bed or stand bolt upright in his simple white shorts and vest. 'Forgive me for not standing to greet you here. I am a spineless man with the vertebrae of an anonymous quadruped in my back,' he smiled mischievously from his iron bed. A small, muscular man, taut liveliness in all his movements, he was proud to tell us he was now seventy-one. Whatever the animal was that donated bones for his back, he delighted in saying it gave him the strength of an ox.

Over the entrance to the community hung a sign: 'CHARITY DESTROYS, WORK BUILDS', very much the sort of thing Amte himself would say. Sheer hard work had built Anandwan into a lush and thriving place served by thirty-five wells, long low bungalows and workshops. People who had struggled to get here to live had done it all, building their own methane gas plant; putting in ten thousand trees; nurturing a garden which boasted over a hundred varieties of rose. Beyond the boundaries, the endless wind blew over the cacti and thornbushes.

So, Anandwan expanded, all this was put together by people who very often had no feeling in their hands or no fingers and eyes. Now the place had grown beyond leprosy, taking in blind or deaf people from across the country. These people were outcasts in their home villages, often the source of fear that shot through their communities. Anandwan was a haven and one supported by international agencies in recognition of that.

Down the avenues, blind children drove crippled children around in little wooden buggies, the passengers giving their drivers directions, telling them a little slower here, or to speed up on the straights. 'The school bus,' laughed Dr Prakash Amte, Baba's son, who works here with his wife.

'I do not believe in disability,' Baba Amte told us during our stay, 'only that people have different abilities.'

And here, it seemed to us, was a place for those abilities to grow, as if from nowhere. Sculptures, hewn from wood or forged in metals were sold across the country and abroad. There were repeated tales of people arriving here, lost and desperate, then in time filtering into these workshops to discover some talent that had been stamped upon in the outside world of rejection and begging.

Amte stressed to us that any disease which leads to disfigurement, also infects healthy people with fear – the fear that shuts doors, closes ranks and casts people out. In the caste-ridden, hierarchical society beyond the gates of Anandwan, leprosy is the ultimate symbol of the lowliest order. It has been curable for years, but as Amte pointed out, the fear of society needs treating as well. He took a hard look at the outside world and came here, came from it, to provide an alternative for people with or without the disease to work and live beyond the fear.

As the slogan over the main entrance indicated, Baba Amte and his medical team had little time for self-pity. Anandwan was, powerfully, a place of self-help against appalling odds, and an extraordinarily happy one. 'You lose a finger,' said Amte chirpily, 'you lose seven fingers and so what? You still have others – work with them!'

'You can do that here,' I said to him, 'but what about the world beyond?'

'See,' he said, flat on his back with one arm outstretched, 'our target for treatment has to be society itself, out there beyond here. But we have had to come from it to build this place up into something,' there was a rare pause, 'something which can live as an example to the outside world. This is a struggle here, a shared struggle of creativity. Nothing less will make people forget leprosy, blindness, whatever. To live and work with others, to help and be helped, that's our way. You can live without fingers, but not without self-respect.'

His arm grasped the special wooden bar over the bed, and, hoisting himself up, ignoring the evident pain, he looked directly at us:

'My friends – your journey means much to me. ... I am growing old and my last harvest will soon come.'

He paused again. There was silence. Our journey was absurd, irrelevant against all this. 'I shall remember you,' he said quietly, 'the two white bicycle men.'

Glossary

alu gobi	spicy mix of potato (alu) and cauliflower (gobi), two things very seldom seen growing in India, but the staple of northern dhabas
auto-rickshaw	three-wheeler taxi scooters with motorcycle engines, they have meters which most drivers won't use, sometimes have mirrors which no drivers ever use, you sit in the back, driver in front and haggle a fare.
backsheesh	a tip, a bribe, a solution, a way of getting something done, a way of life
bazaar	market/market town or simply main street of a town, not a place to cycle through.
betel	the nut from which pan is produced, a modest little nut but the source of widespread stains on city streets (see pan)
Bhagavad Gita	or just the Gita, a Hindu holy book containing Krishna's lessons
bidi	small cigarette with no filter but distinctive flavour – when you can keep them alight long enough
bourkha	loose black headdresses worn by Moslem Kashmiri women with slits for the eyes and gauze for the nose and mouth
Campa Cola	what happened when India became one of the few countries in the world to dispense with the services of Coca Cola Ltd
chai	tea … ubiquitous and excellent, in spite of what Rossiter and the rest of the West will tell you
chalo chalo!	what people shout when they're tired of waiting and want to get moving on the bus/train/rickshaw/cycle-rickshaw/traffic jam/queue

chana	spiced chickpeas
chapatti	unleavened bread in the form of a saucer-sized pancake, slapped onto the side of a clay oven to cook
charpoy	rope bed, usually slung with tough hessian, groups of them lie outside dhabas for passing punters in the country, beware of plastic cheapo versions
charas	ganga, dope, cannabis resin, man
chaval	rice
curd	yogurt
dal	thick, thickish or thin lentil soup most people's staple diet
dhaba	roadside shack housing enormous clay ovens for feeding whoever stops
dharma	natural law of Hinduism defining total harmony of the universe, castes and the caste system and the moral code of actions one should follow
dhobi	washerman who collects house to house, smashes your clothes against a washing stone and returns them to you, identifying them by the dhobi system of intricate marks and symbols put on the hem of garments
dhobi ghat	where the smashing happens, at the side of the lake or river
dhoti	white loin cloth wrapped around the legs and thighs then ingeniously drawn up between the legs like an ultra-baggy pair of shorts, but far more comfortable, commoner in the south
dosa	southern lentil-flour pancake (although they do occur elsewhere), wrapped round spiced vegetables to make a masala dosa
ghat	hill, ridge of hills or steep river bank often used for washing or bathing with steps running down below the water

gopuram	high pyramid over the gates of a Davidian temple in the south, often completely encrusted in statues
hookah	water pipe from which several people can smoke at once
hotel	what dhabas are often called in the south, though they tend to be cleaner
howdah	saddle for carrying several passengers on an elephant's back, with a canopy if you're perched in a posh one
idli	kind of rice pancake, often eaten for breakfast with vegetables or spicy sauce
jackfruit	enormous pod – two feet long or more – filled with little sachets full of custard-like liquid, much prized in the south where people will travel miles to hunt down a jackfruit tree
jaggery	tough brown sweetener made from kitul palm sap, but the word is also used to refer to raw cane sugar
jelabi	pancakes in syrup
kirtipan	sword carried as a religious symbol by Sikhs, usually it's represented by a tiny symbol on the comb also carried by Sikhs and refers to their military traditions
kongri	Kashmiri firepot containing live coals in a clay pot which is then held under your clothes to keep the warmth in and winter out
kurta	long-sleeved collarless cotton shirt
lassi	yoghurt and ice whisked together with fruit flavourings, sweet or sour but very refreshing
lathi	policeman's best friend – long, thick, heavy bamboo stick with fillings of various hardnesses and a leather loop at one end to whirl it during a lathi-charge
Limca	lemon fizzy version of Camp Cola, marginally less sickly

lungi	long loin cloth, often brightly coloured, much more common in the south
mahout	elephant trainer and handler, both often grow up together
maidan	open space covered in yellow grass, except in the monsoon
masala	mixture, particularly of spices e.g. garam masala
nahin	no: chowkidar's and official's favourite phrase
namaste	hello, or goodbye
nullah	dried-up riverbed, usually of smaller streams
octroi	barrier for collecting tolls and road taxes at state or regional frontiers
paise	100 paise make one rupee
pan	betel nut plus wide variety of chewing additives wrapped in a leaf and popped into the mouth to round off a meal and aid the digestion. You chew it all around for what it's worth then spit out the red, gooey mass to make yet another red stain on the pavement
papaya	kind of giant tree-melon, very popular for breakfast but often grown for seed as well
paratha	flour and water pancake basted in butter or, more likely, ghee, or more likely still, any old fat available
ponchkai	thick woollen ponchos worn by Kashmiris in winter, plenty of spare room under the folds for a kongri or two
puri	flour and water pancake deep fried – delicious for breakfast
resthouse (P.W.D.)	place where various officials are allowed to stay as they tour the country on business, chowkidars lurk around them, somewhere. . . .
sabze	spiced vegetables – what goes inside a samosa
sadhu	wandering (or rolling) holy man
Sahib	'Lord' title still sometimes applied to Europeans

sal	valuable timber tree, resembling teak
samosa	sabze, wrapped in pastry triangle and deep fried
shalwar kameez	long kurta worn over skin tight trousers
shamiana	brightly coloured tent erected for ceremonies like mass weddings, single weddings, or feasts after police firearms courses
shikhara	Kashmiri version of a gondola
sweeper	low-caste job of sweeping things clean but also entails removing night-soil, experts in the art of dust-creation
tank	water reservoir, much used by water buffaloes and dhobi-wallahs
thali	all-in-one vegetarian meal, the thali is actually the metal plate it comes on, full of dimples called katoris into which various chutneys, rice and vegetables are repeatedly tipped – best in the south
tiffin	Raj term for elevenses – now used to mean any snack with little metal tiffin-tins to put the snacks into
toddy	alcoholic drink tapped from palm trees
Vedas	ancient Hindu texts, the orthodox religious scripts

Travel/Adventure in Paladin Books

Journey Through Britain   £2.95 ☐
John Hillaby
It was a magical idea to walk through the over-industrialised land of
Britain from Land's End to John O'Groats, avoiding all centres of
population. Britain's master walker made his reputation with his
book. Illustrated.

Journey Through Europe   £2.95 ☐
John Hillaby
John Hillaby gives a splendid pot pourri of factual account, lively
anecdote, mythology and private comment in this account of his walk
from the Hook of Holland via the Alps to Nice. Illustrated.

Journey to the Jade Sea   £2.50 ☐
John Hillaby
Tired of city-living and ashamed of his toleration of boredom, John
Hillaby made a three-month safari from the Northern Frontier District
of Kenya to the legendary Jade Sea. Illustrated.

Tracks   £2.50 ☐
Robyn Davidson
Robyn Davidson went to the dead heart of Australia in pursuit of a
dream – to cross the desert alone. Her voyage opened tracks to the
discovery of self as well as to the profound beauty and nobility of a
threatened land and its indigenous people. Illustrated.

Hamish's Mountain Walk   £3.95 ☐
Hamish Brown
No one had ever climbed all 279 Scottish Munro peaks in a single
journey, until Hamish Brown embarked upon his magnificent mountain walk. This is not only an unforgettable account of one particular
journey, but the result of a lifetime spent on the mountains, in
contemplation of the scenery and in deep conversation with the
people of the Highlands.

Hamish's Groats End Walk   £2.50 ☐
Hamish Brown
For five months, the author and his collie Storm walked the length
and breadth of the British Isles, taking in the highest peaks in
Scotland, England, Wales and Ireland.

Beyond the Mexique Bay   £2.50 ☐
Aldous Huxley
A fluid and lucid account of Huxley's travels in Central America.

To order direct from the publisher just tick the titles you want
and fill in the order form.   PAL16182

Travel in Paladin Books

The Quest for Arthur's Britain   **£3.95** ☐
Geoffrey Ashe
The examination of the historical foundations of the Arthurian
legend with archaeological chapters presenting the results of exca-
vations at Cadbury, Tintagel, Glastonbury and lesser-known sites.
Illustrated.

The Secret Country   **£3.50** ☐
Janet and Colin Bord
An exploration of folklore, legends and hauntings surrounding the
standing stones, earthworks and ancient carvings of Britain.

A Guide to Ancient Sites in Britain   **£4.95** ☐
Janet and Colin Bord
Each site is illustrated with photographs and maps and gives accurate
basic archaeological information, precise instructions on how to get
to each site, and the folklore, ghost stories and unusual theories
connected with them.

A Guide to Anglo-Saxon Sites   **£2.95** ☐
Nigel and Mary Kerr
The first comprehensive gazetteer of Anglo-Saxon Sites in Britain.
Illustrated throughout.

A Guide to the Hill Forts of Britain   **£3.95** ☐
A. H. A. Hogg
Hill forts are among Britain's most spectacular monuments. Here is a
'gazetteer' of 160 of Britain's most notable sites.

Mysterious Britain   **£4.95** ☐
Janet and Colin Bord
All over the British countryside are totems and indications of lost
civilizations and knowledge, scattered in a rich profusion if only the
eye can see. This book looks into the past while suggesting startling
research for the future. Illustrated.

Mysterious Wales   **£2.50** ☐
Chris Barber
Wales is the Celtic land of mystery par excellence. This is a
beautifully illustrated treasure trove of extraordinary tales and magical places, complete with map references and directions.

To order direct from the publisher just tick the titles you want
and fill in the order form.

Folklore in Paladin Books

A Dictionary of British Folk Customs   £2.95 ☐
Christina Hole
Every folk custom, both past and present, is described with its history, development and present-day usage. The book includes a nationwide calender showing what happens, where and when.

The Classic Fairy Tales   £3.95 ☐
Iona and Peter Opie
Twenty-four of the best known stories in the English language are presented in the exact words of the earliest surviving text or English translation. Lavishly illustrated.

The People of the Sea   £1.95 ☐
David Thomson
The haunting record of a journey in search of the man-seal legends of the Celts. 'Enthralling, spine-tingling, cliff-hanging'. *Financial Times*

To order direct from the publisher just tick the titles you want and fill in the order form.   **PAL6082**

Anthropology in Paladin Books

Humankind   £2.95 ☐
Peter Farb
A history of the development of man. It provides a comprehensive
picture of how we evolved to reach our present state, and analyses
the remarkable diversity of human beings.

Shabono   £2.95 ☐
Florinda Donner
'A masterpiece . . . It is superb social science because in describing
her experiences among the Indians of the Venezuelan jungle Florinda
Donner plummets the reader into an unknown but very real world.'
Carlos Casteneda.

The Mountain People   £2.50 ☐
Colin Turnbull
A remarkable and gripping account of two separate periods in which
Turnbull lived with a declining African tribe, the Ik, in a mountain
area on the borders of Uganda and Kenya.

The Forest People   £2.50 ☐
Colin Turnbull
A fascinating study of the Pygmies of the Ituri Forest – a vast expanse
of dense, damp and inhospitable forest in the heart of Stanley's 'Dark
Continent'.

The Human Cycle   £2.95 ☐
Colin Turnbull
An illuminating comparison of Western industrial society and smal-
ler-scale societies elsewhere in the world. Far from believing in the
superiority of 'advanced' societies, Turnbull shows how we could
refashion our own ways by learning from them.

Lucy: The Beginnings of Humankind   £2.95 ☐
Donald C. Johanson and Maitland A. Edey
'A riveting book that is at once a carefully documented report, an
exciting adventure story, and a candid memoir of a brash young
palaeoanthropologist . . . What Lucy suggests about our forebears
will keep palaeanthropologists arguing for years.' *Publishers Weekly*.
Illustrated.

Social History in Paladin Books

The Common Stream   **£2.95** ☐
Rowland Parker
The history of a Cambridgeshire village from the first traces of human settlement to the present day, and the common stream of ordinary men and women who have lived and died there. 'Beautifully written, imaginative and truthful.' *Ronald Blythe*

Men of Dunwich   **£3.95** ☐
Rowland Parker
An imaginative reconstruction of the life of an ancient community in East Anglia, which, over the centuries, took its living from the sea, until finally the sea assailed, eroded and then engulfed the community. Illustrated.

American Dreams: Lost and Found   **£3.95** ☐
Studs Terkel
From Miss USA to an unknown New York cab driver – these frank confessions, woven together by a master craftsman, represent the authentic voice of America. A rum and original piece of social history that will surprise, shock and move you.

The Fields Beneath   **£2.95** ☐
Gillian Tindall
The absorbing history of a London village – Kentish Town – as it is gradually absorbed into Greater London, and its final emergence in the late sixties as a richly variegated and human triumph against ruthless landlords and didactic town planners. Illustrated.

To order direct from the publisher just tick the titles you want
and fill in the order form.   **PAL7382**

All these books are available at your local bookshop or newsagent, or can be ordered direct from the publisher.

To order direct from the publishers just tick the titles you want and fill in the form below.

Name _____

Address _____

_____

Send to:
Paladin Cash Sales
PO Box 11, Falmouth, Cornwall TR10 9EN.

Please enclose remittance to the value of the cover price plus:

UK 60p for the first book, 25p for the second book plus 15p per copy for each additional book ordered to a maximum charge of £1.90.

BFPO 60p for the first book, 25p for the second book plus 15p per copy for the next 7 books, thereafter 9p per book.

Overseas including Eire £1.25 for the first book, 75p for second book and 28p for each additional book.

Paladin Books reserve the right to show new retail prices on covers, which may differ from those previously advertised in the text or elsewhere.